Great British Family Names & Their History

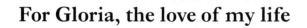

For Gloria, the love of my life

Great British Family Names & Their History

What's in a Name?

John Moss

PEN & SWORD
HISTORY

AN IMPRINT OF PEN & SWORD BOOKS LTD.
YORKSHIRE – PHILADELPHIA

First published in Great Britain in 2019 by
Pen and Sword History
An imprint of
Pen & Sword Books Ltd
Yorkshire - Philadelphia

Hardback ISBN 9781526722805
Paperback ISBN 9781526751553

Typeset in INDIA By IMPEC e Solutions

Printed and bound in the UK by TJ International Ltd.

Pen & Sword Books Ltd incorporates the Imprints of Pen & Sword Books
Archaeology, Atlas, Aviation, Battleground, Discovery, Family History,
History, Maritime, Military, Naval, Politics, Railways, Select, Transport, True
Crime, Fiction, Frontline Books, Leo Cooper, Praetorian Press, Seaforth
Publishing, Wharncliffe and White Owl.

For a complete list of Pen & Sword titles please contact

PEN & SWORD BOOKS LIMITED
47 Church Street, Barnsley, South Yorkshire, S70 2AS, England
E-mail: enquiries@pen-and-sword.co.uk
Website: www.pen-and-sword.co.uk

or

PEN AND SWORD BOOKS
1950 Lawrence Rd, Havertown, PA 19083, USA
E-mail: Uspen-and-sword@casematepublishers.com
Website: www.penandswordbooks.com

Contents

A map depicting the regions of Great Britain.

Foreword

Some places are named after people; some people are named after places. Many ancient family names predate Norman times, and are veiled in long forgotten nomenclatures and spellings. Some names bear little resemblance to those we learned in childhood; Latin, Brythonic Celtic, Welsh, Anglo-Saxon, Germanic, Norse and French names – many barely in a form of English that we might recognise.

Names that are built into the history and topography of the land, and that provide an insight into who we are and why the place where we live came to be. Names that hold mysteries and often come as revelations when their meanings are unlocked.

They reflect the long and chequered history of Great Britain and the numerous invasions and incursions that have taken place over the centuries. Romans, Angles, Saxons, Jutes, Danes and Normans. They all came. They settled here and made us what we are, and the melting pot of dialects and languages they brought with them has been synthesised over time into what has by now become an international language – a complex, eloquent tongue that the rest of the world seems eager to learn.

Surnames are a relatively recent occurrence. Before the Norman Conquest, people did not have them as such; they were known by a personal name or nickname. After 1066 however, Norman overlords introduced surnames as a way of identifying the subjugated people over whom they ruled. So the practice gradually became commonplace, and old Saxon and Celtic names fell out of use.

Of course, the origin of many common surnames is straightforward, as they are derived from specific occupations, of which Baker, Tailor, Weaver, Smith, Thatcher, Tanner, Butcher, Carpenter, Carter, Shepherd and Fletcher are examples. There are innumerable others. Many surnames are derived from the more obvious British counties and cities, (Chester, Poole, York, Devonshire and Hampshire, for example). Therefore, I have not included any of these, because their sources are so self-evident as to require no explanation.

Furthermore, most of the names I have included originated long before the structure of the English language was established. Variations are more often the rule than the exception. Even within close blood ties, members of the same family frequently used different spellings for their surnames. Names also tend to evolve naturally, so that over time the final version often bears scant affinity with its original form. Therefore, wherever possible, I have tried to include some of the variations that exist.

Many old Norman names include the prefixed preposition 'de', (from the French, meaning 'of' or 'from'), indicating their place of origin, as in examples like De Boynton, De Mowbray or De Conyers. Many constituted the embryonic forms of surnames, which became necessary when detailed accounts of landownership were drawn up, as was the case of the 1086 Domesday Survey. However, over time, as people assimilated into English culture, with very few exceptions, these tended to be dropped.

In addition to a comprehensive bibliography of sources used in compiling this book, I have included details of those websites which I have found particularly helpful. There are far too many possible names to include them all, but I believe these websites will go some way to facilitate further investigation by the reader. They have proved especially useful in relating to the ancient Scottish and Irish clans and families.

Northern Ireland, (or Ulster), posed its own particular problem, since it did not exist as a clearly defined entity until the twentieth century, since when the Republic of Ireland, (or Eire), has no longer been part of Great Britain. Nevertheless, many of its ancient family names stem from a time when the whole island of Ireland, both Eire and Ulster, were part of a unified nation. Therefore, I felt obliged to disregard its more recent political partition and include family names no matter in which part of Ireland they originated.

Despite the fact that the twenty-first century has seen so much material readily available online, and it has proved to be a great time-saver, I have made references wherever possible to reliable entries in the *Anglo-Saxon Chronicles*. I have also used as a starting point, the Roll at Battle Abbey, which includes the names of all the knights, dukes, counts and barons who attended William at Hastings, as well as those who had furnished the expedition with ships, horses, men, finance and supplies for the venture.

History shows that the transition from Saxon to Norman Britain was painful and protracted. William brooked no opposition to his new order and dealt brutally with any form of dissent, allowing his barons a free hand in their pillage of England. Lands that had been held by Saxon thegns for many years were confiscated and distributed liberally among the so-called Companions of William. Peasants fared no better than their masters. In the year 1067, the *Anglo-Saxon Chronicles* recorded that 'the king set a heavy tribute on poor folk, though still nevertheless let his men harry all that they went over'. It also records that in 1070, 'the king allowed all the monasteries in England to be plundered'. In 1082, it declared that 'there was much famine'.

I have also made numerous references to the *Domesday Book*, William the Conqueror's great audit of 1086, so-called because in its day it was likened to the final day of judgement. The implications, the scope and extent of the survey were also described in the *Chronicles*. In 1087, a year after *Domesday*, it recorded that 'there was not a hide of land in England that he [William] knew not what he had from it, and what it was worth, after it had been set down in his document'.

Certain other information has been based on early taxation documents, including Pipe Rolls, medieval treasury financial records, (also known as Great Rolls); Hundred Rolls, (a census of landownership in England and Wales); Poll Tax Rolls, (a fourteenth century individual head tax); and Subsidy Rolls, (feudal county taxation records).

At best, this book can only be snapshot. It is also a personal selection. Doubtless there are others who would have made different choices from those I have made. Be that as it may, it was not feasible to include every possible name or to satisfy every viewpoint. So, I have chosen those that may be considered important or unusual in some way – the ancient, historic and noble names – those that interest me most, that are somehow pivotal in the development of our history or made significant contributions to the social and political development of the nation.

What follows, therefore, are some of the explanations and derivations of over three hundred of the ancient family names in Great Britain. And, while much of the material that I have included may be available elsewhere or hidden in the terra incognita regions of the public domain, I hope that in its totality, this book provides a valuable resource that has the benefit of being all in one place – here – as a concise reference document, written in plain English.

John Moss
December 2018

Part One

North-East England

Family Names in County Durham, Northumberland,
Tyne & Wear and Yorkshire

The Aske Family of Aughton

The Askes are an old family whose origins can be traced to the eleventh century in Aske, a township in the Parish of Easby, near Richmond in the North Riding of Yorkshire. They held the land as tenants from the Earl of Richmond following the Norman conquest of 1066. Formerly, they had belonged to a Saxon named Thor.

According to the *Domesday Book*, the estate was known as Alreton, 'in the hundred of Land of Count Alan', and had just 'five villagers, three smallholdings and four ploughlands'. The first record of the surname was in Cumberland, (now Cumbria), though the main body of the family lived in Aughton in Yorkshire. Variations on the surname include Askey, Askew, Aiscough and Asker.

The church at Aughton bears brass effigies of Richard de Aske and his wife, who died in the fifteenth century. Later, Robert Aske, (1500-37), a lawyer and Fellow at Gray's Inn, objected to the king's Dissolution of the Monasteries, and was a protagonist in the insurrection known as the 'Pilgrimage of Grace', during the reign of Henry VIII. He was beheaded for treason at York in 1537.

There is an alternative variation of the surname – that of Asker, derived from the Old Norse 'askr', which translates as 'the ash tree', and probably describes a specific location, where a branch of the family lived. It was possibly at a special place or a district boundary of some kind. In early times, the ash tree had mystical significance and was often planted at the outskirts of a settlement or at an important meeting place.

In 1922, Sir Robert William Aske was created Baron Aske of Aughton. A barrister and decorated Lieutenant Colonel in the Territorial Army Reserve, he was a Liberal Member of Parliament on two occasions for Newcastle-upon-Tyne.

At the time of writing, Sir Robert John Bingham Aske, the third Baron, is the incumbent, and lives in Exeter, Devon.

The Belasis Family of Durham

The surname derives from the Manor of Belasis near Billingham in County Durham, which along with the Lambtons and Edens, was once the family seat of the Belasis family. It is a Norman-French name, which comes from 'bel', meaning beautiful, and 'assis', to sit. Hence the name means 'beautiful seat'. In this case, the word 'seat' almost certainly pertains to the place, eg. a country or a family seat.

Rowland de Belasis, (sometimes spelled Belasyse) was the first known holder of the surname and took it directly from the placename. By 1264, he was a knight of the Bishop of Durham and lived at Cowpen Bewley. Although the family continued their association with the area, the Manor of Belasis later passed into the ownership of Durham Cathedral.

Between 1270 and 1280, John de Belasis held land around Wolviston and may have exchanged part of the Belasis estate for territory at Henknowle near Bishop Auckland, where the arms of the Belasis family are located in the church of St Andrews. The Belasis family also had strong connections with Coxwold near Thirsk in Yorkshire.

In 1611, Sir Henry Bellasis was made Baronet Belasyse of Newborough in Yorkshire, and his son, Thomas, the second Baronet, was created Viscount Fauconberg of Henknowle in County Durham in 1642. He was member of Parliament for Thirsk in 1624.

John Belasyse, the Baron of Worlaby, (1640-89), became a distinguished Royalist commander during the Civil War and fought at the Battles of Newbury, Naseby and Edgehill, with many honours being initially heaped upon him, including the Lord Lieutenancy of Yorkshire, as well as the Governorship of Hull and of Tangiers. However, in a somewhat chequered career, he was later impeached and imprisoned in the Tower of London. Finally, after release, he spent his latter days restored in status as Lord of the Treasury.

Another notable member of the Belasis family was Miss Mary Belasis of Brancepeth Castle near Durham, who lived in the eigtheenth century. She fell in love with a County Durham Member of Parliament by the name of Robert Shafto. She reputedly was heard to sing what became a well-known folk song, 'Bobby Shafto', which went thus:

> 'Bobby Shafto's gone to sea,
> With silver buckles on his knee,
> When he comes back, he'll marry me,
> Pretty Bobby Shafto.'

Unfortunately for the lovelorn Miss Belasis, when Shafto did finally return from sea, he married someone else. Mary is said to have died of a broken heart.

When Henry Belasyse, the second Earl of Fauconberg of Newborough, died in March 1802, without male heirs, the peerage passed through his eldest daughter, Lady Anne Belasyse, to her husband Sir George Wombwell, and the Belasyse title became extinct.

The Blenkinsop Family of Blenkinsopp

The Blenkinsop surname, (usually spelled with one 'p', but occasionally with two), derives from Blenkinsopp Castle, which is located at Haltwhistle in the Tyne Valley, near Hadrian's Wall. The land and castle were held by the Blenkinsops from the thirteenth until the early nineteenth century.

The family traces its ancestry to one Richard Blenkinsoppe, grandson of Ranulfus, who held the manor in 1240. Later records show that Thomas de Blencansopp was licenced to fortify it in 1399, and that by the year 1416, the building was listed as a castle.

Explanations of the name's meaning are obscure, though most authorities suggest it means 'Blenkin's hill', probably after a man called Blenkin. An alternative interpretation of the Blenkinsopp name may have originated in the early medieval Cumbric language, where 'blaen', meant 'top', and 'kein', meant 'back' or 'ridge'. Hence, 'top of the ridge'. To this was later added the Old English element 'hop', meaning 'valley'. Variants of the surname include Blenkinship, Blenkinshopp and Blenkenshippe.

A celebrated military member of the family was Major General Sir Alfred Percy Blenkinsop, (died in November 1936), who became a Knight Commander of the Order of the Bath and a Companion of the Order of St Michael and St George.

Later in the twentieth century, Blenkinsopp Castle served as a hotel, but major damage was caused by a fire in 1954, and large parts of the property were demolished on safety grounds. Today it is part home and part ruin. What remains is a Grade I Listed Building and a Scheduled Ancient Monument.

The Boynton Family of Sedbury

Bartholomew de Boynton was made Lord of the Manor of Boynton within a year of the Conquest of 1066, his family taking possession of land previously owned by Torchill de Bovington, in the East Riding of Yorkshire, which the *Domesday Book* refers to as Bouintone. Alternative spellings of the name include Boyntun, Bointon, Byington and Bointen.

The name probably came from the Old English personal name 'Bofa', plus 'ing', meaning 'people' or 'family', and 'tun', signifying a settlement or farmstead. Loosely translated it might mean 'the settlement of Bofa's people'. Alternatively, the name may have arisen from Boyton in Wiltshire or from Boyington Court in Kent, which was recorded in 1207 as Bointon.

Either way, the family seem to have taken their surname from the place, and the first persons known to use it were Walter, Adam and Gilbert in the early twelfth century. Walter de Boynton was actively involved in the building of Bridlington Priory.

Sir Matthew Boynton, (1591-1646), was created Baron Boynton of Barmston in 1618 and held the office of Sheriff of Yorkshire from 1628 to 1629 and was Governor of Scarborough.

By the sixteenth century, the Boyntons had become one of the ten richest families in the East Riding. However, they failed to produce male heirs and through marriage, their estates passed to the Del See family. By the middle of the seventeeth century, members of the family are known to have emigrated to America, sailing from Hull on the ship *John of London* and settling in Massachusetts.

In more recent times, Sir Griffith Wilfred Norman Boynton was a Lieutenant Commander in the Royal Navy and was the thirteenth Baronet until his death in 1966.

The Chaytor Family of Croft

See: The Clervaux Family

The Clervaux Family of Croft

The Clervaux family name, (sometimes Clairvaux, Clerevaulx, Clervoe or Clairvo), first appears in the North Riding of Yorkshire shortly after the Battle of Hastings, when they held a family seat as Lords of the Manor. It is thought to have derived from Sir Hamon de Clervaux, who probably came from Clervaux Castle in Anjou, and is recorded as having fought at Hastings with William of Normandy. However, apart from its derivation from a placename, opinions differ as to the exact origin of the surname. It may possibly have originated in Clervaux in neighbouring Luxembourg, or from Clairvaux-les-Lacs in the Jura Region of France, or from Clairvaux, near Rodez in Aquitaine - no definitive source seems to exist. According to contemporary accounts however, Hamon de Clervaux came to England in the train of Alan Le Roux of Brittany and received the honour of Richmond from the Conqueror himself.

An account of 1290 declares that the Clairvaux were freemen, and thereby excused the manorial duty of ploughing. Clearly, they soon gained status and influence in the county. Sir John Clervaux of Croft, (c.1400–43), for example, was High Sheriff of Yorkshire, as were many of his succeeding generations. The family also consolidated its power by marriage into influential families like the Neviles, the Belasyse, the Mortimers and the Vavasors, even though, as a result, some of their property passed out of Clervaux hands. Nevertheless, when Sir Richard Clervaux, who was a courtier of Henry VI, died in 1490, a plaque was placed above his tomb in Croft Church depicting the arms of Clervaux impaling those of the Vavasours, suggesting a higher status position.

During the reign of Elizabeth I, the family's heiress, Elizabeth Clervaux, married Christopher Chaytor of Butterby in County Durham. He served as Surveyor General for Elizabeth and was granted arms in 1571. By descent, their son, Anthony Chaytor, inherited both the Chaytor and Clervaux estate at Croft.

William Chaytor, (1639-1720), was created Baronet Chaytor of Croft Hall, near Darlington, and the title passed to succeeding generations thereafter, culminating with William Henry Clervaux, the seventh Baronet Chaytor of Croft, who died as recently as 1976, when Sir George Reginald Chaytor succeeded as the eighth Baronet in September of that year.

Several family ancestors had military careers, with Major Henry Chaytor, (1686-1717), serving in the British Army under the Duke of Marlborough, as did his son, Thomas.

The Clervaux connection has been maintained throughout the centuries, being frequently incorporated as a middle name for many of the family members. Clervaux James Chaytor, (born in 1967), and Frances Alexandra Clervaux Chaytor, (born in 1961), demonstrate that the Clervaux family name survives right up to recent times.

The Constable Family of Burton Constable

Burton Constable was recorded in the Domesday Survey as Santriburtone and occupied by an unnamed knight on behalf of the Crown. It seems he was succeeded by Erneburga of Burton, who married Ulbert, the Count of Aumale's constable. Their son, called Robert Constable, had land at Erneburgh Burton before 1190, and by the thirteenth century, the family held substantial areas of the Count's estate. By then the place had beome known as Burton Constable.

Sir Robert Constable, (c.1478–1537), eldest son of Sir Marmaduke Constable, was married to Jane Ingleby of Ripley, daughter of Sir William Ingleby of Ripley. He fought alongside Henry VII to quell the Cornish rebels at the Battle of Blackheath in 1497. However, after a dispute, he fell out of the monarch's favour, and in 1537 was arrested, tried for treason, and hanged the following year at Hull.

The Constable surname comes from the Old French word 'conestable', (or 'cunestable'), derived from the original Latin word *'comes'*, meaning a count and *'stabuli'*, meaning a stable. Hence, an 'officer of the stable'. Also in the thirteenth century, the Constables added their name to the Manor of Burton, (the placename meaning 'settlement at a fortified dwelling'), and the estate at Burton Constable in North Yorkshire came into being.

The oldest part of the manor house dates from the reign of Stephen in the twelfth century, but in the late fifteenth century a new brick house was built by Sir John Constable, (born around 1400, son of William IV, known as 'le constable'), replacing Halsham as the family's principal seat. This was replaced again in 1768, by a Palladian villa designed by John Carr for Sir Marmaduke Wyvill.

Sir Philip Constable, born around 1595, gained the title of Baronet Constable of Everingham, but with the death of Sir Frederick Augustus Talbot Constable in 1818, the baronetcy became extinct.

The Conyers Family of Durham

Conyers, (sometimes De Conyers), is a name of Anglo-Norman origin and derives from the Old French word 'coignier', that is, a person who mints money – as in the English word 'coin'. The family were originally from the town of Coigners in Normandy and moved to live at Sockburn, where the Bishop of Durham, Ralph Flambard, granted the manor and estate of Sockburn-on-Tees near Middleton St George to Roger de Conyers at the end of the eleventh century. Conyers was appointed Constable of Durham Castle.

The first recorded spelling of the family name in England is that of John le Conyare, dated 1327, in the Sussex Subsidy Rolls, during the reign of Edward II.

The village of Norton Conyers, north of Ripon, takes its name from the family, and has been associated with the Conyers for centuries. The village was mentioned in *Domesday Book*, but there was probably a habitation of some kind there in Viking times.

In June 1509, William Conyers was created Lord Conyers, and his descendant, Sir John Conyers, (1599-1664), became Baron Conyers of Horden in County Durham. However, with the family's inability to produce male heirs, in the eigtheenth century the baronetcy passed through marriage of the female line into the Darcy family.

In the early twentieth century, David George Conyers, who fought in the Great War, was forced to sell his home at Castletown Conyers in County Limerick, Ireland, and died childless in Canada in 1952, bringing the main family line to an end.

Norton Conyers House, a Grade II Listed mid-fourteenth century house with Tudor, Stuart and Georgian additions, has been the home of the Graham family since 1624. The novelist Charlotte Brontë is said to have based Thornfield Hall, in her novel *Jane Eyre*, on the house at Norton Conyers.

The Fenwick Family of Northumberland

The first record of the Fenwick surname occurs around 1220, when Robert de Fenwicke is known to have lived in the Scottish border region. Later, a Walter del Feneweke is recorded in Lincolnshire in 1275, and Thomas de Fenwyck of Northumberland in 1279. Nicholaus Fynwyk was provost of Ayr in 1313, and Reginald de Fynwyk, (sometimes Fynvyk), appears as bailie and alderman of the same borough in 1387 and 1401.

The name is usually pronounced 'Fennick', and comes from Old English, meaning, simply, 'the farm on the fen'.

The Fenwicks achieved notoriety throughout the north and were frequently involved in the border troubles of Tudor times. They held strongholds at Kirkharle, Bywell-on-Tyne and the original peel tower at Wallington; this later became Wallington Hall, near Morpeth. In fact, the Fenwicks were found on either side of the English–Scottish border and are thought to take their name from Fenwick near Kyloe in Northumberland.

During the Civil War, Sir John Fenwick was killed at Marston Moor, and his descendant, another John Fenwick, was beheaded for high treason after conspiring to murder the Dutch-born protestant William of Orange. Fenwick's property and estate were confiscated by the Crown, as was his horse, Sorrel. This was the same horse that threw William as it stumbled over a mole hill in the grounds of Hampton Court. Ironically, shortly afterwards the king died from his injuries.

The Fulthorpe Family of County Durham & Halifax

The Fulthorpe surname, (sometimes Folthorpe or Foulthorpe), is of northern origin and most prevalent in County Durham, where the family became known as the 'The Filthy Foulthorpes'. The surname comes from Old Norse and has many other alternative spellings and variants, including Farlesthrop, Farlestorp, Fullthropp, and Fawthropp.

It derives from the village of Farlethorp in Lincolnshire, and was recorded in the 1190 Pipe Rolls, (the annual financial records of the Exchequer), during the reign of Richard I. Another recorded spelling of it as a family name is that of Mary Fawthropp, whose baptism was recorded at Halifax Parish Church in Yorkshire in 1577.

In the mid-fourteeth century, one branch of the Fulthorpes was absorbed into the De la Dale family. Sir Thomas de la Dale, (who died in 1396), was a relative of John of Gaunt, Duke of Lancaster, and sometimes went by the alternative surname, Fulthorpe. He was succeeded by his son, yet another Thomas de la Dale, and thereafter that family branch retained the new surname. The last of the De La

Dales male line died out in the sixteenth century, and when Anne de la Dale married Alexander Fettiplace in 1537, her family's estate passed to her husband.

The Gascoigne Family of Ravensworth

The Gascoigne Family name, (sometimes Gascoign, Gascoyne, Gaskain, Gaskin or Gasking), first appears with the name of William Gascoigne, who was born around 1089 in Lasingcroft, Yorkshire. Later, a Bernard Gascon appears in Northamptonshire in 1206, and in 1208, another William le Gascun also lived in the West Riding of Yorkshire. In the thirteenth century, other lines of the Gascoigne family included Philip le Gascoyn of Shropshire and Geoffrey Gascoyne of Norfolk. By the fourteenth century this surname had appeared in Yorkshire as Gasqwyn.

The name is of Norman French origin and simply refers to 'Gascon' – a native of Gascony. This in turn derives from the Latin 'Vasco-Onis', which means 'boasting'. It has a similar root as the origin for the name of the Basque Country of Spain, (in Spanish: 'Païs Vasco').

In the sixteenth century, Isobel Boynton, a descendant of the Lumleys and heiress to the Ravensworth estate near Gateshead, married Sir Henry Gascoigne of Gawthorpe in Lancashire, and the family acquired Durham Ravensworth Manor, which they sold to the Liddell family in 1607. The Liddells went on to build Ravensworth Castle in the eigtheenth century, but it was demolished in 1953.

It was in 1635 that Sir John Gascoigne, (1556-1637), was created first Baron Gascoigne. The line of the peerage continued until Sir Thomas Gascoigne, the eighth Baronet, died in 1784, at which point the title seems to have disappeared, as his son Thomas, (1786-1809), did not apparently succeed to the title.

The last known member of this Gascoigne line is Richard Edward Gascoigne, third son of William Harcourt Crisp Gascoigne, who was born in 1989.

The Hylton Family of Hylton

Hylton, (sometimes Hilton), is of old Anglo-Saxon origin, and probably derives from a village of that name, as there are several in Dorset, Staffordshire and County Durham. The surname self-evidently translates as 'hill town'. The place called Hylton in the north-east region was, as the name implies, a small enclosure, located on a hill upstream from the Monastery of St Peter at Monkwearmouth on the River Wear.

There are several claims as to who was the progenitor of the family. One account maintains that the Hilton family are first recorded in 924, when Adam de Hylton presented a silver crucifix, weighing twenty-five ounces of silver and bearing the family arms, to the monastery at Hartlepool. Another early record appears in Durham, when in 1157, Romanus de Hilton made a written agreement with Absolum, Prior of Durham. Later, Robert Hylton, first Baron Hylton, is recorded, as is his son, Alexander, who was a Member of Parliament in 1332.

Hylton Castle was built by Sir William Hylton some time around 1400, but the family also held extensive estates in Yorkshire, Durham and Northumberland. By the thirteenth century they had assumed the title of a barony within the Bishopric of Durham.

Descendants of the Barony of Hilton are recorded in the fifteenth and sixteenth centuries in London, where William Hilton was recorded as body tailor to Henry VIII and his daughter was seamstress to Elizabeth I.

One of the so-called Pilgrim Fathers, who set sail for the New World aboard the ship *Fortune*, was William Hylton of Biddick Hall, often referred to as the 'Biddick Pilgrim Father'. As a consequence, many descendants of the Hylton family are to be found in America.

From 1772 to 1746, John Hylton was Member of Parliament for Carlisle. Upon his death in September 1746, the peerage fell into abeyance, and was not reinstated until 1866, when Sir William George Hylton-Jolliffe was made Baron Hylton of Hylton. He was the son of William Jolliffe and Eleanor Hylton, and thereafter, the family surnames were combined as Hylton-Jolliffe. Eleanor's father, John Hylton, had been a captain in the 15th Hussars, whose regiment took part in the infamous St Peter's Field incident in Manchester in 1819, (known as the Peterloo Massacre).

Hylton-Jolliffe descendants were politically active throughout the nineteenth and twentieth centuries, as successive Members of Parliament for Wells in Somerset. From 1949 to 1967, William George Hervey Jolliffe was Lord Lieutenant of that county, and in 1999, Raymond Hervey Jolliffe was elected as an hereditary peer.

Audrey Pellew Hylton-Foster, of another branch of the family, was created Baroness Hylton-Foster for life in December 1965, but on her death in October 2002, the peerage became extinct.

The Liddell Family

See: Part Eight: Scotland: The Liddell Family of Roxburghshire.

The Lumley Family of County Durham

The Lumley family traces its ancestry to Liulf, (or Ligulf), de Lumley, born in Northumberland in 995, who died in Gateshead, (or possibly in West Yorkshire), in 1080. His son, Uchred de Lumley, was born in Lumley in Durham in 1140.

The surname is variously recorded as Lumbley, Lumly and Lumby, and eventually was to become the family name of the Earls of Scarbrough. It may have originated in the village of Castle Lumley in County Durham or from Lumby, an old township in Yorkshire. It was recorded in 963 in the *Anglo-Saxon Chronicles* as Lundby, possibly from the Old English 'lumleia', signifying an enclosure near water.

The Lumleys lived mainly in County Durham, though other branches are found in Yorkshire and further south in the eastern counties, as evidenced by Roger de Lumelye, recorded in the Leicestershire Hundred Rolls of 1273.

Ralph de Lumley was summoned to Parliament as Lord Lumley in 1384, but somehow fell foul of the law; he was attainted and his peerage forfeited in 1400. In 1547, John Lumley was created Baron Lumley.

The title of Viscount Lumley of Waterford was created in the Peerage of Ireland in 1628 for Sir Richard Lumley, who later fought as a Royalist in the Civil War. By 1689, a descendant, yet another Richard, was created Earl of Scarbrough to add to the family Baronetcy and Viscountcy.

Richard Lumley, first Earl of Scarbrough, (1650-1721), was a celebrated soldier and statesman who took part in the Battle of the Boyne in 1690 and afterwards saw action in Flanders. He also undertook extensive development of the family seat at Lumley Castle.

Richard Aldred Lumley, born in 1932, was a godson of the then Duchess of York, (later Elizabeth II), and Lord Halifax, former Viceroy of India and later Foreign Secretary.

The present incumbent is Richard Osbert Lumley, thirteenth Earl of Scarbrough, known as Viscount Lumley until 2004, when he succeeded his father. In 2011, he was appointed Deputy Lord Lieutenant of South Yorkshire.

The Manners Family of Etal

The Manners Family, (sometimes De Manners), arrived in Northumberland with the invasion of 1066. They originated in the village of Mesnieres, near Roan in the Seine-Maritime department of France, where they had lived since it was first held by Rollo, a Viking ancestor (c.846–c.932). The surname is thought to have derived from the Latin word 'manere', meaning to remain or abide, and was recorded in the thirteenth century as Maneria.

The village of Mannor near Lanchester in County Durham was named after the family, who, over time were to hold the Earldom and Dukedom of Rutland as well as the Marquessate of Granby. One of the earliest written records of the name is that of Sir Robert de Manners, who held the land in 1165, and another was of a Reginald de Meiniers, dated 1180.

The Scottish form of the name is Menzies, and the first known bearer north of the border is Robert de Meyners, (or de Meyneiss), who was the Great Chamberlain of Scotland some time between 1217 and 1248. Branches of the family were scattered far and wide over

England, with a record of Reginald de Meiniers, in Sussex in 1188, Walter de Maners, documented in 1230 in the County of Cornwall and Edward Manners, listed in the Yorkshire Poll Tax of 1379.

Etal Castle was founded by the Manners family in 1341, when Robert de Manners received licence to crenelate his manor, permitting him to designate it as a castle.

Thomas Manners, (c.1492-1543), succeeded as twelfth Lord de Ros of Helmsley in 1513. He was appointed Keeper of Sherwood Forest and became a Knight of the Garter in 1525. As Lord Chamberlain to Anne of Cleves, he was granted extensive lands in Yorkshire and Leicestershire, including Abbeys at Croxton, Beverley and Riveaux, during the Dissolution of the Monasteries, and went on to become the first Earl of Rutland.

By the mid-eigtheenth century, Sir William Talmarsh, (known as Lord Huntingtower), son of Sir John Manners and Louisa Tollemache, was created first Baron Manners of Hainby Hall in Lincolnshire. His successors held the peerage up to modern times and were Members of Parliament for various constituencies in Yorkshire, Leicestershire and Lincolnshire. His children also inherited the Earldom of Dysart.

Charles John Montage Manners, born in 1999, the son of the eleventh Duke of Rutland, is the current Marquess of Granby.

The Maynard Family of Darlington

The origin of the name Maynard probably arrived with the Normans in 1066, as Maginhard, (sometimes Mainard or Meinhard), which is a personal name derived from two Germanic words, 'magin', meaning 'strong and brave', and 'hard', simply meaning 'hardy'. A variation of the name, possibly a forerunner, appears as Meinardus in the Norfolk section of the *Domesday Book*. The first recorded current spelling of the family name appears in the Pipe Rolls of Suffolk in 1195, during the reign of Richard I.

The main branch of the Maynard family settled at Hoxne Hall on the south coast of Sussex. However, another breakaway branch migrated north into Yorkshire. It is recorded that Sir Richard Maynarde of Kirklevington fought at Agincourt in 1415.

The Maynards were originally cattle breeders. Some time in the sixteenth century, a branch from Eryholme, near Darlington, rose to become important members of county society in Harlsey Hall near Northallerton.

A notable family member was William Maynard, first Baron Maynard, (c.1589-1640), a politician who became Lord Lieutenant of Essex, as did several of his descendants. Another branch of Maynards lived at Wass in the Parish of Kilburn.

Over the eigtheenth and nineteenth centuries, the family saw many migrations to Canada, Australia, New Zealand and America. In this connection, a notable emigré Maynard was Brigadier Francis Herbert Maynard, born in Ottawa, Canada in 1881. He fought in the First World War and was decorated with the Military Cross in 1916. He also fought in the Third Afghan War in 1919. He was made a Companion of the Order of the Bath in 1937, the same year that he won the Distinguished Service Order. He died in March 1979 at the age of ninety-seven.

The Mowbray Family of Yorkshire

The Mowbray family name, (sometimes De Mowbray), arrived after the Conquest of 1066 with Geoffrey de Montbray, (died 1093), who lived in Northumberland. He was Bishop of Coutances and personal assistant to William the Conqueror. According to an entry in the *Domesday Book*, he moved to live in a castle he had built in Bristol. Other variants of the family name spelling include Moubray, Mowbrey and Moubrey.

Roger de Mowbray, the first Lord Mowbray, (1254-97), had also built a castle at Thirsk in the North Riding. Unfortunately, he sided with the Scots in a land dispute and his castle was demolished by the Crown as a result.

The family had a country seat in Kirby-Malzeard in the West Riding, but when Thomas Mowbray was created first Duke of Norfolk by Richard II in 1397, it became the property of the Norfolks.

John de Mowbray, the fifth Lord Mowbray, succeeded as sixth Lord Segrave in 1368, and in 1377 was created the first Earl of

Nottingham. His son, also named John, was a Knight of the Garter and a Privy Counsellor. He fought in the Hundred Years War and became the second Duke of Norfolk on the death of his father in 1425.

As of 2015, Sir John Robert Mowbray, (born in March 1932), was the sixth Baronet Mowbray of Mortimer, Berkshire and Bishopwearmouth in County Durham. He held the office of Deputy Lieutenant of Suffolk in 1993.

The Neville Family of County Durham

The Neville family name, (sometimes Neuville or Nevill), is thought to have originated in the township of Neuville in Calvados or in Néville in the Seine-Maritime Region of France. Both names come from the Old French 'neuf', meaning 'new', and 'ville', signifying a town or settlement. The family can be traced back to the Earl of Northumbria, a great-grandson of the Saxon King Ethelred II and to Uhtred, whose son Dolfin is recorded in 1131 as holding the Manor of Stainthorp in County Durham from the prior of Durham, a territory which remained in the hands of the family for over four centuries. It was there that John, the third Baron Neville, was to build Raby Castle in the thirteenth century, reputedly on the site of an earlier mansion constructed by King Cnut, and which became the family's principal country seat.

One of Dolfin's grandsons, Robert, son of Meldred, married the heiress of Geoffrey de Neville, who inherited the Bulmer lordship of Brancepeth near Durham through her mother's line. Brancepeth Castle became another seat of the family, and it was there that they adopted the Norman surname of Neville.

Over the following century, the Nevilles gained power and wealth in the county, and Hugh de Nevill was mentioned by name in the Great Charter, (Magna Carta), in 1215. His son, also named Hugh, went on to become Baron Nevill of Essex in 1311.

By 1294, Ranulf, (sometimes Ralf), de Neville had been elected to Parliament with the rank of Baron. The third baron, John Neville, was a warden of the Scottish Marches, Lieutenant of Aquitaine and a notable soldier in the Hundred Years War. He strengthened the family's position by the marriage of his sisters into the Percy and Latimer families.

In 1397, Lord of Raby, Ralph Neville, was created Earl of Westmorland by Richard II. His eldest son, also called Ralph, (1364-1425), married a daughter of John of Gaunt and their sons included peers of the realm and a bishop of Durham, while their daughters included the Abbess of Barking, Duchesses of Norfolk and of Buckingham, as well as Cicely Neville, who was the mother of Kings Edward IV and Richard III. The Nevilles were closely connected to the houses of Lancaster and York and had by that time arguably become the most important family in England.

Unfortunately for them, when in 1569, Charles Neville, the sixth earl, took part in an abortive northern uprising, he was punished by having all his estates, including the castles of Brancepeth and Raby, forfeited to the Crown. When Charles died abroad in 1601, that branch of the family line became extinct, and the lands and titles went to the Latimer branch, one of whom, Edmund, claimed the barony. In 1604, following a longstanding dispute regarding entitlement, James I granted Edward Neville the Barony of Abergavenny.

In 1784, Lord Abergavenny was made an earl. His descendants built a house at Eridge in Sussex, which remains the seat of the family to the present day. The Marquessate of Abergavenny and the Earldom of Lewes were conferred on the family incumbent in 1876. Other branches of the family still reside in Berkshire and Essex.

The Osborne Family of Yorkshire

The Osborne family name comes from an Old English spelling of Osbern, as recorded in the *Domesday Book*, and probably derived from an earlier Norse personal name, 'Asbjorn', from 'as', meaning god, and 'bjorn', meaning bear, hence 'bear god', or perhaps 'divine bear'. The Anglicised version, Osbeorn, translates more precisely as 'god warrior'. Spelling variations include Osbourne, Ausburn and Osborn.

Early family members settled in Normandy some time around 1028. Two of the family were guardians of William the Conqueror and appear in records as Seneschal and Herfast Osborn. William FitzOsborn, (William 'son of Osborn'), fought at Hastings and tradition has it that William the Conqueror offered him his daughter in marriage along with a gift of the Isle of Wight. It is no coincidence that Osborne House, the favourite residence of Victoria, is a major tourist destination on the island.

An early American settler, Richard Osborne, born in London in 1612, sailed to the New World aboard the *Hopewell* in February 1634 and settled in Hingham, Massachusetts, before later moving on to Windsor, Connecticut.

Kyneton House in Kington was the family home of the Osborne family from the early 1700s. In the nineteenth century, it passed to the Maclaines through the marriage of Martha Osborne and Hector Maclaine. Both these families were major landowners in and around Thornbury.

Sir Edward Osborne, (c.1530-92), was an important London merchant in the sixteenth century. He was Governor of the Turkey Company, trading with Spain and Turkey and became Lord Mayor of London in 1586. In 1620, another Sir Edward Osborne, (c.1596-1647), was made Baronet of Kiveton, and was elected to Parliament in 1628.

Sir Edward's son, Thomas Osborne, second Baronet, (1631-1712), was created Viscount Osborne of Dunblane in 1672, and was Lord High Treasurer between 1673 and 1679.

In 1837, Sir Daniel Toler Osborne succeeded as twelfth Baronet Osborne of Ballintaylor and Balleylemon in County Waterford, Ireland. These titles descended down the family line until Elizabeth Charlotte Eden married Baron Francis Godolphin Osborne. With the ninth Baronet's daughter, Ada, succession continued down the Godolphin line until relatively recent times when the Osborne name was resumed.

George Gideon Osborne, (born in 1971), was a Conservative Member of Parliament for the Tatton Constituency in Cheshire until 2016 and served as Chancellor of the Exchequer under Prime Minister David Cameron. In 2017, he gave up his career in politics to become editor of the *London Evening Standard* newspaper.

The Percy Family of Alnwick

Yves de Vescy, the Norman Baron of Alnwick, erected the first parts of Alnwick Castle in Northumbria, (now called Northumberland), in about 1096, to guard the strategic road crossing the River Aln from Scottish incursions. The castle was already sturdily fortified when it was captured by David I of Scotland. Later, in 1212, Eustace de Vesci, Lord of Alnwick, was accused of plotting with Robert FitzWalter against John. As a result, the king ordered the demolition of the Castle as well as Baynard's Castle, though this was never actually carried out.

The last of the Vescy family bequeathed Alnwick to the Bishop of Durham, and in 1309 it was purchased by Henry Percy, first Baron Percy, (1273-1324), along with the Barony of Alnwick. He set about reinforcing the castle further and turning the living quarters into what were described as 'palatial'. In 1345, the Percys also acquired Warkworth Castle in Northumberland, and the family moved to live there.

The Percy surname derives from the Old French verb 'percer', meaning 'to pierce', and 'haie' signifying an enclosure. Hence, the name was often given to a soldier who was noted for breaching a fortification or barricade. It is recorded that one William de Percy, (1030-96), accompanied William the Conqueror to England in 1066.

A family descendant, also named Henry Percy, first Earl of Northumberland, (sometimes known as 'Hotspur'), was instrumental in deposing Richard II. The Alnwick estate was subjected to frequent engagements during the Wars of the Roses, and after the execution of Thomas Percy, the seventh Earl of Northumberland, by Lancastrian victors, it became an uninhabited ruin. It was not until the mid-nineteenth century that the castle was refurbished by Robert Adam in an Italianate style. The current Duke of Northumberland still lives in the castle, which is open to visitors.

The Roos Family of Yorkshire

The Roos family, (sometimes Ros, Roose, Ruse or Ross), is first recorded in East Yorkshire shortly after the Norman Conquest. Roos was originally thought to be a Norman French name which over time may have transcribed into the Old English word 'rouse', meaning red or red-haired. An alternative view suggests the name is derived from an ancient British or Gaelic word 'ros', meaning a hillock or a promontory. Yet another has it of Dutch descent and defines it simply as a corruption of the word 'rose'.

Both the townships of Roos in Yorkshire and Roose in Lancashire are mentioned in the *Domesday Book*, but the first known record of it as a surname was that of Godfrey de Ross who obtained lands in Stewarton in Cuningham, probably some time before 1086.

According to records, the Manor of Roos was the seat of the Roos family since the reign of Henry I, whose members had led the English army during the Battle of Crecy in 1346.

The present incumbents go by the name of De Ros.

The Teasdale Family of County Durham

The surname Teasdale is simply an alternative spelling of Teesdale. It is of Anglo-Saxon origin and a regional surname from County Durham. Recorded as Tesedale in 1139, it is a combination of 'Tees', (the River name), and the Old English word 'dael', meaning a valley. This suffix, and its derivations, is widespread throughout the region (eg. Wharfdale, Ainsdale, etc). A Walter de Tesdale is mentioned in the Assize Rolls for Durham in 1235 and a Mariota de Tesdale in the Subsidy Rolls of Cumberland in 1332. Other early examples of the name include Alan de Teysedale, (1292, in Northumberland), and Thomas Tesdall, (1525, in Sussex).

Teasdales are still found commonly around Coverdale and Otley in Yorkshire, though branches are known to have moved to live in Sussex.

The Tempest Family of Skipton

The first known spelling of the Tempest family name is that of Roger Tempeste, dated 1120, during the reign of Henry I, in the Records of Skipton & Craven. Later, Richard Tempest appears in the 1222 Pipe Rolls of Yorkshire, and in the Poll Tax Returns of 1379 there is a record of Isabella Tempest. The name derives from the Old French 'tempeste', self-evidently meaning 'a violent storm'.

The Tempest family have occupied a residence on the site of Tong Hall, in the former West Riding of Yorkshire, for more than 750 years and are recorded as owning more than 2,000 acres of land in the surrounding region.

A branch of the Tempest family of Holmside, County Durham, descended from Nicolas Tempest, (1486–1539), and went on to have considerable interests in the Newcastle-upon-Tyne coal trade in the late sixteenth and seventeenth centuries.

Another Sir Nicolas Tempest, (1553–1625), was created first Baronet of Tempest in December 1622 by James I, and lived at Stella Hall, a former monastic property in Blaydon, County Durham, which had been granted to the family by Elizabeth I in 1600. His grandson, Richard Tempest, the third Baronet, (c.1620-1641), was a Colonel of Horse, fighting for the Crown during the English Civil War.

Henry Vane-Tempest, (1771–1813), succeeded as the second Baronet Vane of Long Newton in County Durham in June 1794. By this time, he had already changed his surname to Vane-Tempest, as his uncle's will had specified this as a condition for his inheritance of the properties of Brancepeth Castle, Old Durham and Wynyard. He was Member of Parliament for Durham in 1794 and was the ancestor of the Vane-Tempest-Stewarts, Earls Vane and Marquesses of Londonderry. On his death, with no male heirs, the baronetcy became extinct, and his daughter Lady Frances Anne Vane-Tempest, married into the Stewart family, taking their surname for a time, before reverting to Vane in 1821, after which she was titled the Marchioness of Londonderry.

The Tyrwhitt Family of Northumberland

The Trywhitt family name comes from the village of Trewhitt in Northumberland. It first appears in the mid-twelfth century as a parish in Rothbury, originally recorded as Tirwit, which might have meant 'a river bend where wood is cut'. An alternative explanation is that both the family and placenames come from the Old English 'tyri-pvit', meaning either a meadow or a pine forest.

Records show Hurculus de Trywhitt being knighted by William the Conqueror in 1086 and granted the lands of Terwith, (or Tirwit).

A branch of the family removed to live in the Parish of Stainfield in Lincolnshire. Variants of the spelling include Terwitt, Trewitt, Truitt and Truet.

In the late sixteenth century, through marriage into the Hastings family of Leicestershire, and the failure to produce male heirs, the main family line and its name seem to have become extinct.

The Vavasour Family of Hazelwood

The Vavasours date back to Norman times, and are descended from William le Vavasour, who is recorded in the Roll at Battle Abbey as a knight who fought alongside William at Hastings. The family originated in Le Vavassour in Normandy, from where they adopted the family name. Vassyr is a shortened form of the name. In Old French it signified a so-called 'under vassal', that is, a servant's servant, or a person having other vassals serving under him. Other spelling variations include Vavasor and Vavazor.

An early family member was Maud le Vavasour, born about 1105, daughter of Robert le Vavasour, who was Sheriff of Lancashire in 1150. Maud inherited the family estates at Edlington in Yorkshire and Narborough in Leicestershire. She married Theobald Walter who was Butler of Ireland in 1192 and High Sheriff of Lancashire in 1194.

Yet another Sir William Vavasour was a judge in the reign of Henry II and was an adviser to Matilda, Countess of Warwick. By 1217, Robert Vavasour was Sheriff of York and was influential in the enlargement of York Minister, where a statue of him can be found over the West Door.

In 1299, another Sir William le Vavasour was summoned to Parliament as Lord Vavasour, and later, Nicholas Vausour was listed in the 1379 Poll Tax Returns for Yorkshire.

In 1581, as head of a devout Catholic family, Sir John Vavasour was brought before the Commissioners as a recusant, refusing to attend Anglican services. However, Elizabeth I exempted the family from the penal laws against Catholics out of fondness for Ann Vavasour, who was one of her ladies in waiting. She also highly regarded Sir Thomas Vavasour, who sailed in the fleet which fought the Spanish Armada.

Sir Edward Marmaduke Vavasour was made first Baronet Vavasour of Hazelwood in 1828. He died on a pilgrimage to Rome in 1847.

Sir William Edward Joseph Vavasour, the third Baron, inherited the Hazlewood estate in 1885 and was the last of the family to live there. Mounting maintenance costs and large mortgages made its possession untenable, and it was sold off, complete with castle, church and sixty acres of land, into the Stourton family. Spaldingham Hall, an Elizabethan manor house in the East Riding of Yorkshire, was another of the family seats until it was demolished in 1838.

In 1985, the Vavasours established a vineyard in the Awatere Valley of Marlborough, New Zealand. Sir Eric Michel Joseph Marmaduke, the sixth Baron Vavasour, (born in 1953), is the present incumbent and lives in Leicestershire.

Part Two

North-West England
Family Names in Cheshire, Cumbria, Greater Manchester,
Lancashire & Merseyside

The Acker Family of Little Moreton

An Anglo-Saxon surname, which derives from the Old English word 'aecer', meaning a ploughed field or cultivated land. Later, it became acker, (possibly the origin of the imperial land measure acre). There are a number of variations, including Acres, Ackers, Acors, Akers, Akess and Akker.

The first recorded spelling of the family name is that of William de l'Acre in the 1214 Curia Regis Rolls of Sussex, during the reign of John. Jean de Brienne, (c.1241-96), also known as John of Acre, was Grand Butler of France in 1258 and was Ambassador to Castile in Spain in 1275. Joan of Acre, (also known as Joan Plantagenet), born in 1272 in Acre, was the daughter of Edward I and Eleanor of Castile, and was married to the Earl of Gloucester, a title which her children bore thereafter.

Much later, another family member, George Ackers, born 1788, owned Little Moreton Hall near Congleton, and his son, George Holland Ackers, was High Sheriff of Cheshire in 1852.

James Ackers, (1752-1824), described as the 'father of the silk trade', built Lark Hill Mansion on the site of what is now Salford Museum and Art Gallery in Lark Hill Place. He moved from Little Moreton to live there around 1809. In 1792, James was Borough Reeve to the City of Manchester, later Deputy Lieutenant for Lancashire and in 1800 was appointed High Sheriff of the County.

The Ainsworth Family of Halliwell

The surname is of Anglo-Saxon origin, 'Ain', 'Aegen' or 'Hain', probably referring to a man's name, and 'worth', being the old word for an enclosure, hence, 'Ain's enclosure or field'. The place was recorded in the 1200 Pipe Rolls of Lancashire as Hainewrthe, and later that century as Aynesworth.

The earliest recorded use of the surname was by Robert de Aynsworth, who was named in a charter in 1212. He and subsequent Ainsworths were landed gentry, probably of Norman descent. They came into possession of the Manor of Pleasington, (modern day Plessington), during the reign of Henry VI.

Peter Ainsworth was a master bleacher who moved into the Halliwell district of Bolton in 1739 and set up the Halliwell Bleachworks, rapidly becoming wealthy and influential in the area, and leased surrounding estate lands from Captain Roger Dewhurst. Later, the family bought other lands in Halliwell and in 1801 purchased Smithills Hall. The district of Ainsworth and the Ainsworth Road are named after them.

Richard Ainsworth was largely responsible for the building of Jubilee School, and his father, John Horrocks Ainsworth, was instrumental in building St Peter's and St Paul's churches, as well as many farms and other buildings in Halliwell.

A branch of the family hailed from Cumberland. Thomas Ainsworth, (1804-37), of The Flosh in Cumberland, was High Sheriff of the County and a Justice of the Peace. His son, Sir John Stirling Ainsworth, was a Lieutenant Colonel in the Volunteer Battalion of the Borders Regiment in 1898, served as a Liberal Member of Parliament, and was made Baronet Ainsworth in 1917. His son, also named John, was a lieutenant in the 11th Hussars and was killed in action during the First World War.

Anthony Thomas Hugh Ainsworth, born in 1962, is the fifth Baronet Ainsworth. He was also a lieutenant in the Royal Hussars before going into business as a consultant.

The Anderton Family of Lostock

The first record of the Andertons was at Euxton, (pronounced 'Exton'), near Chorley in the fifteenth century, though their ancestry goes back much further. Little is known about their time there, other than their building of Euxton Hall.

The Anderton family name was taken from a place of that name near Ince in the old Parish of Standish in Lancashire. It originated in Old English, a combination of the personal name 'Eanrad' and 'tun', meaning 'the settlement of a man called Eanrad'.

In 1542, James Anderton was born at Clayton Hall. He was to become a lawyer at London's Gray's Inn, and by the age of twenty had built Lostock Hall near Bolton. His cousin was reputed to have farmed for Elizabeth I. Despite this, the family were devout Catholics at a time when, following the Reformation, it was seen as treasonous. Out of favour for their support of Catholic Stuarts during the seventeeth century, they were ultimately reduced to poverty after most of the Anderton estates were sold to the Marlboroughs and Molyneux families.

However, the estates were restored to them in 1677, when Sir Francis Anderton of Lostock Hall, (c.1628-1678), was created Baron Anderton. The title descended through the family line thereafter, until, following his part in the Jacobite Rebellion and the Battle of Preston in 1715, Francis Anderton was convicted of high treason and the estates once again sequestered. The Andertons separated into the two noble families of Euxton and Lostock and the baronetcy became extinct in 1760.

The Antrobus Family of Lymm

The ancient Antrobus family's principal seat was at Antrobus Hall in Great Budworth, near Lymm in Cheshire. The family name probably arrived with the Normans in 1066. Early records mention Edward Antrobus in Yorkshire in 1185, and yet another man of that name in Lancashire in 1273. The family name is recorded in the *Domesday Book* as Entrebus, possibly from the Old Norse personal name 'Andri' and 'buski', meaning a thicket. An alternative derivation may come from the Norman-French 'entre-bois', which can be interpreted as 'within (or between) the woods'.

Antrobus Hall was sold to Thomas Venables in 1460. Shortly thereafter, Joseph Antrobus is known to have married Ann Parr on the 27 August 1572, during the reign of Elizabeth I.

In 1815, Sir Edmund Antrobus was created Baronet Antrobus of Antrobus in the County Palatine of Chester. John Coutts Antrobus, (1829-1916), was a County Councillor for Cheshire and held the rank of Honorary Lieutenant Colonel in the Earl of Chester's Yeomen Cavalry.

Variants exist including Anthrobus, Antrobuss and Entrobus. Branches of the family emigrated to America, with Joan Antrobus settling in Massachusetts in 1635.

The Arden Family of Bredbury

The Arden family, (sometimes Ardern, Arderne or Harden), trace their ancestry to the twelfth century, when they held substantial properties throughout the north of England. They had originally moved to Chester from Warwickshire, when Sir John de Arderne of Alvanley married Joan de Stokeport, (Stockport), daughter of Richard de Stokeport in 1326. William Shakespeare's mother, Anne Arden, also came from the Warwickshire branch.

The family intermarried with local nobility, particularly the Davenports, Leghs and Dones. Their Cheshire estates were in Alvanley, Bredbury, Harden, Tarporley, and Utkinton, as well as lands in Haughton, Lancashire.

Perhaps the most celebrated family member was Richard Pepper Arderne, born in 1745, a lawyer, politician and friend of Prime Minister William Pitt. Richard became Attorney General, was knighted in 1788 and created Baron Alvanley of Alvanley in 1801.

The fifteenth century-built Underbank Hall in Stockport was the town house of the Arderne family until it was sold in 1823, and eventually purchased by a banking company as a commercial premises.

The Ardens also purchased other important properties in the region, including Pepper Arden Hall in South Cowton, Yorkshire and Ardene Hall in Tarporley, Cheshire.

The Assheton Family of Downham

The Asshetons date back to the Norman Conquest, with ancestors fighting at Hastings. The name simply means 'ash town', describing the ancient topography of Ashton, (formerly known as Assheton-under-Lyne), from where the family took their surname.

Ralph de Assheton of Great Lever in Lancashire, (1421–86), was knighted by Richard III in 1483. A reportedly cruel and tryranical man, he was subsequently known as 'The Black Knight of Ashton', and an effigy of him is still paraded annually through the town of Ashton-under-Lyme. His son, also named Ralph, served as Receiver of the Revenue for the Duchy of Lancashire and was Member of Parliament for Liverpool in 1553.

Yet another Ralph was High Sheriff of Lancashire in 1579. By 1620, the family had been created Barons Assheton of Lever, but when the fourth Baron, Sir John Assheton, died childless in 1624, the baronetcy became extinct.

The Asshetons formed an alliance by marriage with the Hothams. Later they were members of the so-called Long Parliament, of which Oliver Cromwell was a member. Sir John Assheton was also knighted by the king on the battlefield at Northampton.

The family acquired many lands throughout Lancashire, including Middleton, Downham, Cuerdale, Clitheroe and Rochdale. A branch of the family also purchased lands in Whalley Abbey following Henry VIII's Dissolution of the Monasteries. They formerly lived at Middleton Hall, but had built a new country seat at Downham Hall near Preston and lived there from 1558. Lord of the Manor, Ralph Assheton, took the title of Lord Clitheroe when he was knighted in 1955 and remains the present owner of Downham Hall.

The Asshetons had many disparate branches spread throughout Lancashire, including at Penketh, Preston, Glazebrook and Croston.

The Baguley Family of Worsley

Places called Baguley occur as far apart as Berkshire, Shropshire, Somerset and Cheshire, and appear to be of Anglo-Saxon origin. The name is recorded in 995 as Bacgan leah and as Bagelei in the *Domesday Book*. There are several confused explanations of the origin of the placename, but most authorities seem to prefer the Old English 'Bacga', a man's personal name, and the suffix 'leah', meaning a woodland clearing. Hence, 'Bacga's wood (or clearing)'.

The family took their surname from the ancient district of Baggiley in Cheshire, which, during the eleventh century, was held by Hamo Massy, (sometimes Masci), who was created Baron of Durham Massey by William of Normandy for his support in the Conquest.

In the early thirteenth century, during the reign of John, a family descendant, Matthew Massy de Bromhale, (Bramhall), was given lands in Baggiley, (in present day Wythenshawe), and his heirs adopted the family name.

Later, Sir William de Baggiley was knighted by Edward I and married one of his daughters, (possibly Lucy Corona, though some have it as Isabel). This saw the Baguley family highly promoted in English aristocracy.

Sir William built Baguley Hall in 1320 when he was Lord of the Manors of Hyde and Levenshulme. Through marriage, in 1353 these lands passed to Sir John Leigh of Booth, in whose family they remained until the late seventeeth century, when the line terminated in Edward Leigh. It finally passed into the hands of the Tattons in 1825.

Over time, the surname gradually morphed from Baggiley into Baguley, and is now marked by a district of the same name in South Manchester.

Bigalow, a fairly common name in many colonial countries, particularly in America, is a derivation of Baggiley.

The Barlow Family of Chorlton

The Barlow surname may derive from places of the same name in Derbyshire and Lancashire and may either be Anglo-Saxon meaning 'bare hill', (in reference to people who may have lived there), or else come from the Old English 'bere', meaning 'barley', and 'leag' or 'leah', indicating a clearing. This last explanation may therefore be taken to signify a woodland clearing where barley grew. In 1086, the *Domesday Book* listed a Berleie in Derbyshire, Berlie in Shropshire, and Berlai in Yorkshire.

The township of Barlow also appears as Berlawe in the 1260 Assize Court Rolls of Lancashire. The family held the Manor of Barlow in Chorlton-cum-Hardy after Thomas de Barlow set up in residence around 1200 and adopted it as his surname. By 1389, Roger de Barlow was also in possession of lands in Chorlton, Hardy, and Withington, where the family built Barlow Hall and a small half-timbered chapel.

Alexander Barlow, who was Lord of the Manor in 1567, was also a devout Catholic and fell foul of the religious changes made by Elizabeth I. He was committed to prison, where he died in August 1584. Another notable family member was Edward Barlow, known as St Ambrose Barlow, who also became a Catholic martyr as a result of his missionary work in Lancashire, which saw him repeatedly imprisoned, before he was finally executed on the instructions of Parliament at Lancaster on 10 September 1641.

In 1773, the family estates, including Barlow Hall, were sold off and became the property of the Egerton family of Tatton. In March 1879, the west wing of Barlow Hall was almost entirely destroyed by fire; all trace of the great hall was lost, while other parts of the building sustained extensive damage. What remains of the Hall is a Grade II Listed Building, and in recent times has been converted into a golf club house. Barlow Moor Road in south Manchester is named after the family.

The Barton Family of Smithills

The Bartons were a wealthy family of sheep owners, who over successive centuries, extended considerable influence over the Smithills (sometimes Smethells) Deane district of Bolton. The name Barton comes from the Anglo-Saxon 'bere', meaning barley, and 'tun', an enclosure or settlement. The name is recorded in the *Domesday Book* as Bertone, a township in Preston Parish. One of the earliest known spellings of the name appears in the name of Aelfric aet Bertune in the Anglo-Saxon Name Register during the reign of Ethelred Unraed in 1015.

William Radclyffe, (or Radcliffe), obtained the Manor of Smithills from the Hultons in 1335. However, the family failed to produce male heirs, and in 1485, Cecily, the last of the Radclyffes to own the estate, married her second cousin John Barton, through which his family came to own Smithills Hall.

In 1516, John Barton gave the lands to his son Andrew, and he lived at the Hall with his wife Agnes, as did their descendants. Finally, Grace, the only heir of Thomas Barton, married Henry, first Lord Viscount Fauconberg, whose descendants sold the Manor to the Byrom family in 1721.

Sir Roger Barton, a celebrated magistrate in Bolton in the mid-sixteenth century, was renowned for sentencing George March, the heretic cleric, to be burned at the stake in 1554.

In 1801, the Hall and estate were sold to the Ainsworth family, who extensively rebuilt and extended it. In 1999, Smithills Hall was taken over by Bolton Council, having been a restaurant for many years in the late twentieth century. Latterly its outbuildings have become home to an animal farm attraction which is open to the public, while the original hall remains private property.

The Baskervyle Family of Chelford

The Baskervyles, (sometimes Baskervilles, Basquevilles or Baskervyyles), almost certainly acquired the surname from their place of origin, which has been identified as either Boscherville in the Eure region of Normandy, Basqueville in the Pays de Card, or Bosherville near Rouen. Whatever its origin, the name was brought to England from France after the Conquest. It derives from two old northern French words: 'bochet', meaning a copse or a thicket, and 'ville', a town. It may be interpreted therefore as 'a township in a copse'.

The *Domesday Book* records Sir Robert de Baskerville living at Eardisley Castle in Herefordshire, possibly granted to him by the

Conqueror. Indeed, this may have been the family's first settlement in England, though they held yet another castle near the River Wye at Bredwardine, on the Welsh-English border.

The northern branch of the De Baskervyle family lived at Baskerville Hall, sometimes known as 'Old Withington', near Chelford in Cheshire, which Sir John Baskervyle acquired from Robert de Camville, along with its estate, in 1266. According to the Prestbury parish records, the Baskervyles lived there till around 1570. An influential family, they held other substantial lands in the county and on the Wirral Peninsula.

A branch of the family, the Baskervyle-Gleggs, moved to Goostry in Cheshire around 1737, where they remained well into the 1890s.

There is an account that, during the building of the Hooton to West Kirby branch railway in the nineteenth century, the landowner, a member of the Baskervyle-Glegg family, insisted upon a station being built at Thurstaston, much against the railway company's wishes. However, due to his status in the local area, the railway acceded to his condition.

Some time around 1865, Lucy Baskervyle-Glegg of Withington Hall, married the son of the third Viscount St Vincent of Norton Disney and Sutton-in-Derwant in Yorkshire. In 1906, John Baskervyle-Glegg of Withington Hall and Egerton Leigh of Jodrell Hall were joint Lords of the Manor of Goostry. Both of these families are listed in the 1937 edition of *Burke's Landed Gentry*. Withington Hall was demolished in 1958.

During the mid-1950s, another John Baskervyle-Glegg attended Rugby School, and yet another of that name played in the England Cricket team in 1962. More recently, the 2000 Edition of the Royal Horticultural Society's yearbook *The Garden* contained a chapter entitled 'A Rector's Pastoral: Adam's Apples' by Diana Baskervyle-Glegg.

The Birch Family of Rusholme

The Birch family traced their lineage back to the twelfth century and are best remembered for Birch Hall and Birchfields Park in Rusholme.

Walter de la Birch is one of the earliest known bearers of the name, it being recorded in a charter of 1182. There is also a Richard de Birches recorded in the Lancashire Assize Court Rolls in 1246. The family were granted lands in the district of Hyndley Birch, for service in the Crusades, where they built Birch Hall as well as a small family chapel on the site, which they dedicated to St James.

The name is a modern derivation of the Old English word 'birce', which literally means a birch tree.

The family sided with the Parliamentarian faction in the Civil Wars and were principal agents in securing Manchester against the Earl of Derby.

In 1689, John Birch was the High Sheriff of Lancashire. In latter days the estate passed to Manchester businessmen John Dickenson and then to the Anson family. Birch Hall was demolished in 1926 and the site is now in the grounds of the Manchester Grammar School.

The Bold Family of Bold

The Bold family, (sometimes Boulde, Bowld or Bould), trace their origins back to Anglo-Saxon times, but the earliest written record in 1154 is of one William de Bold, (c.1130-1160). Later, Geoffrey de Bolde was listed as a witness at the Assize Court of Stafford in 1199.

The name has three possible origins: first, an Anglo-Saxon word 'bold', meaning a 'small farm'. Second, simply meaning, as it says – bold, or brave. Third, and most likely, the family adopted its surname from the village of Bold in Lancashire.

It was in 1402 that John de Bold was the garrison commander who defended Caernarfon Castle against Owain Glyndwr. He was subsequently knighted, made Constable of the Castle and was granted five thousand acres at Bold. In 1407 he became the High Sheriff of Lancashire, and held the post until his death in 1410, the first of six Bold family descendants to do so. Earlier, in 1406, he had founded the Chantry, now the site of Bold Chapel in St Luke's Farnworth in Widnes, (formerly St Wilfrid's). Later, in 1415, his son Thomas fought alongside Henry V at Agincourt.

By 1588, Bold family estates extended as far as Buckinghamshire and Yorkshire, and minor branches of the family also had holdings in Ireland.

In more recent times, Jonas Bold became the Lord Mayor of Liverpool in 1802. In 1829, Sir Henry Bold-Hoghton was High Sheriff of Lancashire. The family had royal connections in the personage of Mary Patten-Bold, (1795-1824), daughter of Peter and Mary Patten-Bold. Mary was married to Prince Sapieha, (Ostafi Eustace Sapieha Rozanski) of Dereczym in the Duchy of Lithuania.

The Bolds are represented in the Knowsley, Halton and old St Helens coats of arms. Liverpool's Bold Street is named after them.

The Booth Family of Dunham Massey

The Manor of Dunham is recorded in the *Domesday Book* as having belonged to Aelfward, a Saxon thegn before the Norman Conquest, and to Hamo de Massy, (sometimes Masci), afterwards. The Barons de Massy also had control over the surrounding manors of Baguley, Bowdon, Hale, Partington, and Timperley. They remained Lords of Dunham until the fourteenth century, when the family's male line became extinct and in 1409 the Booth family inherited most of the estate. The Booths trace their ancestry back to early medieval times when their name appears in several different forms, including Bouth, Booths and Bothe.

By Tudor times, the family had intermarried with neighbouring aristocratic families, as did George Booth, (1515-43), who married Elizabeth de Trafford, and Sir William Booth, (1540-79), who married Elizabeth Warburton of Arley.

The unfortunate Lady Jane Grey, the great-neice of Henry VIII, who fell prey to Queen Mary's axeman in 1554, was a daughter of the Booth family.

Later, another Sir George Booth fought for the Parliamentarian cause during the First Civil War. He was elected Member of Parliament for Cheshire in May 1645 and to the First Protectorate Parliament in 1654, before being commissioned to assist the major generals in

Cheshire. However, he fell out of favour when he described them as 'Cromwell's hangmen'. By 1659, he was plotting with Royalists to bring about the Restoration of the monarchy, and headed an abortive insurrection during the summer of 1659. Defeated, Booth was arrested and imprisoned in the Tower of London, but was eventually released on bail.

Ironically, in 1660, Booth was elected to the Convention Parliament. He was one of twelve MPs appointed to facilitate the return of Charles II to the throne. At the king's coronation in April 1661, Booth was made Lord Delamere. In the eigtheenth century, the Booths were also created Earls of Warrington.

The Bostock Family of Cheshire

The Bostocks trace their ancestry back to Osmer, a Saxon Lord who was Thegn of the Manor of Bostock in Cheshire. After the 1066 Conquest, Osmer was dispossessed of the land in favour of a new Norman overlord, Hugh d'Avranches, (known as Hugh the Fat), who became Earl of Chester. He ceded the land to the Vernon Family, who shortly after taking possession, adopted the family name De Bostock, in keeping with Norman tradition.

The Bostocks went on to hold extensive lands throughout the region, including Great Budworth, Warmingham, Church Coppenhall and Church Minshull.

The village of Bostock was recorded in the *Domesday Book* as Botestoch. Later, in 1260, it was recorded as Bostoc in the Cheshire Pipe Rolls. The name derives from the Old English personal name 'Bota' and the suffix 'stocc', or 'stoche', the latter usually taken to indicate a council meeting place or holy place.

The name of William de Bostock, (sometimes known as Lord of Bostock), is found in documents relating to Middlewich and the salt industry between 1255 and 1295. It was this same William who fought against Simon de Montfort at the Battle of Evesham in October 1265.

By the time of the Reformation, the family were strict Puritans and, dissatisfied by intolerance of Catholics, Arthur Bostock emigrated to America around 1640 and established a large Connecticut-New Hampshire Bostock ancestry. The surname is sometimes written as Bostwick or Bostick in America.

The Bostocks built Broadbottom Hall in 1680 and occupied it until the nineteenth century. It has been scheduled as a Grade II Listed Building of architectural and historic interest since 1990.

The Bradshaw Family of Wigan

It is thought that Sir William Bradshaw was first user of the surname, having taken it from the earlier form of the placename 'Bradshaigh', (sometimes Bradishaigh or Bradshagh). The family owned the districts of Haigh and Blackrod for many years, but these were eventually given to the Crown in exchange for a knighthood. The aforesaid William was known for his participation in the Crusades to the Holyland in 1314, when, failing to return, his wife Mabel supposing him dead, married Sir Osmond Nevile. When William did actually return after ten years' absence, following a prolonged chase after his usurper, he killed the unfortunate Nevile. The event is commemorated by a stone monument at Mabel's Cross, (known locally as Mab's Cross), in Standishgate, Wigan.

The placename is recorded in the Lancashire Assize Rolls of 1246 as Bradeshaghe, and means 'the broad wood or grove', from the Old English 'brad', meaning broad or wide, combined with 'sceaga', indicating a thicket.

Following the Civil War, in 1649, John Bradshaw was appointed as president of the High Court and presided at the trial of Charles I for high treason. Many other eminent lawyers had refused to sit in judgement of the king, and Bradshaw was virtually unknown at the time of his appoinment. Formerly, he had been Attorney General for Cheshire and Flintshire. The warrant for the king's execution was signed at Bradshaw's own house in Walton-on-Thames and his was the first of the named signatories to appear on the death warrant. After the execution, Bradshaw accrued many honours and acquired considerable wealth, becoming President of the Council of State, at that time the highest office in England. Later he became Chancellor of the Duchy of Lancashire.

The Bradshaw family continued to reside at Haigh Hall, as they had done since the time of Edward II. The Hall eventually became the seat of the Earl of Balcarres.

The Brereton Family of Handforth

The Brereton family line begins in 1175 with William de Brereton, who arrived in England with William the Conqueror. Initially, Duke William granted the land to Hugh the Fat, who became Earl of Chester. He parcelled out portions of land to others, including one Gilbert Hunter, who in turn gave portions to his subordinates, one of whom was possibly William, who began to use the placename as his family surname De Brereton, a common custom at the time.

When they became Lords of the Manor of Bosden in the early 1500s, the Breretons established Handforth Hall as their country seat.

Later, a less fortunate family member, also named William, along with four companions, was sent to the Tower charged with high treason as lovers of Anne Boleyn. Despite protestations, they were sentenced to death and beheaded on Tower Hill in 1536. Anne was herself beheaded two days later.

Yet another William Brereton, (1604-61), was created Baron Brereton of Hanforde (Handforth) in Cheshire in 1626. He was Commander-in-Chief of the Cheshires at the Battle of Middlewich and in the Siege of Nantwich in the Civil War. Later, he went on to serve twice as a Councillor of State.

Some argue that the surname is of probable Norman French origin and means the 'place of the brier rose' or 'a place covered with briers'. Others that it is derived from the township of Bretune in Brittany. Whichever, it was entered in the *Domesday Book* as Bretone, held by Gilbert, (known as 'the Huntsman'), after it had been confiscated from a Saxon called Wulgeat.

Over the centuries, the family exerted power and influence widely over Cheshire, with holdings in Handforth, Malpas, Cheadle and at their later country seat at Brereton Hall. Sir Richard Brereton was the last owner of Tatton Park before the Egerton family took possession in the sixteenth century.

The Bulkeley Family of Cheadle & Beaumaris

The Bulkeley family, (sometimes Bulkelegh or Buckley), derives from the Anglo-Saxon township in the Parish of Malpas in Cheshire, from where they took the name. It comes from the Old English 'bulluc', meaning a bullock, and 'leah', indicating a woodland clearing. This suggests that at one time the place was a clearing in which bulls were kept. The earliest record of the name was that of Robert de Bulkelegh in Cheshire in 1259.

They were for many years an important land-owning family of south Manchester. As early as 1326, part of the Manor of Cheadle was known as Cheadle Bulkeley, having been acquired by Richard de Bulkelegh through marriage. He also inherited a part of neighbouring Cheadle Mosley, which in the late nineteenth century became the district of Cheadle, in Stockport. Thereafter, the estate passed to succeeding generations until, through wastefulness, they were forced to sell off the estate to the Reverend Thomas Egerton in 1756.

In another branch of the family, Sir Richard Bulkeley of Beaumaris, (c.1500-47), was Chamberlain of North Wales. His great-grandfather was Sir William Troutbeck, a descendant of Edward I, and later family members were made Viscounts Beaumaris.

In the seventeeth century, Humphrey Bulkeley served in the Parliamentarian army during the English Civil War and succeeded to the Cheadle estates. He died unmarried aged sixty and is buried, along with several other members of the Bulkeley family, in St Mary's Parish churchyard in Cheadle.

St. Mary's still displays the Bulkeley coat of arms, as well as stained glass commemorating the marriage of the third Sir Richard Bulkeley in 1577. The Bulkeleys of Beaumaris are today one of the leading families in North Wales, and still live in Anglesey.

The Byrom Family of Manchester

The surname relates to the word 'byre' an old word for a barn, and the Old English word 'byrum', meaning 'people who live by the cattle shed or barn'. The surname Byron, best known in the person of the celebrated poet Lord Byron, is a variant on the name. One of the first recorded spellings of the name is one Roger de Birum, who was listed as a witness in the Yorkshire Fines Court Rolls of 1240.

The Manchester Byroms were a prosperous and influential family in the city, and they owned several substantial houses around the region. Their considerable wealth had been gained from dealing in linen drapery. Most of the district of Royton was held by the family during the thirteenth century and remained so until the early seventeeth century.

By 1585, it is recorded that Sir John Byrom, first Baron Byrom of Rochdale, lived at Royton Hall, having sold the family estates in Ancoats to the Moseley family. He was High Sheriff of Nottinghamshire, served as Lieutenant of the Tower of London and was an Officer of the Royal Bedchamber. During the Civil War, in 1642 he commanded Royalist forces at the Battle of Edgehill.

A timber-framed sixteenth century monastic building in Kersal known as 'the Kersal Cell' was purchased by the Byrom family in the 1660s, but subsequently fell into disrepair and was demolished. In the eigtheenth century, Byrom Hall became the ancestral home of the celebrated poet John Byrom. Tradition has it that it was there, in 1749, that he wrote the hymn *Christians, Awake*.

The Chadderton Family of Chadderton

The Chadderton family take their name from the district, which is now in the Metropolitan Borough of Oldham in Greater Manchester. The name is of Anglo-Saxon origin and has been recorded as both Chaderton and Chaterton, comprised of the Old Welsh word 'cader', meaning a hill fort, and the Old English 'tun', indicating a settlement.

Some of its most notable family members were High Sheriffs of Lancashire, and others governed the Isle of Man for the Earl of Derby. They came into ownership of the lands of Chadderton under a medieval system of land tenure, whereby the district was sublet to the De Trafford Family, and in about 1235 Richard de Trafford gave the lands to his son Geoffrey, who became the founder of the Chadderton family. Geoffrey had Chadderton Hall built and became Lord of the Manor of Chadderton.

By 1367, the manor had passed into the possession of the Radclyffe family, who were one of the most illustrious families in England. John de Radclyffe, Lord of Chadderton, fought at Agincourt in 1415, and was knighted by Henry V. William Chadderton, (c.1540-1608), born in Moston, was a Professor of Divinity, an academic and onetime Bishop of London and of Chester.

The Oldham Metropolitan Borough coat of arms still bears the griffin, a device taken from that of the Chadderton family. Chadderton Hall was demolished in 1939.

The Charnock Family of Astley Hall

The family took their name from Charnock Richard near Chorley, where they had their original home, an area now famed as the home of the Camelot Theme Park. The name was originally of probable Welsh origin; it was variously written as Chernoc and Chernoch and comes from the word 'carn', Old Welsh for a rock or stone; hence 'a rocky district'.

Robert Charnock rebuilt Astley Hall, married five times, firstly to Isobel Norris of Speke Hall in Liverpool, and promoted the building of the first school in Chorley in 1611.

The family had a somewhat chequered history, with Robert's younger brother, John, being executed for high treason in 1586, following an abortive attempt to overthrow Elizabeth and replace her with Mary, Queen of Scots, known as the Babington Plot. Robert Charnock died in 1616.

By 1624, Thomas Charnock was Member of Parliament for Newton-in-Makerfield. Royalists to a man, like many other

Lancashire families who followed the old religion, after the Civil Wars ended the family was heavily fined by Parliament for their support of Charles I.

Robert Charnock, the last of the family male line, died in 1653. His daughter and sole heir, Margaret, married Richard Brooke from Mere in Cheshire and thereafter Astley Hall passed through marriage to the Brooke family and thence to the Parkers. In the early twentieth century it went to the Tattons.

The Cheetham Family of Stalybridge

The Cheetham surname was first found in the district of that name in north Manchester and dates back to the twelfth century. The name is comprised of two elements: 'ced', a Celtic name meaning 'forest', and the Old English word 'ham', signifying a settlement of some kind. The name may therefore be translated as 'the settlement or homestead in a wood named Chet', (or belonging to a man called Chet) – either is possible. One of the earliest recorded occurrences of it as a surname is that of Geoffrey de Chetham in the Lancashire Assize Rolls of 1246; he is known to have held lands in Allerton in Yorkshire, which was entered in the *Domesday Book* as Alretone and Alreton.

In the late sixteenth century, Sir Humphrey Chetham, (1580-1653), was a Manchester merchant, who was responsible for the creation of Chetham's Hospital, (now Chetham's Music School), as well as the adjacent Chetham's Library, one of the oldest public libraries in the world, and the place where Karl Marx and Friedrich Engels did much of their writing. Born in Crumpsall and educated at Manchester Grammar School, Chetham developed a profitable textile manufacturing business from which he acquired considerable wealth. He became High Sheriff of Lancashire in 1631.

The Cheethams remained an important textile family, and were major employers and benefactors in Stalybridge, where in the late eigtheenth and early nineteenth centuries they built the Castle Street and Bankwood Mills. The Cheetham Park & Eastwood Nature Reserve, which is one of the nation's oldest RSPB areas, was presented to Stalybridge by the Cheetham family. John Cheetham, (1802-86), a local philanthropist, helped establish local libraries and art galleries, and was at one time the Member of Parliament for Salford.

The Chorlton Family of Chorlton

The Chorlton Family name is evident in districts of Manchester like Chorlton-cum-Hardy and Chorlton on Medlock and traces its history back to 1546, during the reign of Henry VIII, when George Chorlton is reputed to have been granted the family coat of arms.

The surname is an Anglo-Saxon locational name, there being several places called Chorlton in England. It is derived from two words, the Old English 'ceorla', (plural of 'ceorl' or 'churl'), meaning 'peasant', and 'tun', meaning an enclosure or settlement. The parish of Chorlton near Nantwich in Cheshire was recorded in the *Domesday Book* as Cherletune, and as Cheluerton in the 1259 Lancashire Assize Court Rolls for Manchester. Charlton is another probable derivation of the surname.

By the late eigtheenth century, Dinah Chorlton lived at Withington Old Hall, in Manchester, and her farmlands extended for well over a thousand acres. It was the only manor house in Manchester boasting a moat at that time. In total, the Chorltons held nineteen farms, including Dog House Farm, Chorltons Farm, and Catch Croft Farm.

In more recent times, Squire Robert Chorlton had been a technical author for A.V. Roe & Company, manufacturing aeroplanes in Manchester, and was a founder member of the Manchester & Lancashire Family History Society.

The Clayton Family of Clayton-le-Moors & Adlington

Robert de Clayton, (sometimes Cleaton or Claiton), came to England with William the Conqueror and was granted lands known as Clayton-le-Moors for his military service during the 1066 invasion. The name derives from Ancient British words 'clog' and 'tun', meaning, literally 'village on the clay'.

In the twelfth century the family built Clayton Hall, where reputedly, Oliver Cromwell billeted his troops before the assault on Manchester in the Civil War.

When Adam de Grimshaw, (born in 1313), married Cicely Clayton, he adopted the Clayton surname and moved to live with her at the Hall, while the remainder of the Grimshaws continued to live at Crowtree near Blackburn.

The Manor of Adlington in Lancashire was purchased by Thomas Clayton some time around 1688. He also bought the adjoining Manor of Worthington, whereafter both were passed by descent to members of the Clayton family. Most notable of these was Richard Clayton, who became Lord Chief Justice of the Common Pleas in Ireland, a post he held from 1765 until his death in 1770.

Later, another Richard Clayton served as Recorder of Wigan from 1815 until his death in 1828, and was Constable of Lancaster Castle, as well as being the British Consul at Nantes in France. He had been created a Baronet in 1774 and died while serving at Nantes, after which time his brother, Robert, succeeded to the baronetcy and estates.

Richard Browne-Clayton died in 1886 and the Adlington Hall estate, comprising one hundred and twenty-nine acres was sold off. In 1921 it was purchased by Wigan Corporation.

The Clowes Family of Broughton

The family emerged as major landholders in the Broughton district of Salford in the early eigtheenth century. First mention of the surname occurs in 1721, when John and Helen Radcliffe sold Booths Hall to Samuel Clowes, a Manchester merchant, who systematically bought land and property in the area, including the Tyldesley Manor, which was part of the Lordship of Tyldesley.

Clowes bequeathed land holdings to his grandson, also named Samuel, (an appellation continued in the Clowes family). On Christmas Day 1782, he leased two farm holdings to Warrington School. He also made a great deal of money out of the construction of the many canals that were being dug in the region. Records show a bill and receipt to the value of £257 12s 1d, for purchase of land in Boothstown, taken for the Leigh Canal, 'paid to Sam Clowes, Esq., by His Grace the Duke of Bridgewater'. Another sum of £97 5s 10d was paid by one John Coupe, for use of the land in Boothstown in Worsley, for rights to build a canal.

Through numerous land deals, the family grew rich. By 1840, Broughton consisted of just over a thousand acres, of which some eight hundred and seventy were owned by the Reverend John Clowes, a notable gardener and botanist. It was under his stewardship that St John's Parish Church on Wellington Street was built, entirely from family funds. Reverend Clowes was its rector for sixty-two years and was buried there when he died.

The family developed Broughton Park for housing in the early nineteenth century, specifying that all the dwellings should be of substantial rateable value. Many still stand there as well as in nearby Higher Broughton.

When a turnpike road was proposed to run from Manchester through Clowes land to Strangeways, bitter negotiations took place with the family. Their insistence on Toll Bars was very controversial, but the completion of Bury New Road added even more money to the family coffers.

Great Clowes Street in the Higher and Lower Broughton districts of Salford was named after the family.

The Dacre Family of Greystoke

There is an opinion that the origin of the Dacre family name was probably d'Acre and derived from a member of the family who reputedly served during the Third Crusade at the siege of Acre in 1191. However, this is unsubstantiated.

The family was first found in Dacre, a village near Penrith in Cumberland, and listed in a document of 1125 as Dacor. The village name was most likely derived from the Welsh word 'deigr', or from the Old Norman 'dacr', (meaning a 'tear'), and referring to 'a trickling stream'.

According to the Domesday Survey, Dacre was originally held by Uctred, and the manor subsequently passed to William de Dakyr, which he held under Thomas, Earl of Lancaster. The Dacres also held the Greystoke and Gillesland baronies, as well as many other estates in Cumberland, Northumberland and the adjoining counties.

Later, in 1278, another William Dacre was made Sheriff of Cumberland, during the reign of Edward I. In 1321, Ralph Dacre was summoned to Parliament as Lord Dacre, and within the year was appointed High Sheriff of Cumberland and Governor of Carlisle. He was married some time in the fourteenth century to Margaret, second Baroness Multon of Gilsland, and heiress of a large estate around Naworth Castle in Cumbria, as well as lands in North Yorkshire. She built Dacre Castle as her home shortly after the death of her husband. With no issue, after her death Margaret's estates passed in their entirety to the Crown.

Humphrey Dacre was created Lord Dacre of Gildland in 1473, a title that descended down the family line until recent times, when, upon the death of John Thomas Archibald Douglas-Home, the twenty-eighth Baron, in 2014, his daughter, Emily Douglas-Home became twenty-ninth Baroness Dacre.

Other variants of the surname include Dacker, Daker, Dakre, and Dakers. Greystoke was also the noble family name that author Edgar Rice Burroughs chose for his eponymous hero, Tarzan.

The Davenport Family of Bramhall

The Davenport family originally lived in Astbury, near Congleton in Cheshire. Their origins can be traced back to Ormus de Davenport at the time of the Norman Conquest. He was given the Manor of Davenport from the Venables of Kinderton, the original Norman feudal Lords. The name is recorded at the time of the *Domesday Book* as Deneport, held by Gilbert, and previously posessed by the Saxon, Godwine. It is almost certainly named from the River Dane, ('Dauen' or 'Daan' in Old English), that runs through the local landscape.

In 1166, Ormus' son, Richard, became the chief forester of Leek and Macclesfield. Later the family acquired the hereditary status of Magistrate Sergeants of the Forest of Macclesfield. Branches of the Davenport family lived at Calveley, Wheltrough, Woodford, Capesthorne and Bramhall.

Some time around 1590, Sir Humphrey Davenport was Lord Chief Baron of the Exchequer, and was married to Mary Sutton of Sutton Hall

Bramall Hall was the grand home for the Davenport family in Stockport. It is recognised as one of Greater Manchester's grandest timber framed buildings and dates back to the fourteenth century. The Davenports resided there for five hunded years. Subsequent owners carried out substantial refurbishment in the nineteenth century. It now belongs to Stockport Metropolitan Borough Council and is open to the public. Bramhall Park used to be the parkland and woodland estate attached to Bramall Hall.

Capesthorne Hall in Cheshire is stilled owned and occupied by the Bromley Davenport branch of the family, who have resided there since the eleventh century.

The De Lacy Family of Clitheroe

The Lacy family name is first recorded for Hugh de Lacy, (1020–85). Alternative spellings of the family name include Laci, Lacy, and Lascy. Their possession of the town of Clitheroe began when it was granted to Lord Roger de Poitou, (sometimes Pictou or Potevan), by William, following his support in the invasion. Lacy had also been a hero at Hastings, as was his brother Ilbert, both of whom were from the town of Lassy in the Calvados region of Normandy, and from where they acquired the surname.

In 1121, Poitou passed the territory on to Hugh's son Gautier (or Walter) de Lacy. They held it for almost 200 years and built Clitheroe Castle, possibly the oldest surviving building in Lancashire, some time around 1186.

Ilbert was rewarded for his part in the invasion with a gift of the district of Blackburnshire, with 170 lordships, of which 150 were in

Yorkshire. He also held the Manor of Rochdale, the town and castle of Pontefract, and extensive lands in Lincolnshire and Nottinghamshire. Part of the Burnley Borough Council coat of arms still bears the Lacy Knot. Large areas around Pendle and Rossendale were for many centuries the family's private hunting grounds.

The Yorkshire branch of the family took the name 'de Pontefract', while others were Earls of Lincoln. Walter de Lacy seems also to have acquired lands in Shropshire, where he developed Ludlow Castle. The hamlet of Stanton Lacy, (originally the Saxon hamlet of 'Stantun'), in Ludlow was renamed after him. From around 1086, Walter's sons, Roger and Hugh, built the earliest surviving parts of the castle and the De Lacy family retained the Lordship of Ludlow until the end of the thirteenth century.

Many succeeding generations married into county aristocracy, particularly its female members. Roger de Lacy was constable of Chester between 1193 and 1211. Walter de Lacy's great granddaughter, Elizabeth de Burgh, married Robert the Bruce, of Scotland.

The De La Warre Family of Manchester

In 1204, King John granted John de la Warre the Lordship of Bristol and in 1206 he was made Lord of the Manor of Wickwar in Gloucestershire. The ancient market town of Wickwar, derives its name from 'wick', (meaning 'a turn in a stream'), and 'war', from the manor having belonged to the De la Warre family.

On the death of Thomas Greddle, (sometimes Grelley or Grelly), the eighth Baron of Manchester in 1347, the vast estates of the family passed, through the marriage of his sister Johanna, to John de la Warre. The De la Warre family held the Manor of Manchester thereafter for over a century.

During the reigns of Edward I, Edward II, Edward III and Richard II, successive members of the De la Warre were called to be Members of Parliament. Sir Roger de la Warre, the third Baron de la Warre, (1326-70), had distinguished himself during the Hundred Years War at the Battle of Crecy in 1346.

In 1422 Lord of the Manor, Thomas de la Warre, (1359-1426), founded a college, granted by royal licence, (now 'Chets' music school and Chethams Library), and a collegiate church, (now Manchester Cathedral). Thomas was a priest in the parish of Ashton-under-Lyne from around 1371, and afterwards became rector at Manchester, though he did not inherit the title of Baron until the death of his elder brother John, who died childless in 1398.

De la Warre maintained his interest and patronage in the collegiate church until his death in 1426. There is a statue of Thomas La Warre on the facade of Manchester Town Hall.

Later, another celebrated family member, Thomas West, Baron de la Warre, is recorded as having married Cecilia, daughter of Sir Thomas Shirley the proprietor of the Virginia Company, in 1596. Thomas was Virginia's first governor and became immortalised in giving his surname to Delaware Bay, (initially Delawarre), as well as to the river and state in America.

The De Trafford Family of Trafford Park

The De Trafford family were one of the foremost Catholic families in Victorian Britain, and trace their ancestry back well before Norman times. A member of the family is said to have served King Cnut. Radulphus, an early forebear, died in about 1050, during the reign of Edward the Confessor.

The surname is a direct corruption of 'Stratford', from the Old English 'straet', indicating a Roman road, and 'ford', a river crossing.

The family's long association with Trafford Park dates at least from the late twelfth century and an early bearer of the family name, Sir Henry de Trafford, who died in 1334. Nowadays the name is perhaps best known for the Trafford Centre, Old Trafford and Trafford Park. Over time, they acquired power and influence throughout north-west England, so that by the seventeeth century they were knights of the realm with many generations serving as High Sheriffs of Lancashire.

In 1841, Sir Thomas Joseph de Trafford became the first Baronet de Trafford of Trafford Park and the baronetcy was inherited by his successors up to modern times, when in 2010 Sir John Humphrey de

Trafford, (born in 1950), became the seventh Baronet. He was also appointed a Member of the Order of the British Empire at that time.

In 1882, their estates at Trafford Hall were threatened by the projected Manchester Ship Canal, which was intended to run round its north side. The plan was vehemently opposed by Sir Humphrey de Trafford right up to the time of his death in 1886.

In 1898, after numerous abortive attempts by Manchester City Council to convert the estate into a public park, Sir Humphrey Francis de Trafford sold the land in its entirety to Trafford Park Estates, who turned it into the first, and the largest industrial estate in Europe. The Metropolitan Borough of Trafford is, of course, named after the family, and Trafford Metropolitan Borough coat of arms still bears the image of a griffon, emblem of the De Traffords.

The Downes Family of Shrigley

The Downes family of Shrigley Hall, Macclesfield, held the estate for over five hundred years until the early nineteenth century. Shrigley and Worth were in the ancient parish of Prestbury, in the Diocese of Chester, a branch of Downes of Sutton-Downes and Overton-in-Taxall.

The estate dates back to the De Shrigley and De Macclesfield families of around 1313 and was for some time the home to the Downes, who held the estate thereafter, when documents show William, son of Robert de Downes, in occupation.

Other branches of the family were at Butley and Tytherington in Cheshire, and at Wardley and Chorley in Lancashire. There is also documentary evidence of a branch of the Downes Family at Nantwich from 1596 to the early nineteenth century.

The family line is now extinct; the last of the male line of succession, Edward Downes, died on 30 December 1819. However, before his death he sold the family estates. Worth-in-Poynton was sold to Sir George Warren of Poynton, and that of Shrigley to William Turner of Mill Hill in Blackburn. Turner built St John's & St Gregory's Church in Bollington in 1834, which contains murals of the Downes family.

Shrigley Hall reopened as a hotel in 1989 and was carefully restored to retain its original character.

The Duckenfield Family of Dukinfield

The district of Dukinfield dates back to the twelfth century, and was probably known as Dokenfield, from the Anglo-Saxon English words 'duce' and 'feld', simply meaning 'a field where ducks are found'. The Duckenfield family, who almost certainly took their surname after the district which predated their occupation, were Lords of Dukinfield from the thirteenth century until the mid-eigtheenth century.

The most celebrated of the Duckenfields was Robert Duckenfield, a Puritan soldier who distinguished himself in battle for the Parliamentarian cause. In 1651, he commanded the forces which secured the Isle of Man, and two years later he was appointed to Cromwell's Barebones Parliament. During the Civil War, he was appointed High Sheriff of Cheshire and played an active role in the defence of Stockport Bridge against Prince Rupert. He was also an important figure in the siege of Wythenshawe. In 1650, he was made Governor of Chester.

Robert Duckenfield is buried at the Church of St Lawrence in Denton. The family amassed a great deal of land and property throughout Cheshire and by the mid-seventeeth century they owned the whole of Dukinfield, now part of the Tameside Metropolitan Borough.

The Dutton Family of Dutton

There are several places called Dutton in Cheshire and Lancashire. Possibly known as Duntun and recorded in the *Domesday Book* as Duntune, previously held by Edward, a Saxon freeman, but later by William de Mallbank for Odard. The placename comes from the Old English 'dun' meaning a hill and 'tun' signifying an enclosure or settlement. Other sources use the Saxon name Duddatune or 'Dudda's farm', suggesting an alternative interpretation.

Records show that Odard accompanied William in his conquest of England and had been rewarded by a gift of Dutton land. His son,

Hugh, inherited the land and it passed in turn to his son, also named Hugh. It was this latter Hugh de Dutton who married the daughter of Hamo Massy, Baron of Dunham Massey, and who extended the Dutton estates by purchasing several nearby townships, including Little Leigh, Barnton, and Preston-nigh-Dutton. In 1236, Hugh also purchased land in Aston and built a chapel on land between the River Weaver and Dutton Park at Poos-eye.

The family lived for many years in the old manor house at Dutton, but in 1539 Sir Piers Dutton built a new half-timbered house overlooking the Weaver valley.

Eventually, without male heirs, the estates passed through marriage of the female side to the Warburtons and Hattons, and possibly the Leghs and the Daniels, who were all major ruling families of Cheshire.

The Duxbury Family of Standish

The Duxbury family name first appears in the parish of Standish in Anglo-Saxon times, some time between 600 and 900. Various alternative spellings of the surname include Dukesbury, Ducksbury, Dukesbery, Deuxberry and Duxberry. The name probably derives from the Old English personal name 'deownc' and 'byrig', meaning a fort; hence, 'Deowue's fort'.

It is known that Magnei de Duxbury acquired the land around 1135. An early documented occurrence of the family name, in 1549, is shown to be that of Isabella Duckesbere of Great Harwood.

The family seat was at Duxbury Hall, but they also owned lands in Adlington, Standish and Chorley. However, during the so-called Banastre Rebellion of 1315, Henry de Duxbury was imprisoned for his part and the Manor of Duxbury was seized. This rebellion had been closely associated with Standish Parish and was led by Sir Adam Banastre, against Thomas, Earl of Lancaster.

Duxbury Manor eventually passed to the Standish and Mayhew families. In the late nineteenth century under Standish ownership, the estate comprised over six thousand acres, with nineteen hundred more in the mid-nineteenth century. In 1932 the manor finally reverted into the ownership of Chorley Corporation.

The Eaton Family of Stockport

The Eatons, (sometimes De Eaton or Eyton), were a powerful family during the medieval period and through intermarriage with other Cheshire families accrued wealth and influence throughout the region. The family name comes from two Old English words 'ea', meaning 'river, and 'tun', an enclosure or settlement. In the *Domesday Book*, several places of this name are recorded, spelled variously as Etune, Etone, Eitone, Eitune and Ettone. At that time, the lands of Eaton in Cheshire were held by Earl Hugh, having previously belonged to Earl Edwin. One of the earliest known spellings of the name is Peter de Eton in the 1273 Hundred Rolls of Huntingdonshire.

Later, in 1311, it is recorded that Nicholas de Eaton and his wife Joan, (daughter and heir of Richard de Stokeport), were tenants of Birkdale Hall in Lancaster. The marriage inextricably tied the Eaton family into the continuing history of Stockport, and the Stockport coat of arms still bears the double headed eagles from the De Eaton family arms.

In 1369, Isabel de Stokeport, heir to her brother Richard, died childless and the estate reverted to an aunt, Cicely de Eaton who married Sir Edward de Warren, (sometimes Warrene). This ended the Eaton line of the Barons of Stockport, and succession fell to Sir John Warren, the second husband of Cecily de Eaton. Subsequently, family descendants went on through the Warren line.

The Egerton Family of Tatton

The Egertons, (sometimes Eggerton), were an influential family, at both national and county level. The name appears in the *Domesday Book* as Eardingtun, and later in 1206 as Ediardinton. It is thought to have derived from a personal name, when one Ecghere, (or Ecgheard), founded a settlement, (a 'tun'); hence, 'Ecghere's settlement'. The earliest known spelling of the surname is that of David Eggerton, who was a witness to the 1282 Assize Court Rolls of Cheshire.

Tatton is recorded in 1086 as Tatone, held by William Mallbank for Earl Hugh. It had been the possession of Erchenbrand, a Saxon freeman before the Conquest.

In the sixteenth century, Sir Philip Egerton, (died in 1563), married Eleanor Brereton, the daughter of Sir Randle Brereton of Malpas. Sir Thomas Egerton, Viscount Brackley, (1540-1617), purchased Tatton Park from his half sister Dorothy Brereton, and it remained in the Egerton family from 1598. Thomas had served at the court of Elizabeth I, and later in 1603, was appointed Lord Chancellor of England by James I.

The Egertons continued in their ownership of Tatton Park, despite serious financial difficulties in the early eigtheenth century, when Elizabeth Egerton was widowed and forced to contemplate the sale of the estate. However, in 1758, her son, Samuel, inherited a large legacy and secured the future of Tatton for the next two hundred years.

In 1784, yet another Sir Thomas Egerton was made Baron Grey de Wilton, and in 1801 became Earl of Wilton. He was responsible for the raising and funding of the Royal Lancashire Volunteer Regiment. His volunteers trained on Drill Field, located between High Bank, now Nazareth House in Sedgley Park, Prestwich.

In the late eigtheenth century, Francis Egerton, third Duke of Bridgewater, (the 'Canal Duke'), held extensive properties and coal mines in Worsley and built the Bridgewater Canal. Francis died childless and bequeathed his canal property to Lord Francis Leveson-Gower, who subsequently changed his name to Egerton. He was made Earl of Ellesmere in 1846.

During the late Victorian period, Tatton flourished, reaching the height of its status under the ownership of Wilbraham Egerton.

Maurice, the last Lord Egerton, died in 1958, leaving Tatton Hall and its extensive Park to the National Trust.

The Ellesmere Family of Worsley

The family name comes from the village of Ellesmere in Shropshire, which is recorded in the *Domesday Book* as Ellesmeles, held by Earl Roger in 1086, previously in the posession of the Saxon Earl Edwin, and may simply mean 'Elli's lake'. The nearby lake, or mere, (also known as Aelsmere), gave its name to the township. The Ellesmere family name is first recorded in 1377, by which time David Ellysmere lived in Warwickshire.

They were related to the Egertons through the third Duke of Bridgewater, and were influential benefactors around Salford, Worsley and Walkden. The Earl of Ellesmere, Francis Leveson-Gower, third son of George Leveson-Gower, Duke of Sutherland and Elizabeth Gordon, nineteenth Countess of Sutherland, (known as Francis Egerton), inherited his father's substantial estates on his father's death in 1833. Thereupon, Francis assumed the surname of Egerton in lieu of Leveson-Gower.

Worsley Court House, a Grade II Listed Building, was built by the Earl of Ellesmere to house the manorial court of Worsley, (the Court Leet), which last sat in 1888. He also built the Packet House on the Bridgwater Canal and endowed the local church. It still carries his coat of arms as does the nearby M60 Motorway bridge. Ellesmere Shopping Centre in Walkden is named after the family.

The Entwistle Family of Entwistle

One of several theories concerning the Entwistle family name has it as French in origin, and that the early family members acquired their lands as Norman barons after the 1066 invasion. Some authorities suggest the name came from Estouteville, and others that it comes from the Old English 'twisle' or 'twisla', meaning 'a piece of land at the confluence of two rivers', a feature of the local Entwistle landscape.

Many alternative spellings of the name existed in early medieval times, including Antwysell, Antwisel, Hennetwisel, Ennetwysel and Entwissell.

The village of Entwistle is named after the family, who held these lands for many centuries. It is located between the towns of Bolton, Darwen and Bury, and surrounded by the villages of Edgworth, Quarlton and Turton.

The township dates from the early thirteenth century, when it was part of the Manor of Entwistle. Entwistle Halland, originally built around the year 1200, was the original family seat. Its most famous resident was Bertine Entwistle, who was reputedly knighted in 1415 by Henry V at Agincourt.

Entwistle Hall was built later, in the early seventeeth century. The Entwistles also inherited Castleton Hall from Dorothy, daughter of Robert Holt, who married into the Entwistle family in 1649.

In 1949, Sarah Spencer-Churchill, daughter of Sir Winston Churchill, married Antony Beauchamp Entwistle and took the married surname Entwistle.

The Fazakerley Family of Kirby

The first recorded reference to the De Fazakerley family, (sometimes Fazakerleigh or Fasakerlegh), occurs in 1276, when Henry de Fasakerlegh is listed in the Lancashire Assize Rolls. Much later, in 1412, it is recorded that Robert de Fazakerley married Ellen de Walton and arrived at the Manor of Walton, accompanied by a sizeable armed contingent, to dispossess his new father-in-law, John de Walton, of goods and chattels in lieu of the dowry which had not been paid. That dispute was not settled until 1426, when a third part of the manor was awarded to Robert de Fazakerley and Ellen as her belated marriage portion.

The Fazakerley name is of Anglo-Saxon origin, derived from three Old English words, 'faes', meaning a border or fringe, 'accer' or 'acre', meaning a field, and 'leah', signifying a wood or clearing. It may be loosely translated as 'a place on the edge of a field near a wood clearing'.

As Catholics, the Fazakerleys were Royalist supporters during the Civil War, and paid dearly for their convictions. The possessions of Nicholas, and his father Robert Fazakerley, (both of whom died during the wars), were confiscated by Parliament, on a posthumous charge of high treason.

However, other Fazakerley family members had distinguished themselves over the years, including Thomas de Fazakerleigh, who was Coroner for Lancashire in 1379, and John Fazakerley who was Governor of the Isle of Man from 1418 to 1422. Two members of the family were Mayors of Liverpool: John de Fazakerley in 1428, and Roger Fazakerley in 1530. Another Nicholas Fazakerley was Member of Parliament for Preston from 1732 to 1767. John Nicholas Fazakerley, (1787-1852), was the Member of Parliament for Great Grimsby in 1818, for Lincoln in 1826, and for Peterborough from 1830 to 1841.

The family name is nowadays immortalised in the Liverpool district of the same name and by at least two local schools bearing the name Fazakerley. Until 1850, High Street in Prescott was known as Fazakerley Street.

The Foden Family of Cheshire

The Foden family name appeared in Cheshire during Anglo-Saxon times, possibly originally derived from Odin, the pagan god of the Saxons. There are several alternate spellings, including Fodin, Fowden, Fodon, Vodden and Voden. Later, as surnames tended to indicate place of birth, it simply meant someone who came from the village of Foden, in Prestbury.

The earliest written record of the name is of Philip Fowden, who married Katherine Broke at Prestbury Church in 1563. Shortly after, in 1568, Hugh Fowden and Mary Stubbs were married at the same church.

By the 1700s, they held significant farming lands around Astbury and Prestbury, though there were migrations of family members to both America and Australia in the eigtheenth and nineteenth centuries.

Foden and ERF lorries, founded in Sandbach by Edwin Foden, (1841–1911), became a major local employer. The celebrated Foden's Brass Band is still based in Sandbach and were British Open Brass Band Champions in 2008.

The Gerrard Family of Brynne & Wigan

The Gerrards are an ancient and influential landowning Lancashire family, particularly around the districts of present day Wigan. The name Gerrard, (sometimes Gerard, Garret, Garrett, Jarrard or

Gerart), is an old Anglo-Saxon name derived from Old German, meaning 'spear carrier' and a Gerard is recorded in the Domesday Survey and identified as Lord Chancellor of England. However, the FitzGerrards of Brynne boasted an ancient ancestry going back to the time of Alfred the Great.

DeBretts identifies the Gerrard family as deriving its origin from the same ancestor as the Duke of Leinster, the Marquess of Lansdowne, the Lords Windsor, and many others. The descendants of Gerald, (or Gerard), third son of Walter FitzOther, continued the surname of Gerrard, and settled at Brynne in Lancashire.

Some time around 1250, William Gerrard inherited Brynne Hall by marriage to the daughter and sole heiress of Peter de Brynne. The family seat at Brynne Hall, (sometimes Bryn), dates from the fourteenth century.

Documentation shows that the family owned lands around Winwick, Standish, Hindley and Ashton-in-Makerfield in the mid-sixteenth century.

In 1544, Thomas Gerratt had been made Earl of Hertford at Leith in Scotland, and by 1555, William Garrett was Lord Mayor of London. Subsequent family members became Attorneys General and Chancellors of Ireland.

The family name is still recorded by Gerrard's Bridge on the nearby Leeds & Liverpool Canal. The Gerrard family tomb is at All Saints Church in Wigan.

The Glassbrook Family of Glazebrook

Six miles from Warrington, in the most easterly township in the West Derby hundred, with its southern boundary at the River Mersey, is the village of Glazebrook. The parish is listed in 1227 as Glasbro, thought to be derived from 'glaze brook (or broc)', a Celtic river name meaning 'grey-green'. This was the Earldom of the De Glasebrook family, (sometimes Glasebrook). Other derivations include Glazebrook and Glasbrook. Their lands were originally bestowed by William the Conqueror upon his illegitimate son, Galfe, as recorded in the *Domesday Book*.

The township's existence predates the County Palatine of Lancashire, which was not created until 1297. Glassbrook lands included the village of Glazebury, from where their name derives, as well as the River Glazebrook, a tributary of the Mersey.

The family successfully defended their territory against the advancing Scots, whilst the Grosvenors held the west against the Welsh, and the De Traffords the east. Ten other families held the line, including the De Botteliers of Bootle.

In the 1800 survey, the district was known as Glassbrook. Nowadays, the township comes under the administrative authority of Cheshire.

The Grelley Family of Manchester

In the Roll of Battle Abbey at Hastings, the family name first appears as 'Greile'. In the *Domesday Book* it is shown as Greslet, but many other subsequent alternatives exist, including Grelle, Gressy, Greslé, Grelly, Grelley, Gredley, Gradley, Gredlai, Gresley and Greddle, among others. The name probably comes from the Old French word 'greslet', meaning pockmarked or pitted, no doubt a physical attribute of one of the family's early progenitors.

After the 1066 invasion, the old Salford Hundred and the extensive lands between the Rivers Ribble and Mersey, as well as the Manor of Manchester, were given by William the Conqueror to one of his favourite barons, Roger de Poitevin (sometimes 'de Pictou' or 'Poitou').

Later, de Poitevin, in turn, granted Manchester to one of his own supporters, Albert de Greslé, who had accompanied him at Hastings. Greslé thereby became the first Baron of Manchester, a manor which his family held for the next two hundred years. The family lived in Grelley Manor, (now Chethams Library), adjacent to Manchester Cathedral. In 1276, a descendant, Peter de Gresley, was patron of the rectory of Manchester.

The last of the family to bear the title was Thomas Greddle, the eighth Baron of Manchester, and when he died in 1347, unmarried, the vast estates of the family passed, through the marriage of his sister Johanna with John de la Warre, into the De la Warre Family.

By the eigtheenth century, branches of the family, notably the Gradells of Ulneswalton, settled in Clifton near Kirkham, and continued under the name Gradwell to the present day. There are Gresleys known in Derbyshire and Greasleys in Nottinghamshire, but whether or not these are related is open to question.

The Grimshaw Family of Crowtree & Sabden

For much of the nineteenth century the Grimshaws were an influential family in Barrowford. Their history dates back to 1276, when Richard de Grymishagh inherited the tenement of Crowtree near Blackburn from his father, Walter. The main branch of the family continued to live into the later years of the seventeeth century. They had probably taken the surname from the local district, originally spelled Grymishagh or Grymishaw, meaning 'an open wood'.

In the fourteenth century, Adam de Grimshaw had married Cicely de Clayton, and thereafter this branch of the family resided at Clayton Hall, Clayton Le Moors. The rest of the Grimshaw family lived at Sabden, which was to be their family home from around 1594 to 1800 when Nicholas Grimshaw sold it. Another Nicholas Grimshaw, (of Heyhouses), lived in Sabden during the reign of Elizabeth I.

The tragic Moorfield Pit disaster of 7 November 1883 saw sixty-eight men and boys killed and injured, many of the Grimshaw men among them. A plaque on the A678 bridge over the Leeds and Liverpool Canal near the Moorfield Colliery site commemorates the event.

The Grosvenor Family of Eaton Hall

Eaton Hall in Cheshire has been the family home of the Grosvenor Family since the fifteenth century. The surname originally comes from one Hugh le Grande (or 'Gros') Veneur, (meaning 'master huntsman'), who accompanied William in his conquest of England.

Some time during that century, Raufe, second son of Sir Thomas Grosvenor of Hulme, near Northwich, married Joan de Eton, heiress to the Eton estate.

By 1601, Richard Grosvenor had acquired lead and coal mines as well as stone quarrying interests in Denbighshire, Coleshill and Rhuddlan in Flintshire. Richard's son, Roger, was killed in a duel in 1661, and upon his death the baronetcy went directly to his grandson, Thomas, then aged just eight years.

A descendant, also named Richard, was created Baron Grosvenor of Eaton in 1761, and Earl Grosvenor and Viscount Belgrave in 1784. The first Earl's only son, Robert, succeeded to the title in 1802. The family acquired the Manors of Holywell, Fulbrook and Greenfield in 1809. In 1831 he was created Marquess of Westminster.

A later descendant, Hugh Lupus, (named after the Norman Earl of Chester), became third Marquess in 1869, and was elevated to the Dukedom in 1874. Successive dukes have held the estate until the present day. Eaton remains the seat of the sixth Duke of Westminster, and the family still has great wealth and many holdings throughout the UK including large areas of central London

The Halsall Family of Halsall

In 1066, the township of Halsall was held by a man named Chettel. Following the Conquest, the Barony of Warrington included the northern portion of the parish of Halsall, as well as Barton and Lydiate. By 1212, Robert de Vilers was the Lord of the Manor of Halsall and the family name of 'de Halsall' was adopted some time shortly thereafter, when Gilbert de Halsall was a prominent figure in the region.

In 1395, Henry de Halsall, who had embraced an ecclesiastical career, was presented by his father to the rectory of Halsall, which in 1413 he exchanged for the archdeaconry of Chester. A great deal of county intermarriage followed, amongst them the Heskeths, the Molyneux of Sefton and the Stanleys of Weaver.

A prominent Halsall of the early fifteenth century was Sir Gilbert Halsall, who fought in the Hundred Years War and was Bailiff of Evreux.

In the late sixteenth century, Edward Halsall founded the school at Halsall. A Henry Halsall was made a knight in Dublin on 22 July 1599 and was probably sent to prison for debt in 1631, whereupon the estates passed into ownership of Sir Charles Gerard, who had married Penelope, daughter of Sir Edward Fitton of Gawsworth, near Macclesfield.

The Harrison Family of Warrington & Samlesbury

The Harrison family name has existed since Anglo-Saxon times, and occurs in many early manuscripts, with various spellings, including Harryson and Harieson. The name simply means 'son of Harry', a diminutive form of Henry. Some alternative sources have it that the first Harrisons came from Cumberland, possibly as early as the eleventh century.

Around 1390, Thomas Heryson was born in Greystoke, and a Stephen Harrison is recorded living in Kendal in the early 1400s. The Harrisons of Bankfield in Lancashire date from the early 1500s.

Samlesbury Hall near Clitheroe has long been associated with the Harrison family name. The manor house had been originally built in 1325 by Gilbert de Southworth and was the home of the Southworth family until the early seventeeth century. In recent years it had stood empty, and was in danger of falling into dereliction, before it was purchased by Joseph Harrison of Galligreaves Hall. Harrison was a prominent Blackburn industrialist, who substantially renovated the Hall in November 1862, investing large amounts of money in its restoration.

Although it continued to be owned by the Harrisons, Samlesbury Hall was tenanted for a number of years by Frederick Baynes, a one-time Mayor of Blackburn. More recently, the Hall has been fully restored by local volunteers and is open to the public. It is a Grade I Listed medieval manor house.

The Hatton Family of Tabley

A branch of the Hatton family, who had taken their surname from the Cheshire village of that name, moved to settle in Longstanton during the reign of Elizabeth I. These Longstanton Hattons were related to the famous Sir Christopher Hatton, (1540-91), the queen's Lord Chancellor. Later, in July 1641, another Christopher Hatton was created Baron Hatton. He was also made Governor of Guernsey, and his son, (yet another Christopher), became the Viscount Hatton. However, the family failed to produce male heirs and by 1812 the peerage had became extinct.

The surname is mainly found around Lancashire and Cheshire, and probably comes from the Old English, 'heath', and 'tun', meaning a 'heathland settlement'.

The name Tabley comes from the Anglo-Saxon 'tabban-leah' meaning 'Tabba's clearing or meadow'. The township of Tabley was held by William FitzNigel in the time of William the Conqueror and is recorded in the *Domesday Book*.

Hatton lands descended from William FitzNigel, who died without male heirs, and passed through marriage to the Duttons, Warburtons and Hattons, and possibly the Leghs and the Daniels families. All these were major ruling families of Cheshire throughout the centuries right up to modern times.

Notable family members were Captain Edward Allen Smeathman Hatton, of the Royal Marine Light Infantry, who was killed in action in April 1915 at Gallipoli, and Major General Villiers Hatton, (1852-1914), an officer in the Grenadier Guards, who fought in the Sudan campaign in the 1890s.

The Heaton Family of Deane

The first appearance of the family name is of Randle de Heton, of Heaton-under-the-Forest, around 1135. Heaton was created a township in the twelfth century and was in the ancient ecclesiastical parish of Deane in the Salford Hundred. Its name derives from the Old English 'heah' and 'tun', meaning 'enclosed ground on high land'; it was recorded as Heton in 1227 and Heton under Horewich in 1332.

In 1199, John granted land to Roger de Heton around the River Lune in North Lancashire in the Manor of Heton-in-Lonsdale. Many sub-branches of the family followed, including the Heatons of

London, of Billinge, of Clouch and of Ravenhurst. The name also appears as far south as Heaton Moor, Heaton Mersey, Heaton Norris and Heaton Chapel.

The family came to live in the Bolton Parish of Deane and gradually expanded its possessions over two centuries, holding public appointments and growing in influence.

In the thirteenth century, two heads of the family received knighthoods. Later, the estates were divided amongst several sons and on the death of William de Heton in 1387, most of the lands in Lancashire were inherited by his two daughters, and subsequently through marriage, passed out of the hands of the Heaton family.

The Hesketh Family of Rufford

The placename Hesketh comes from the Old Norse words 'hestr', meaning a horse, and 'skeid', signifying grazing land. It may also have referred to a horse racing course. The family took their surname from the village of that name in Lancashire.

The Heskeths acquired the Manor of Rufford through intermarriage with the Fitton family, when in 1275 Maud Fitton married Sir Thomas Hesketh of Holmeswood, and half of the Rufford estate came as her dowry. Their grandson, Sir John de Hesketh, married Alice Fitton and thereby secured the rest of the estate to become Lord of the Manor of Rufford.

The family were great benefactors of the Church of St Lawrence at Great Harwood, where Thomas Hesketh founded a chantry in 1521 and bequeathed it an endowment of land. His son, (also called Thomas), was knighted at the coronation of Mary Tudor in 1553.

Despite being a fervent supporter of Mary and himself a Roman Catholic, Thomas managed to retain some status when the Protestant Elizabeth I came to power in 1558, and went on to serve her with distinction, becoming High Sheriff of Lancashire in 1563.

Subsequent generations married into other powerful Lancastrian families and several became Members of Parliament and High Sheriffs for Lancashire.

In 1593, Richard Hesketh was involved in the plot to place the fifth Earl of Derby on the throne, in succession to Elizabeth, but was betrayed and sentenced to death. Their family house at Martholme eventually passed by marriage to the De Hoghtons.

In 1761, Sir Thomas Hesketh, (1726-78), was created Baron Hesketh of Rufford, and the baronetcy remained in the family line until recent times.

During the early nineteenth century, family fortunes fared badly as mechanisation hit the farming and weaving industries hard, markets fell and rents went unpaid, so that in 1819, the third Baronet, Sir Thomas Dalrymple Hesketh, (1777-1842), sold the estate to Richard Grimshaw Lomax of Clayton-le-Moors for the sum of £75,000. This sale ended Hesketh influence in Rufford, their Lordship of the Manor having lasted over five hundred years.

The Heywood Family of Heywood

By the twelfth century, Heywood was identified as a hamlet in the township of Heap in Bury. The Heywood Family can be traced back to 1164, when a Peter Heywood was living there. There are two possible explanations of the origin of the surname. One has it coming from the Old English 'heah', meaning 'high', and 'wudu', meaning 'wood'. Simply 'high wood'. Another cites the Old English 'haga', as more likely, and meaning a hedge or animal enclosure (in a wood). Whichever is true, the family almost certainly took their name from the place.

In 1286, it was recorded that Adam de Burgo (or de Bury), 'granted land in Heywood, in the parish of Bury county of Lancaster' to Peter de Heywood.

It was another Peter Heywood who was one of the officers who apprehended Guy Fawkes in the vault of Parliament House, thereby foiling the gunpowder plot of 5 November 1605. Yet a further Peter Heywood was a midshipman on board HMS *Bounty* when the crew mutinied in 1789. A model of the ship is in Heywood Library.

Heywood Hall, the family seat, was built in the thirteenth century and rebuilt in 1611. The Heywoods were Royalists in the Civil War and their fortune was much reduced thereafter. As a result, in 1717, the Hall was sold to John Starkey of Rochdale.

St Luke's church in Heywood started life as a chantry chapel for the family, and Robert Heywood rebuilt it in 1640. Regrettably, though later owners, the Starkeys, left Heywood Hall to the local council, it was demolished in 1960.

The Hibberd Family of Over Alderley

Hibbard, (sometimes Hibberd), is a surname of Norman origin which arrived with the Conquest of 1066, though a reference is made to an Archbishop Hibbert during the reign of Offa in the eighth century *Anglo-Saxon Chronicles*. It is most likely an early English form of the Norman personal name Hildebert or Hilbert. Variants include Ilbert, Hibbert, Hibberd, Hibbard, Hibberte, Hileberd, Heebarde and Hibot.

An alternative explanation of the name's origin is that, following the Conquest, the Normans adopted an old Germanic given name 'Hildeberht', from 'hild' and 'berht', somewhat crudely translated as 'battle famous'. The personal name is also recorded in its Latin forms as 'Ylebertus' around 1150 and as 'Hildebertus' in 1160 – both occurrences in Lincolnshire.

The Yorkshire Poll Tax records of 1379 list Johannes Frere et Hibbott; an Edward Hibberte appears in Yorkshire in 1400; William Hhibert was documented in Lancashire in 1473.

St Catherine's Church in Over Alderley, Cheshire, was built as a private chapel by Thomas Hibbert in 1840, where he assembled valuable oak carvings, stained glass and brass objects, much of it older than the building itself. It became the parish church of Birtles and Over Alderley in 1890, is a Grade II Listed Building, and features in Simon Jenkins' book *England's Thousand Best Churches*.

Birtles Hall is an impressive Grade II Listed country house which was built in 1790 for the Hibbert family. In more recent times the Hall has been sympathetically restored, retaining most of its original features and has been converted into six 'luxurious' apartments.

The Hoghton Family of Hoghton

The country seat of the De Hoghtons, (or Houghtons - pronounced 'Horton'), Hoghton Tower, (sometimes known as Hoghton Castle), dominates the central Lancashire landscape around Darwen and Preston. The family traces its lineage back to the 1066 invasion, when an early Hoghton crossed in the same ship as William the Conqueror himself. Consequently, the family coat of arms is the oldest in Lancashire and the second oldest in England.

The Hoghtons were substantial Lancashire landowners during the reign of Stephen in the twelfth century, and by the fourteenth century they were hereditary knights of the shire. It is believed that William Shakespeare stayed with the Hoghtons for a while in the role of school teacher.

Sir Richard Hogton, (who died in 1630), was created Baron Hoghton of Hoghton Tower and Walton le Dale in May 1611. The second Baronet represented Clitheroe and Lancashire in the House of Commons and was a Royalist leader during the Civil Wars. In 1643, during that conflict, Hoghton Tower was damaged by Parliamentary forces. From 1692 to 1702, Sir Charles de Hoghton carried out substantial repairs but the family ceased to live there from 1768, and it was rented out to local farmers.

By the middle of the nineteenth century, the Tower had long been derelict, but when Sir Henry de Hoghton, the ninth Baronet, inherited the estate in 1862, he began restoration.

Sir Richard Bernard Cuthbert de Hoghton, born in January 1945, succeeded as the fourteenth Baronet Hoghton in 1978. In 1980, he was made a Knight of the Sovereign Military Order of Malta, and in 1984 was awarded the Constantinian Order of St George of Naples and Parma. He was Deputy Lieutenant of Lancashire in 1988 and held the office of United Nations Special Ambassador in 1995. He still lives at Hoghton Tower.

Hoghton Tower and the Great Barn were designated as a Grade I Listed Buildings in October 1952, the coach house, stables and the gate piers on the drive to the west of the house are listed as Grade II.

The gardens are listed at Grade II on the National Register of Historic Parks and Gardens.

In 1978, the Hoghton Tower Preservation Trust was established as a charity for the preservation of the house, and to encourage education and research.

The Holden Family of Rossendale

Records show Robert de Holden, (sometimes Houlden), owning lands around Haslingden in Rossendale from the thirteenth century, and that the family remained prominent and influential in Lancashire until the nineteenth century. The name comes from the Old English words 'hol', meaning deep, (as in a hole), and 'denu', signifying a valley. Hence, the name may be taken to mean 'deep valley'.

Their fifteenth century home at Holden Hall in Haslingden was the residence of Robert de Haslingden, who lived there with his family for over five centuries until Ralph Holden, the last male heir of the family line, died in 1702. The Hall was demolished at the beginning of the nineteenth century to allow expansion of the adjacent cemetery.

The Holdens of Haslingden were the stewards and wardens of the Royal Forest of Rossendale and the Forest of Boland. Until the sixteenth century the surrounding moorland was forested and used by the monarch for hunting. However, in 1507, Henry VII decreed that the area should be deforested, so that by the middle of the nineteenth century very little woodland was left. The hamlet of Haslingden Grane, including Broad Holden and Holden, are named after the family.

The Holland Family of Heaton & Upholland

The Hollands, (or De Hollands), have a long and influential history around the districts of Clifton and Prestwich, north of Manchester. The name originated in the Netherlands, from where its earliest members had migrated. Until the fifteenth century, the name was spelled Holand (or Holande), and was probably originally associated with the Manor of Upholland, which was in the possession of a man called Steinulf.

In 1341, Sir Thurstan de Holland purchased a piece of land, known as Roden, (or Rooden), in Prestwich, an area nowadays known as Heaton Park. Thurstan founded the line of Hollands of Denton and their branch of Clifton.

In 1666, William Holland of Denton acquired the inheritance of the Reddish family in Great Heaton, and from that time chose Heaton, (or Heton), for the family's principal residence.

During the Civil Wars, the Hollands supported the Royalist cause, and afterwards suffered extreme punishments for their bad fortune.

William Holland was buried in Prestwich in 1682. His daughter Elizabeth inherited the estate and upon her marriage to Sir John Egerton, ownership passed to the Egerton family at Heaton Hall, which was extensively rebuilt in 1777.

The Hollingworth Family of Hollingworth

The name Hollingworth is of Anglo-Saxon origin, derived in part from the Old English word 'hollins' (or 'holegn'), early names for the holly bush. In 1059, the village was listed as Holisurde, a spelling also found in the *Domesday Book* in 1086 when it was held by Earl Hugh d'Avranches, (known as 'Hugh the Fat' or 'Hugh The Wolf'). The 'ing' element of the name refers to 'the people or family of', the name is usually accepted as meaning 'the people or family who live by the holly bushes'.

The Hollingworth family were Lords of the Manor of Hollingworth, (in modern day Tameside), from the mid-thirteenth century until the early eigtheenth century, and had been the most prominent family in the area for more than five centuries.

They owned Hollingworth Hall and the Old Hall, and by the late seventeeth century, held almost seven hundred acres of the surrounding lands, including five farmsteads.

The village of Hollingworth was historically part of Cheshire and gave its name to the Hollingworth family who had owned most of the surrounding area from before the Norman conquest. The *Domesday*

Book shows that the Manor of 'Holyngworthe' was considered barren and worthless. Before 1000, Hollingworth had been in the ancient Hundred of Hamestan.

In 1734, the family influence and prosperity declined and its properties passed to Daniel Whittle in 1831, before being sold to Robert de Holyngworthe, who claimed to be a descendant of the original Lords of the Manor. His ownership was short lived however, and the larger of the estates passed through a variety of hands until in 1924 it was sold to Manchester Corporation Waterworks.

The remainder of the estate, based on the Old Hall, was sold by the Hollingworth family in 1800 to Samuel Hadfield. The Hall was demolished in 1943, having previously served as a school and a mental asylum. Only the chapel still remains.

The Hulton Family of Westhoughton

Hulton is a locational name found in Lancashire and Staffordshire, and is a corruption of two Old English words: 'hyll', simply meaning 'hill', and 'tun', referring to an enclosure or settlement. Hence, 'the settlement on the hill'. Over time the name has been variously recorded as Helghetun and Hilton.

Early records show that Iorweth and Madoc de Hulton, sons of Bleiddyn, came from Wales to live in Bolton in 1167. They were probably expelled from Wales by Lord Robert de Banastre. In 1212, Iowerth de Hulton also held Pendleton in Salford.

In 1304, Richard de Hulton of Westhoughton is recorded as having freehold of lands in Hulton, Ordsall, Flixton and Heaton. He built Hulton Hall, which, by the late nineteenth century, was surrounded by a 1,000 acre park of plantations and pleasure grounds with four acres of water. The estate, which is rich in coal mines, was the sole property of the Hultons of Hulton Park.

The Hultons were devout Catholics, and in common with many Lancastrians, kept the old faith during the Reformation, while remaining loyal and allied to the sovereign. They worshipped at Deane Church and some are buried in its Hulton Chapel. Ironically, it was William Hulton who was the Lancashire magistrate committed to defending Elizabeth I in the Anglo-Spanish War in 1585.

In 1819, at the infamous 'Peterloo Massacre', the magistrate, also named William Hulton, ordered the Yeomanry Cavalry to arrest orator Henry Hunt as he addressed the great demonstration at St Peter's Field in Manchester, thus setting off a train of events which were to go down in history as a less than glorious event.

The last surviving member of the Hulton family, Sir Geoffrey Hulton, died without heir in 1993, marking the end of the Hulton dynasty, after more than eight centuries dominating the land west of Bolton.

The Hyde Family of Denton

The Hyde family name, (sometimes Hide or Hyda), probably derived from the Old English 'higid', which by the time of Domesday had become 'hide', a measurement of land varying from sixty to a hundred and twenty acres.

Not recorded in 1086, the township of Hyde bears the name of one of its oldest and most distinguished families. It began with Matthew de Hyde, (or Mathaeus de Hyde), (c.1170-1211), whose son Robert de la Hyda acquired the title Robert de Norbury from Edward II, as well as Lordship of the Manors of Hyde and Newton in Cheshire, Shalcross in Derbyshire and of Halghton in Lancashire.

During the Civil Wars, Robert Hyde was a zealous Puritan who took part in the defence of Manchester in 1642.

While the family seat was at the sixteenth century Hyde Hall, they rarely lived there, and for much of its history it was occupied by tenant farmers. The Hall was listed as Grade II in November 1967.

An illustrious holder of the family name was Anne Hyde, Duchess of York and of Albany, (1637-71), who was James II's first wife and the mother of Queen Anne.

The Kirkby Family of Kirkby-Ireleth

The Kirkby family have long been associated with the village of Kirkby-Ireleth, a township in Ulverston in Cumbria. The name

Kirkby simply means 'village with a church'. The actual family name can be traced to Orm, son of Ailward, (or Eiward), to whom Albert Grelley, Lord of the Manor of Manchester, granted a knighthood.

By the end of the twelfth century, Roger de Kirkby had ownership of lands at Kirby-Ireleth and was in residence at Kirkby Hall, known at that time as Cross House or Kirkby Cross. This was to be the seat of the Kirkby family for the next ten generations.

Kirkby (or Cherchebi) is recorded in the *Domesday Book*, as is the parish church, dedicated to St Cuthbert, which stands in the hamlet of Beckside, near Ulverston. It may have been founded by Alexander de Kirkby, who lived during the reign of Henry III.

Notable as local benefactors, the family acquired large areas of land in the Dalton and Furness region and bequeathed funds to set up trusts in support of the poor. In the early eighteenth century they fell on hard times, when in 1719 - Colonel Roger Kirkby mortgaged it to a banker, representing the Duchess of Buckingham. When he later became insolvent, the manor fell by default into the possession of the Duchess, in part payment of her claim. It was later sold on to the Cavendish family, the Dukes of Devonshire, who are the owners at the time of writing.

The Langley Family of Agecroft

Agecroft, also known in early medieval times as Achecroft or Edgecroft, was the manor house of Pendleburg, (now Pendlebury), and was the residence of the Prestwich family.

Some time around 1340, Richard de Langley married Joanna, sole heiress of the Prestwich family, and subsequently the Prestwich and Heaton estates came into the possession of the Langleys.

Langley is a common locational surname from several villages called Langley, (or Longley), many found in the *Domesday Book* under various spellings, such as Langelei, Langeleie or Longelei. The name comes from the Old English 'lang', meaning long, and 'leah', meaning wood or glade.

The Langley family took their surname from the place, and are recorded residing at Agecroft Hall in 1389. In that year they also acquired Drinkwater Park in Prestwich, which now belongs to the Forestry Commission.

Langleys married well and propitiously, their sons and daughters married into the De Trafford, the De Hollands and the Assheton families.

By the fourteenth century, the family seat was in Middleton. In 1385, Sir Robert Langley was appointed as Rector of Radcliffe and the following year saw him appointed Dean of York. This appointment was blocked by Pope Boniface IX, for the family's part in the deposition and murder of Richard II. The Langleys had already achieved notoriety by October 1404, when Charles Langley was elected Bishop of London and Archbishop of York, despite opposition from Rome. The Pope excommunicated Langley and Henry IV, the king who had promoted him.

On his death, the larger portion of the manor and estates went to Sir Robert's elder daughter Anne, which subsequently became part of the Reddish estates through marriage, and his extensive land holdings in Polefield, (in Unsworth), passed to his other daughter, Dorothy. Thus, through the female line, the Langleys were subsumed by marriage into other great families.

The family name is still honoured locally by having several streets named after them as well as the large housing estate of Langley in Middleton, Rochdale.

The Lathom Family of Knowsley

Another Old Norse name, Latham comes from the village of that name in Lancashire. It is derived from the word 'hlatha', which is generally translated as meaning a place by a barn. Lathom is recorded as Lathum in the 1201 Pipe Rolls of the county.

The family, (sometimes spelled Latham), date their lineage back to the Norman invasion. An early account tells of Robert, son of Henry de Lathom, who died in 1198, holding the Manor of Woolfall, near Huyton in Merseyside.

Burcough Priory, near Ormskirk, was built in 1190 by Henry de Lathom and in 1189, Robert de Lathom became the first Lord of the

Manor. Records show the construction of the original house on the site of Lathom Hall in the twelfth century as principal residence of the family.

In 1304, another Robert de Lathom was granted a royal charter to hold a market and fair, which survived till the mid-1320s, when it had moved to nearby Prescot.

In the fourteenth century, Lathom Hall passed into the Stanley family by the marriage of Isabel de Lathom to Sir John Stanley, who became Earl of Derby following the Battle of Bosworth in 1485.

In 1496, the Hall was substantially remodelled and fortified in preparation for a visit by the Earl's father-in-law, Henry VII. Later, in the sixteenth century, it was demolished under Henry VIII's Dissolution of the Monasteries.

There being no surviving male heirs of the Lathom line, all their holdings eventually passed by marriage into the Harrington family.

The Lawton Family of Church Lawton

The Lawton family name comes from Old English and means a 'settlement near a hill', or possibly a 'settlement by a burial mound'. It is derived from 'hlaw', meaning hill, (or burial mound), and 'tun', signifying an enclosure or early settlement.

The recorded history of the Lawton family began when lands were given to Hugh d'Avranches, Lord of the Manor of Chester, the brother-in-law of William the Conqueror, for his support in the invasion of England. He built a Norman church to replace the Saxon one in Cheshire - hence the place was named after the family. The estate became the Parish of 'Lauton' and was recorded as such in the Domesday Survey. Later, it became Church Lawton.

An early record of the Lawton name, however, occurs with Adam de Lauton, who lived during the reigns of John and Henry III. Legend has it that he rescued the Earl of Chester from an attack by a wounded wolf, and in gratitude was granted a thousand acres of land stretching from Congleton to Sandbach. The bleeding wolf can still be seen in the arms of the Lawton family, and is also commemorated in the nearby pub, The Bleeding Wolf at Scholar Green.

Maintenance of the estate deteriorated and the family's interest in it diminished over the following centuries, and while it remains in the possession of the Lawton family, members have moved away to live in Kent, America and Spain. Lawton Hall, the country seat, built in the seventeeth century, still stands despite being partly destroyed by a fire in 1997.

During the First World War, the Hall was a hospital and during the Second World War it was used by the local fire service. In the inter-war period it also served as a hotel and a school for the disabled.

In 1952 it was leased by Mr Harrison and became a private school which ran until its closure in 1986. For several years thereafter the property was unoccupied and became derelict, as ongoing disputes over its ownership placed the property in limbo.

By the mid-1990s, the Hall had fallen victim to vandalism and theft, with most of its valuable fittings being torn out or wrecked.

The Legh Family of Adlington

Hamo (or Hamon) de Legh, (sometimes Leigh), was born of Norman descent around 1126 at High Legh near Knutsford in Cheshire. He became Lord of the Manor around 1215. Later, the Legh family moved to Adlington Hall near Macclesfield. This fine half-timbered manor house became home to Robert de Legh and his new bride Ellen de Corona when they moved to live there in 1315.

The name Legh derives from the Old English 'leah', meaning a wood clearing, and the family are thought to be descended from Efward de Lega, a man of Saxon origin.

Sir Piers Legh, (1325-99), was knighted in 1397 by Richard II and executed two years later for his part in Henry Bolingbroke's abortive coup.

His son, Sir Piers Legh II, (1389-1422), was the second family occupant of Lyme Hall. He was wounded in the Battle of Agincourt. It is said that his mastiff stood over his wounded body on the battlefield and protected it for many hours. Later, back home, Legh established what became known as the Lyme Hall Mastiff, the forerunner of the English Mastiff breed.

The Leghs owned the Manor of Newton, (part of the Goldborne district of Wigan), as well as lands in Winwick, where family tombs may still be found. They also held extensive lands throughout Cheshire, Staffordshire and Derbyshire and thereby exerted powerful influence upon the local demography and economy. Their vast estate stretched as far south as Newcastle-under-Lyme. Lyme Hall near Disley was the family's seat for many years, but was bequeathed to Stockport Corporation in 1947. Their present seat is in Lewes, East Sussex.

In 1892, William John Legh was created Baron Legh of Newton-in Makerfield, a title which has passed down the family line to the present day. As of 2017, the fifth Baron is Richard Thomas Legh, who was born in 1950.

The Leycester Family of Tabley

In 1276, Sir Nicholas Leycester, (sometimes Leicester), married Margaret de Dutton and acquired the township of Nether-Tabley near Knutsford. The fourth descendant of Sir Nicholas, John de Leycester, built Tabley Old Hall during the reign of Richard II. Later, Sir Peter Leycester, who was born in 1613, is said to have been a contender as the first historian in the county, having created an early record of the families of Cheshire. He altered and extended the Old Hall between 1656 and 1671. His grandson, Sir Peter Byrne (1732–70), assumed the name of Leicester by Act of Parliament and in 1760 he had Tabley New Hall built to replace the old Tudor building.

Some time in the late eigtheenth century, Viscountess Bulkeley, Anna Dorothea Warren, (heiress to the Warren family of Poynton), left part of her estate to the second Lord de Tabley, on condition that her family name was incorporated as Leicester-Warren. By 1811 the sixth Baronet, Sir George Leicester, had assumed the name and arms of the Warrens, and thereafter the Tabley branch were known by the name of Leicester-Warren.

The Lister Family of Gisburn

The first record of the Listers in the Parish of Gisburn occurs in 1312 when a family member from West Derby married Isabel de Bolton. She is thought to have descended from Leofric, Earl of Mercia, who had married the famous Lady Godiva of Coventry.

The name Lister, (or Litster), referred in ancient times to a dyer of fabrics, the Old English word for a dye was 'litte'. Variations on the name include Lester, Lyster, and Ledster.

In the Domesday Survey, the Manor of Gisburn, (or Ghisebum), was held by the Abbot of Salley, (or Sawley), and which, in 1224, was repossessed by the Crown. In 1613, Gisburn came into the possession of the Lister family.

In 1797, as a result of his having raised troops to fight in the Napoleonic Wars, Thomas Lister was made Baron Ribblesdale of Gisburne Park, and thereafter the family name effectively changed to Ribblesdale. The first Lord Ribblesdale planted more than a million oak trees in the Ribble Valley. The fourth Lord Ribblesdale's sons were both killed in action, one during the Boer War in South Africa and the other in the First World War.

In 1927, part of the estates was sold to pay death duties of the last Lord Ribblesdale, and on the death of his last sister in 1944, the remainder of the Lister-Ribblesdale estates were sold off.

The Mainwaring Family of Peover

The Mainwarings, (pronounced Mannering), held the Manor at Peover Hall in Cheshire from the time of the Norman Conquest. Ranulphus de Mesnilwarin, (1040–86), believed to be the family's ancestor, came to live in Over Peover, (pronounced pee-ver), some time after 1066.

The family name is taken from their birthplace, the ancient village of Le Mesnil Varin, (from the Old French meaning 'the Manor of Warin'), now called Saint-Paër, in Normandy. Over time it corrupted to an Anglicised version of Mainwaring.

The present Hall at Over Peover was built in 1585 by Sir Randle Mainwaring, the first Baron Mainwaring, and had a Georgian extension added later by the second Baron, Sir Henry Mainwaring, the last male heir of the family.

In 1797 the house was purchased by Thomas Wettenhall, who took the name of Mainwaring, guaranteeing that the family name would continue, until 1919, after which it was owned by several other unrelated families.

During its long history, the Mainwaring family counted lords and knights amongst their number, as well as several Sheriffs of Chester and Lords of the Manor. Documents and deeds held at the John Rylands Library in Manchester show their possession of several Cheshire townships, including Allostock, Astley, Baddiley, Goostrey-cum-Barnshaw, Chelford, Knutsford, Nantwich, Over Peover, Great Warford, Little Warford, Waverton, Wharton, Withington and Worleston.

The Malbank Family of Nantwich

The Malbanks are an old family dating from the time of the Norman invasion. They married into the influential Vernon Family of Haddon Hall, and number among their descendants the De Stokeports, as well as the Wilbrahams and the Breretons.

One of the earliest known family members was Hugh Malbedenc, (1100-35), who became Baron of Wich Malbank. Later, William de Malbanke, (sometimes Mallbank), (1089-1130), was made First Baron of Nantwich.

Several variants on the original name exist, including Malbanc, Mallbone, Milbanks, Milbanke and Malbon. The family line continued through to Thomas Malbon, Mayor of Congleton in the late 1600s, at which time a branch of the family moved to Staffordshire.

An influential family in Nantwich, the Malbanks are referred to on the opening page of the very first commissioned parish register of Nantwich, begun in 1539, which describes 'the pairyshe of Wychemalbank', (named after the original Norman Baron William de Malbank).

Part of the family, known by the name Malbon, moved into the Parish of Barthomley, situated on the Staffordshire border, though still lying within the old Hundred and deanery of 'Namptwich' (Nantwich). At that time the parish contained five townships, Barthomley, Alsager, Barterley, Crewe, and Haslington. There are memorials in the local church for the family of Malbon. Other family members moved to Cheadle and Mobberley in Staffordshire.

The Middleton Family of Leighton

There are many villages named Middleton in Britain and the Middleton family of Lancashire are typical of those who acquired the surname from these places. It is a simple locational name, made up of the Old English words 'midel' and 'tun', referring to a middle farm or settlement. Of the many in existence in 1086, the *Domesday Book* uses various spellings, including Middeltune, Middelton and Mideltuna.

An early recorded use of it as a family name is that of Robert de Mideltone in 1166 in Oxfordshire. Much later, records show that Sir George Middleton, (who died in 1673), was the owner of Leighton Hall near Carnforth and was Sheriff of Lancaster. As a mark of the family status, the chantry chapel of St Mary's in St Oswald Parish Church in Warton is dedicated to the Middleton family and their coat of arms is carved on a seat near the lectern. They acquired the chapel along with Leighton Hall, (dating from 1246), by the marriage of Alyson Croft with Geoffrey Middleton in 1438.

The Middleton Baronetcy was first created in June 1642 for George Middleton, but the title became extinct on his death in 1673. This came about at the end of the English Civil Wars, when heavy punitive fines were levied on the Middleton estates. In line with many other Catholic landowners, Sir George had been a staunch Royalist supporter. Sadly, while away fighting battles, his tenants stole many of his possessions and along with post-war seizures and subsequent fines, very little of their once extensive and wealthy estates remained intact.

In 1722, Leighton Hall was sold at public auction, and consequently little survives from the time of the Middleton family tenancy. At the time of writing, Richard and Susan Gillow Reynolds are its owners.

The Middletons have American connections. Edward Middleton emigrated to the United States in the 1600s, and his grandson, Henry Middleton, was elected President of the First Continental Congress on the 22 October 1774. There is a plaque dedicated to Sir George Middleton in the church at Warton, where George Washington's family is buried. The district of Middleton in Lancaster is almost certainly named after the family.

The Molyneux Family of Sefton & Croxteth

William de Moulins, (sometimes Molyneuxes), entered eighteenth on the Rolls of Battle Abbey, was granted the 'Manors of Sephton, Thornton and Kuerdon' by Lord Roger de Poitou, Earl of Lancaster, (sometimes Pictou or Poictiers), as a reward for his support in the Norman invasion. He was a common ancestor of the Molyneux family, who were one of the oldest families in Lancashire. Being of Norman descent, the family were granted the Manor of Little Crosby, which had been previously held by an Anglo-Saxon by the name of Uctred, until it was confiscated after the Conquest.

By 1212, it had passed to Richard de Molyneux of Sefton, whose family by then owned most of the Liverpool districts of Speke and Rainhill.

The Molyneux family grew in power, wealth and influence, and in 1446, Henry VI granted Croxteth Park, an area measuring over nine hundred acres, to Richard Molyneux.

In 1483, Thomas Molyneux was appointed Constable of Liverpool Castle, Steward of West Derby and Salford, and Master Forester of Simonswood, Toxteth and Croxteth. In 1575 the family had begun building Croxteth Hall as their new country seat. The Hall is located just two miles from Aintree Racecourse, which the Molyneux family had owned and developed.

Until relatively modern times the Hall played host to numerous house guests during Grand National week. At other times throughout the year the Park was a venue for pheasant shoots and riding. It was not uncommon for important society figures and royalty to stay for country house parties at Croxteth, particularly during the Edwardian era.

The Molyneux family were made Earls of Sefton in 1771. However, excessive gambling debts forced the family to sell off land and since the last Sefton Lord of the Manor died without heirs in 1972, the estate and Hall has been maintained and administered by Liverpool City Council.

The Mosley Family of Manchester

The Mosley surname originates in the Old English term 'mos-leah', meaning 'mouse wood' or 'small woodland clearing'. Over time, variant spellings have included Mowsly, Moseley, Mowsley, Mosely and Mousley. The family claim to have descended from Ernald de Moseley, who first settled somewhere near Salford Bridge in Manchester during the reign of Edward IV.

Ancoats Hall was the principal seat of this prosperous Manchester merchant family. Sir Nicholas Mosley was the first of the family to be Lord of the Manor of Manchester, and a onetime Lord Mayor of London. He and his brother had set up a business in woollen manufacture at a time when Manchester had a virtual monopoly on that industry. Their business expanded to such a degree that Nicholas moved to London to handle that end of the trade and to negotiate many profitable export agreements for his company.

He was also appointed as Alderman to several London wards, and made Lord Mayor of the City in 1599. He was a great success in this role, carrying it out with enthusiasm and dedication, being instrumental in raising soldiers and money to finance the building of warships for the navy of Elizabeth I to defend England against the Spanish Armada. He also arranged to supply troops, ordnance and provisions to Ireland in support of the campaign by Lord Essex. For this he was eventually knighted, aged 72 years, by the queen.

Sir Nicholas also built Hough End Hall in Withington, in south Manchester, a fine house, largely furnished with gifts from the queen, including most of the oak furniture.

Sir Nicholas retired in 1602, though as Lord of the Manor he presided over local courts. During this time he changed his name from Moseley to Mosley, dropping the 'e', so that his name could be embedded into the family motto, Mos Legem Regit, (which translates as 'custom regulates law'). He died in 1612, aged eighty-five years, and is buried in Didsbury churchyard. Effigies on his grave depict him kneeling in civic robes, accompanied by his first and second wives.

The Mosley family retained Lordship of the Manor of Manchester until 1846 when all the rights were sold for £200,000 by Sir Oswald Mosley to the Corporation of Manchester, which had been newly created in 1838. Mosley Street in Manchester still bears the family name.

In the twentieth century, a much-vilified member of the family, Sir Oswald Mosley, was founder and leader of the British Fascist Party in the 1930s. He became a Conservative MP for the Harrow constituency in 1918, the youngest MP in the House of Commons, and in 1928 was made Chancellor of the Duchy of Lancaster. A dedicated fascist, he actually paid visits to both Mussolini and the German dictator, Adolf Hitler, who was best man at Mosley's second marriage in Goebbel's house in Berlin.

However, the Second World War and the ensuing collapse of Fascism in Europe effectively brought an end to Mosley's career as a politician, and an end to the party's popularity in the western world. Mosley retired to live in France, where in 1968 he wrote his autobiography *My Life*.

By 1977, Sir Oswald Mosley was suffering from Parkinson's disease and died on 3 December 1980 in bed at his home in Orsay. He was cremated and his ashes scattered.

The Norris Family of Speke

The Norris family are thought to have origins dating well before the Norman Conquest, with many variations in the spelling of the surname, including Norrys, Norries, Noris, Norreys, Noreis, Noriss, Norrish, Norie, Norrie, Norse and Norice. It may have been derived from the

Old English words 'nord', (north) and 'hus', (house), indicating that the original family probably lived in a house at the north end of the settlement. Alternatively, it may have come from the Old French word 'norrice', meaning a nurse.

The family is first known at Speke, near Liverpool in 1314, when the region still lay within the County of Lancashire. It was William Norris II who began building Speke Hall over four hundred and fifty years ago, with funds accrued from the spoils of war.

Like many old Lancashire families, the Norrises were staunch Catholics, until Thomas Norris became the first head of the family to convert to Protestantism in 1651. Nevertheless, he was regarded as a Royalist sympathiser during the Civil Wars, which resulted in the punitive confiscation of his estates by Parliament; these were not restored until 1662. Thereafter the Norrises held the Speke estates, on and off, until the mid-eigtheenth century. Some time around 1795, the family moved to live in a fashionable district of London, and the house gradually fell into disuse.

Although several nineteenth century restorations were undertaken to Speke Hall by later owners, the twentieth century saw the Norris estate virtually obliterated. Bordering on the runway of Liverpool Airport, it is an unlikely setting for a fine restored Tudor house, now in the safekeeping of the National Trust.

The Ormerod Family of Whalley & Ormerod

The Ormerod surname probably derives from an old Norse name of 'Ormr', (meaning a serpent, snake or dragon), and originated in Cliviger, a medieval East Lancashire hamlet in the parish of Whalley, originally known as Ormes Royd. A 'royd' or 'rod' had several meanings in early medieval times, including a valley, a clearing, wood, or cultivated area, so the surname could translate variously as 'dragon wood', 'snake valley', 'serpent field' or any other likely combination.

Alternatively, and more probably, it may simply mean 'Orme's clearing' as Orme is known to have held extensive lands in the region.

The *Domesday Book* witnesses that significant areas of land in Northern England were owned by Gamel and Orm, his son; they were probably Christian Vikings who had settled in the Lancashire-Yorkshire borders, and by the middle of the eleventh century Orm was already a man of considerable wealth and importance.

An early Ormerod family member is Matthew de Homerodes, whose name appears on documents some time around 1270. Matthew had, possibly, three sons: Gilbert, Adam and Tille. It is through them that all Ormerods are believed to be descended. The family held the Manor of Ormerod from 1311 until 1793, when Charlotte Ann Ormerod conveyed the estate to her husband, Colonel Hargreaves, and the lands passed out of the family.

The first recorded spelling of the family name is probably that of Peter Ormerod, dated in January 1563. He was married to Agnes Pearson at Burnley.

Ormerod is still a widespread surname throughout Lancashire and West Yorkshire with significant family descendants in Australia and the Americas. Spelling variations of the name include Ormerod, Ormeroyd, Omerod, Omrod and Ormrod.

The Osbaldeston Family of Osbaldeston Hall

The Osbaldeston family traces its roots back to 1063, during the reign of Edward the Confessor, but it is believed to be even older. Several alternative forms of the name have appeared over the years, including Osbaldtun, Osbaldstun, Osberston, Osbaldton and Osbaston, although American branches have also been shortened to simply 'Deston'. All are derived from Old Saxon, which means 'the settlement or homestead possessed by Osbald', (or Oswald).

The family settled in the fertile Ribble Valley, in Osbaldeston village, Balderstone, Salesbury, Walton-le-Dale, Clayton-le-Dale, Samlesbury and Billington. The Domesday Survey shows Osbaldeston and Balderstone as two of the twenty-eight manors held by an ancestor of Ailsi, son of Hugo de Osbaldeston.

In 1387, Thomas Osbaldeston inherited the manor and estate of Cuerdale, near Walton-le-Dale. Then, prior to the Battle of Agincourt, Sir John Osbaldeston was knighted by Henry V and became the Lord of Chadlington Manor in Oxfordshire. Like many noble families, intermarriage with other county families was common and these included the Molyneux, Radclyffes, Duttons and Darwyns.

Osbaldeston Hall, built by Sir Edward Osbaldeston during the reign of James I, was the family seat until around 1750.

By the early twentieth century, Osbaldeston estates were in the possession of the Dugdale family, who sold them on by auction. The Lavery Family owned the Hall from 1942 until it passed into the possession of the Inghams. In 1991, Osbaldeston Hall was purchased by the Walmsleys.

The Penketh Family of Great Sankey

There are several known spellings of this family name including Panketh, Penketh, Pankethman, Panketman, Pankettman, Penkethman, and others. It is an old regional surname derived from the village and former ancient Manor of Penketh in the Lancashire Parish of Prescot and is thought to translate as the 'wood on the hill'.

The family lived in Penketh Hall from around 1216 to 1624, and one of the first mentions of the name was William de Penketh who was witness to a charter in 1240.

In 1280, Gilbert and Robert Penketh became joint Lords of the Manor of Penketh. Gilbert had two sons, Henry and Richard, and it was through them, in 1325, that the inheritance went to seven daughters, or granddaughters. The eldest, Margery, married Richard de Ashton and their descendants retained the lordship of the manor, under the surname Ashton, up to the seventeeth century.

In 1643, during the Civil Wars, Royalist John Ashton was killed at Bolton, and Thomas succeeded to the manor.

Another Thomas Penketh was to become a famous Scottish doctor and a monk of the Warrington Monastery; he is mentioned in Shakespeare's *Richard III*.

In 1656, John Penketh was ordained a Catholic priest, and in 1663, he became a Jesuit. Unfortunately, in 1678 he was implicated in the Popish Plot, betrayed, tried at the Lancaster assizes, and condemned to death. However, he was reprieved, but spent many years in prison before his release on the accession of James II.

The Manor of Penketh eventually came into the Atherton family, and has descended as Great Sankey to Lord Lilford.

The Pilkington Family of Rivington

The Pilkington family have their roots in the ancient Manor of Pilkington, near Whitefield in Bury, and their ancestry goes back to Alexander, (sometimes known as Leonard), de Pilkington who fought at Hastings. It was upon his marriage that Whitefield and Underworth, (later called Unsworth), became part of the Pilkington Estate.

The placename is first recorded in 1202 as Pulkinton. The name may be taken from the Old English to mean 'the settlement of a man called Pilca (or Pileca)'.

The districts of Stand and Outwood, old parts of Whitefield, remained solely in the hands of the Pilkington baronets until the fifteenth century when they were forfeited because of their allegiance to Richard III; Edmund Pilkington had fought alongside the king at Bosworth Field in 1485. The family baronetcy was attainted by the victorious Henry Tudor in retribution, and all their possessions in Lancashire were confiscated and given to the Earl of Derby. Sir Thomas Pilkington later received a royal pardon, fought at the Battle of Bosworth, and was killed at Stoke in 1487.

In the early sixteenth century, James Pilkington, the third son of Richard Pilkington of Rivington Hall, became the first Protestant Bishop of Durham. His brother, Leonard Pilkington, founded a Grammar School in the 1500s at Rivington, near Horwich.

William Windle Pilkington, who was born at Windle Hall, St Helens, on 26 September 1839, the eldest son of Richard Pilkington, was to become one of the founders of the famous Pilkington Glass works in St Helens.

The Pollitt Family of Stockport

The earliest known documentation of the Pollitt family records a man by the name of Henricus filius Ypoliti in Yorkshire in 1171. The most likely origin of the name is that it was the personal name of a man called Pol, from the Greek name Hipolito, related to horses, and from which the word 'hippo' derives. The suffix 'itt' or 'ett' means 'little'. Hence, Pollitt may be translated as meaning 'little horse'. Various different spellings of the name exist, including Pollit, Pollett, Paulet and Pawlet.

In the early thirteenth century, Herriard House in Hampshire had passed by marriage into the Paulet family and by 1493, large tracts of land around Basingstoke were owned by John Paulet, who in 1551 was created Marquess of Winchester.

Basing House, near Basingstoke in Hampshire, was the palace of William Paulet, Marquess of Winchester, a powerful and wealthy Tudor courtier. It was built on the site of a Norman castle and according to some authorities is reckoned to have been the largest private residence in England. Henry VIII and Philip of Spain are said to have dined there.

In the early eigtheenth century Harry Paulet, (1691-1759), was created fourth Duke of Bolton. Branches of the family are found as far apart as Devon, Somerset, Jersey, Staffordshire and Cheshire, with a branch having moved to the North West, notably around Huddersfield in Yorkshire and Wigan, and in the 1830s a contingent of the Pollitt family was living in the Cheadle and Heaton Norris areas of Stockport.

Sarah and James Pollitt ran the Black Boy Public House on Bridge Street in Stockport from 1795 to 1824, on the site of the town's first Sunday School, which began in a room above the pub. John Pollitt and family ran The Grapes Inn in Stockport in the 1800s.

More recently, Pollitts owned and ran a large local vegetable concern on Stockport Road, and George Pollitt was a member of Stockport Council.

The Ponsonby Family of Cumberland

See: Part Ten: Ireland: The Ponsonby Family of County Kilkenny.

The Prestwich Family of Clifton

The now demolished Hulme Hall at Worsley was the one-time seat of the De Prestwich Family and residence of the Lord of the Manor of Manchester. The De Prestwich family were Thegns of Prestwich long before the Norman Conquest. The name is Anglo-Saxon – 'wich' means an enclosure. Prestwich therefore means the 'enclosed land of the priests'.

In 1291, Adam de Prestwich purchased the Manor of Pendlebury, (known also as Shoresworth), later to be passed on to the Radclyffe family of Ordsall Hall. The family were Lords of the Manor of Prestwich until 1362. Some time around 1340, Richard de Langley married Joanna, sole heiress of the Prestwich fortune, and subsequently their Prestwich and Heaton estates came into the possession of the Langley family of Agecroft Hall, who held them until 1561.

The Prestwich family had been wealthy vintners, with extensive land holdings in the north of Manchester as far as Farnworth, but most were lost during the Civil Wars.

The Radclyffe Family of Ordsall

The Manor of Ordsall came into the possession of the Radclyffes some time around 1335, but it was not until 1354 that Sir John Radclyffe established his right of inheritance. In the early fifteenth century, Elizabeth Radclyffe married her cousin Robert Radclyffe and built their first home at Foxdenton Hall.

Of Saxon origin, the surname Radclyffe translates as 'red cliff', as in the township of Radcliffe in the Metropolitan Borough of Bury, named on account of the red sandstone banks of the River Irwell that runs through it, and from where the family originally came.

One of the earliest records of it used as a surname is in the person of Walter de Radcliva in 1182, and shortly thereafter, of William de Redeclive in Lancashire in 1272.

The Radclyffe family, (sometimes Radcliffe or Ratcliffe), were to become major landowners in Ordsall, Prestwich and Salford, and owned Wythenshawe Hall and Park in early medieval times.

The oldest part of Ordsall Hall dates from just before 1361 when Sir John was granted a licence for a chapel. He had fought alongside Edward III in France and was awarded one of the most noble family mottos in the land: 'Caen, Crecy, Calais', reflecting the battles in which he had engaged. He was also responsible for the introduction of Flemish weavers to the north-west's long association with the textile industry.

In 1341, Richard de Radclyffe sold Roden, a piece of land in Prestwich, (sometimes Rooden), now known as Heaton Park. Charles Robert Eustace, who died in 1953, brought the long line of Radclyffes to an end.

The Rigby Family of Standish

The Rigby name comes from the old Norse, meaning 'ridge farm' and almost certainly is derived from the place called Rigby in Lancashire. The earliest known evidences of the surname are those of Gilbert de Rigebi, dated 1208, and of Henry de Ryggeby in 1285.

Records show that in 1339, Ambrose de Wrightington leased a parcel of land at Smithscroft, (Towneley), to Edmund de Rigby and his wife Joan. The Rigbys also appear at Arley in Cheshire as early as 1483, though this was later sold on to the Standish family.

By the sixteenth century, the family held substantial lands around Standish, Coppul, Chorley and Duxbury, as well as Harrock Estate, Wrightington and Parbold.

Alexander Rigby was a member of the Puritan branch of the family from Middleton in Goosnargh near Preston, and in April 1640 he was elected Member of Parliament for Wigan in the so-called 'Short Parliament'. He was re-elected in November 1640 for the Long Parliament, where he sat until his death in 1650. He had been Deputy Lieutenant for Lancashire in 1641 and a colonel in the Parliamentary army in 1643. Ironically, most of the family were staunch Royalists during the Civil Wars, and their estate was confiscated by Parliament, which ruined their fortunes.

The Sandbach Family of Sandbach

The township of Sandbach in Cheshire was probably known as Sanbec or Sandbecd in the *Domesday Book*, Sondbache or Sondebache in 1260, and Sandbitch in the seventeeth and eigtheenth centuries. The name derives from the Anglo-Saxon 'sand bæce', signifying a sandy stream or valley, and was mentioned as having a church with its own priest in the 1086 survey. It is assumed that the family took its name from the town.

During the reign of King John, Sandbach and the surrounding lands were held by Richard de Sandbach, who was High Sheriff of Cheshire in 1230. His brother, Thomas, was also Rector of Sandbach. Thomas's son, Randle, became Lord of Manor of Budenhall near Congleton.

Succeeding centuries saw the ownership of the manor passing out of the family to the Leghs of Booth and then the Radclyffes of Ordsall, who held it for about 250 years.

Some time after 1226, Margaret de Sandbach, daughter of Sir Richard, had married the powerful Sir William de Brereton, (whose family had accompanied William the Conqueror), and thereafter the families were closely linked.

Shortly before 1313, another Richard de Sandbach became rector of the College at Chaplains located in the Church of St Mary and Thomas the Martyr at Upholland, near Wigan. Thereafter the family seems to have been assimilated, along with their lands and wealth, into other noble families of the county through marriage, and subsequent references to the Sandbach family are few and far between.

The Sankey Family of Little Sankey

The Sankey family name has been variously spelled Sonkye, Sanchi, Zanchey or Sanki. Also as Sonchi in 1180, Sanki in the tax rolls and registers of 1202, and as Sonkey in 1228.

Little Sankey Hall was their ancestral seat in Lancashire, though the old manor was transferred to Cheshire when county boundaries were redrawn in 1974.

The family name seems to have been derived from the village of Sankey and the river of the same name. It probably comes from the seventh century English 'sandig', meaning 'a sandy place', or even 'an island of sand' in a fen or bogland.

Gerard de Sanchi, Lord of the Manor of Sankey, was the first known family forebear of any distinction, mentioned in an ancient record, Testa de Nevill, during the reign of Edward I.

In about 1250, Robert Banastre, Baron of Newton, granted land in Lowton to William de Sonkye. One family member is known to have fallen at Agincourt, and another died at Flodden.

As late as 1670, there is an instance of the name being spelled as 'Zanchey'. Individual family members were recorded variously as Roger de Sonky in 1299, John Sankey of Dublin in 1562, and Edward Sankey whose will was probated in Chester in 1609.

The Sankey family arms are found over the doorway to Sankey Parish Church.

The Savage Family of Rocksavage

The first recorded spelling of the Savage family name occurred in the *Domesday Book* in the person of Eadric Saluvage, (known as Edric the Wild, which may have been no more than a nickname). Eadric was an Anglo-Saxon leader who led a rebellion against the Norman invasion. Before the 1066 conquest, he held six manors in Shropshire and one in Herefordshire. The surname comes from the French 'sauvage', meaning 'wild' or 'wilderness'.

From 1368, the Savage family were Lords of half the Manor of Cheadle, (later known as Cheadle Moseley), and were the original owners of Bradshaw Hall, built by Sir John Savage during the reign of Henry VIII.

In 1569, Sir John built Rocksavage House at Clifton, near Runcorn, which became their main county seat. In 1674, this great red sandstone house was listed in the Hearth Tax returns as having fifty fireplaces.

During the Civil Wars, another John Savage, a devout Royalist, lost Rocksavage to Parliamentarian forces, who looted and demolished much of the building. After the war it was restored to the family and completely renovated. His celebrated son-in-law, Sir William Brereton, also built Brereton Hall as a replica of Rocksavage.

Sir Thomas Savage was made Viscount Savage and married Elizabeth Darcy, Countess Rivers, some time in the early seventeeth century, and the title Earl Rivers remained in the Savage family for several succeeding generations.

By that time, Thomas and Elizabeth Savage were members of the court, Thomas being Chancellor to Henrietta Maria, wife of Charles I, and his wife Elizabeth one of her ladies of the bedchamber. Unfortunately, they fell dramatically from grace and they were imprisoned for debt.

The main branch of the Savage family died out in the eigtheenth century with no male heir to continue it, and Rocksavage House ceased to exist two centuries ago.

In 1998, the Queen officially opened Rocksavage Power Station.

The Scarisbrick Family of Ormskirk

There are many variations on this surname, including Scarsbrick, Scarsbrook, Scarasbrick and Scarrisbrick, though all would have originated in the village of Scarisbrick, near Ormskirk in Lancashire. The name is of Old Norse origin, and translates as 'Skar's hill-slope', after the name of the man who owned the land. The suffix 'brick' is a corruption of the Norse word 'brekka', meaning a slope or hill. One of the earliest spellings of the placename was recorded in 1200 as Scharisbrec.

The Scarisbrick family, major county landowners, were once described as 'the richest commoners in Britain'. From 1238, they lived on the site of present day Scarisbrick Hall, and held powerful influences as one of the great families of Lancashire. An early reference to the family name is in 1230, when Scarisbrick was part of the lands which Roger de Marsey sold to Ranulf, Earl of Chester.

Family members intermarried with other notable Lancashire families, including the Heskeths, Halsalls, Bradhaighs and Barlows.

Scarisbrick originally dated back to the time of King Stephen, and the present building of 1867, thought by many to be one of the finest examples of Victorian Gothic architecture in Britain, was designed by Augustus Pugin. The Hall remained in the possession of the Scarisbricks until 1948, when it became Kingswood College. The District of Downholland remained part of the Scarisbrick estate until 1945, when the estate was sold off.

The family business was in the leather and textile trades, as well as having a papermaking business at Milnthorpe in Cumbria. The Scarisbrick vault is in Ormskirk Church, where the last family member, Thomas Scarisbrick, was buried on 26 July 1833.

The Seddon Family of Middleton

The first recorded spelling of the family name is that of Roger Sedan, dated 16 January 1521, when he married Elizabeth Greenehalghe at Manchester.

Sometimes written as Sedan, Sedden, Seden or Seyden, this is an English surname originally associated with the county of Lancashire. The placename is believed to mean 'the broad, wide hill', from the Old English 'side', used in the sense of a hill slope, with 'dun', indicating a hill.

Recordings of the surname from Lancashire church registers include the marriage of Richard Seddon and Alice Scholefield in January 1542, at Middleton, near Oldham.

Richard Seddon, (1845-1906), Prime Minister of New Zealand, was born in St Helens, Lancashire, and served an engineering apprenticeship before going to the Australian gold fields in 1863, and then on to New Zealand.

According to a contributor, Mr Daniel Seddon of Farnworth, the Bridgewater Papers held in the University of Salford state that 'the earliest recording of the family name is that of Thonet and Edward Seddon, who were tenants of The Lords of Worsley in 1446. Richard Seddon of Ringley is also recorded as having married a Joan Standish in 1473'.

The Sherburne Family of Stonyhurst

The Sherburne family's ancient country seat was at Stonyhurst in Lancashire and had been so since around 1246. Variations on the surname include Sherburn and Shyrburne, and the name is derived from the Old English 'scir', meaning 'bright', and 'burna', indicating a stream. Hence, 'bright (or clear) stream'. The name probably originated in the village of Sherbourne in Dorset, which dates back to at least 864, and is recorded in the *Domesday Book* as Scireburne, held by the Norman Bishop of Salisbury, it having been confiscated from the Saxon Bishop Aelfeald.

Richard Sherburne, (1460-1513), is known to have built the choir at Mitton church and was succeeded by his son, Hugh Sherburne, (1480-1528). Thomas Sherburne, (1505-36), was High Sheriff of Lancashire and Richard Sherburne, (1526-94), was knighted and held various public offices including Lieutenant of Lancashire. He enlarged his estates and rebuilt the house at Stonyhurst and Mitton church. He retained his Catholic faith after the Reformation and his son, Richard Sherburne, (1546-1629), bought the rectory of Mitton from James I to avoid problems with non-attendance at church.

In 1540, a Barony was granted to the Sherburnes. The family had close connections with the Isle of Man, where Richard Sherburne was Deputy Governor in 1532, and his son was Governor from 1580 to 1592.

During the 1640s they were forced to flee to York when their estates were confiscated by Parliament on account of their support for the Royalist cause during the Civil War. Their daughter, Anne, married Marmaduke Constable, who was also a Catholic Royalist, and they lived with the couple on their Everingham estates.

Their lands were passed down through the generations until 1702, when the Sherburne estates went to Mary, the young wife of Thomas Howard, eighth Duke of Norfolk, ensuring that they would, thereafter, belong to the Norfolks. Stoneyhurst Hall is now a Catholic college.

The Shrigley Family of Macclesfield

The Shrigley name, originally spelled Shriggelegge, and sometimes Shriggley, comes from the old English 'scric' and 'leah'. Scric is believed to refer to the grey backed shrike, a bird found in the woodland clearings in the Peak District of Pott Shrigley.

The Manor of Shrigley was first given to Horswin, Lord of the Manor and great-nephew of William the Conqueror. Horswin and his five brothers had lands and titles given to them after the Conquest, and many other lands in Cheshire were held by William's extended family. The Macclesfield Forest was itself designated as a royal hunting chase.

Sir John de Shriggeley, who died some time after 1403, was a leading statesman and judge in late fourteenth century Ireland, where he held office as Lord Chief Justice.

Shrigley Hall dates back over five centuries and was originally home to the Downes family until it was sold to William Turner, High Sheriff of Cheshire in 1821. Historically a private family house, Shrigley Hall has been carefully restored to its original beauty and opened as a hotel and country club in 1989.

The Shuttleworth Family of Gawthorpe

The Shuttleworths were an influential landowning family in the Burnley area, whose wealth came from wool weaving. They lived at Gawthorpe Hall for four hundred years and their estates date back to medieval times. The family name reflects a connection with the old woollen weaving tradition of the district, probably derived from the Old English word 'schotil'or 'scyttel', (a shuttle), a device that occurs three times on the family coat of arms, combined with 'worth', meaning an enclosure. The name appeared as early as 1227 as a district in the township of Bury where it was recorded as Suttelsworth.

One of the family's most celebrated members was Colonel Richard Shuttleworth, (1587-1669), of Gawthorpe Hall, who was twice High Sheriff of Lancashire, a Member of Parliament for Preston and commander of the Parliamentarian Army of the Blackburn Hundred during the Civil War. After his death, Gawthorpe was not occupied by a member of the family for 150 years, but several caretaker occupants looked after the estate.

The Shuttleworths numbered novelist Charlotte Brontë as a family friend; she spent some time as a guest at Gawthorpe.

It was not until the 1850s that the Hall would see the family's return, when Sir James Kay Shuttleworth, the great Victorian reformer, commissioned Sir Charles Barry to carry out restoration and improvements to the house.

In 1953, in view of the exorbitant cost of upkeep, Lord Charles Shuttleworth left Gawthorpe and moved to Leck Hall near Kirby Lonsdale. Today the Hall is a National Craft Centre, thanks initially to donations given by the Honourable Rachel Kay-Shuttleworth, (1886-1967), in the 1960s; she was the last of the family to live there.

The Hall is currently maintained by the National Trust and leased to Lancashire County Council, who partly let it as a College of Further Education.

The Stafford Family of Botham & Eyam

The surname comes directly from the county town in Staffordshire, which was recorded in the *Domesday Book* as Stadford, and translates as 'landing place (or mooring) by a ford'. Its origins are Anglo-Saxon and combine two words: 'staef' and 'forda', indicating a shallow crossing place. The De Stafford family took their surname from the place.

Branches of the Staffords and De Staffords of Botham and Eyam are widely spread over many English counties, though they are predominantly a Derbyshire family. They trace their certain history back to Robert de Teoni, who was born in Rouen, Normandy, in 1039, and was standard bearer and cousin of William the Conqueror. He was created Baron de Stafford for services in 1066.

Earlier, less certain sources cite Sviedi Svidrasson, born in 675 at Maere in Norway. Generations of the De Staffords were subsequently born at Stafford Castle, and in the eleventh and twelfth centuries several became Sheriffs of that county. By 1480 the De Stafford surname had been dropped in favour of, simply, Stafford.

Botham Hall in the township of Mellor, about eight miles southwest of Glossop, probably came into the possession of William de Stafford in 1380, through his marriage to its co-heiress, Margaret de Mellor, daughter of Roger de Mellor. The Botham estate was of modest size, and one of the Stafford's traditional country seats.

Another branch, at Eyam in Derbyshire, probably dates from 1200, when Richard de Stafford, a Templar under Henry III, set up a home at Eyam Hall. Richard had been given the land by Sir Eustace de Thorstein, Lord of the Manor of Eyam, in gratitude for services rendered. Eyam stayed in possession of the family until the sixteenth century when it passed by marriage into the Bradshaw family, and was renamed Bradshaw Hall. They were also Lords of the Manors of Calver and Rowland.

In 1787, Botham Hall was purchased by Samuel Oldknow, the celebrated mill owner and cotton manufacturer of Mellor in Marple, now in the Borough of Stockport.

The Standish Family of Standish

The Standish family came into being shortly after the Norman Conquest, when the Bussel family acquired the two adjacent villages of Stanedis and Longetre, (Standish and Langtree), as gifts from a grateful William the Conqueror. They had first settled in Gloucestershire, but a branch moved to the Parish of Standish, in the Leyland Hundred, known then as Stanedich, and since 872, had been one of the largest Saxon settlements in Lancashire. The name comes from two Old English words, 'stan', meaning 'stone', and 'edisc', an enclosed field or parkland.

One of the first recorded spelling of the surname was that of Ralph (sometimes Radulphus or Ranulf) de Stanedis in 1206. Ralph later simplified the name to Standish, when the family held the unbroken Lordship of the Manor until the 1920s.

Their country seat was Standish Hall, first built on its present site in 1574 by Edward Standish. The family held extensive coal mining rights in Adlington, near Macclesfield.

In 1840, Sir Thomas Standish of Duxbury is reported to have sold a coal mine in Duxbury for £8,000. When Henry Noailles Widdrington

Standish, the last Lord of the Manor, died in 1920 without issue at Contreville, France, the Standish line came to an end.

The Stanley Family of Knowsley

Stanley is of Anglo-Saxon origin and appears in several locations around England. It is composed of two elements: 'stan', meaning a stone, and 'leah', signifying a clearing in a wood. The family name derives from Adam de Stanley, (1125-1200), who was Lord of the Manor of Stanley in Staffordshire. They also owned extensive lands in the Isle of Man and, in 1405, Sir John Stanley became First Lord of Man. One of the great families of Lancashire, the Stanleys main houses were at Knowsley, in Merseyside, and Lathom, between Liverpool and Ormskirk.

Sir Thomas Stanley, who was Constable of Chester Castle and Lieutenant of Ireland, was created Lord Stanley in 1455 and two years later was appointed a Knight of the Order of the Garter. His descendants inherited many titles and played important roles in government and diplomacy, including becoming Secretaries of State.

The Stanleys were on the winning Lancastrian side during the Wars of the Roses. In 1485, Sir John had joined Henry Tudor against Richard III, and thereafter received several estates in Cheshire for his support of the new king. In 1508 he was made Lord Lieutenant of Ireland.

Eventually the family possessed extensive lands in Huyton, Prescott, Winwick and Ashton-in-Makerfield, (now in Wigan), as well as being made Earls of Derby. Edward Richard William Stanley, the nineteenth Earl of Derby, born in 1962, is the current incumbent of the peerage.

The Starkie Family of Huntroyde

The Starkie family, (sometimes Starkey), originally came from Barnton in Cheshire. It is recorded that in 1465, Edmund, son of William Starkie of Barnton, married Elizabeth, the daughter and heiress of John de Simonstone, whose family had held land in Simonstone since 1230.

The Starkie surname comes from the Old English word 'stearc', meaning firm, determined or steadfast, and one of its earliest recorded spellings was that of Ranulf Stark, (sometimes Ralph or Ralf), in the Suffolk Pipe Rolls of 1222.

The Starkies were sufficiently wealthy to provide arms for the local militia in 1574, and Edmund Starkie was summoned by the Council to lend money to Elizabeth, to defend the country against the threat of the Spanish Armada in 1588. Already a powerful and influential family by the seventeeth century, it was Roger Nowell Starkie who presided at the trial of the Pendle witches at Lancaster Assizes in 1612.

Edmund was the original builder of the family's country seat at Huntroyde. His grandson, John, (1584-1665), inherited Huntroyde in 1618 and went on to become Chief Justice of the Peace in Lancashire. In 1633, he was appointed Sheriff of Lancaster. John's eldest son Nicholas, a captain in the Parliamentary army, was killed at the siege of Hoghton Tower in 1643. During the Commonwealth period, John Starkie was appointed to the committee responsible for the confiscation and disposal of former Royalist lands.

Later, through marriage, the house at Hall i' th' Wood in Bolton passed into the ownership of the Starkie family. Other inheritances and shrewd purchases added Simonstone, Shuttleworth Hall in Hapton, lands in Osbaldeston and Salesbury, property at Heaton near Horwich and Westhoughton. Other estates were in Pendle, Mearly, Pendleton and Heyhouses and added to the Starkie family's wealth and holdings. By the end of the nineteenth century, the Starkies were the owners of nearly nine thousand acres of land in Lancashire.

Nicholas Le Gendre Starkie, (1799-1865), was Member of Parliament for Pontefract from 1826-1832 and a prominent Freemason, being Provincial Grand Master for the Western Division of Lancashire. Well known and respected philanthropists, later family members donated churches in Padiham, Clowbridge, Higham and Hapton.

In more recent times, Edmund Starkie, (1871-1958), served as captain in the Boer War. He and his wife were prominent local promoters of the Red Cross and St John's Ambulance Brigade, and gave Huntroyde to be used as a hospital for convalescent soldiers during the First World War.

On his death in 1958, the estate passed to his nephew, Guy Le Gendre. The house was partially demolished in 1969 and eventually sold in 1983.

The Stokeport Family of Stockport

The Stockport name existed before the Norman Conquest, and was known as Stocford, derived from two Saxon words: 'stoc' meaning 'a stockaded place (ie. a castle or fort)', and 'port', indicating a wood; literally meaning 'a castle in a wood'. Alternative variants on the name include Stopforth and Stopford. There is sufficient evidence that a fortified stronghold existed in ancient British times, and that in 79 the Roman General Agricola fortified Stockport to guard passage across the Mersey.

After the 1066 invasion, one of the Norman feudal barons, Sir Robert de Stokeport, (c.1160-1206), was created Baron de Stokeport. His daughter Margaret may have married into the influential De Vernon family, and his son Robert would be largely responsible for the development of the town of Stockport, after which the family acquired its name. It is not certain, but this may have been the same man, sometimes known as Roger de Stokeford, who is recorded in Cheshire records of 1295.

The De Stokeport family virtually controlled the township over the next six hundred years, obtaining a Charter in 1220 granting the burgesses of Stockport the right to elect their own mayor, without interference from their Earl or Baron.

The Sudell Family of Blackburn

Although the Sudell family, (sometimes Sudel), came from peasant stock, they have been associated with the development of the Borough of Blackburn for more than four hundred years. The name is thought to have originally come from the township of Sud Hill in East Yorkshire, spelled Suddale in the twelfth century. It derives from two Old English words, 'sud', meaning south, and 'doel' (or 'dael'), meaning a valley (or dale). Hence, 'south dale'. Other variant spellings have included Soudale, Suddell and Soudell. One of the earliest known uses of the name was that of Robert de Sudale, recorded in the 1201 Fine Court Rolls of the County of Norfolk.

John Sudell, who held chantry lands at Oozebooth in 1548, is another early example, as is William Sudell, who was living in Blackburn during the reign of Elizabeth I.

Another William Sudell was elected Governor of Blackburn Grammar School in 1714. Around 1799, Henry Sudel purchased the Woodfold estate and built Woodfold Hall in Mellor. It was to develop into an extensive estate, well stocked with deer and wildfowl.

Several local estates were also purchased, so that by 1820 Henry Sudell was a millionaire. However, ill-advised speculation in continental and American markets led to major financial losses and in 1827 he was declared bankrupt. Thereafter, the family left Woodfold Hall to live at Ashley House near Bath, bringing Sudell family influence in Lancashire to an ignominious end.

The Talbot Family of Bashall, Salesbury & Carr

The Talbot family trace their origins back to Richard de Talbot, who is mentioned in *Domesday Book* as holding land from Walter Giffard, Earl of Buckingham. The name is a combination of the Old French words, 'tal', meaning to destroy, and 'bod', meaning messages or tidings; hence, (possibly), 'messenger of destruction'. The name arrived with the Normans in 1066, and later one Talebod de Neweham was recorded in the Book of Seals for Essex in 1146.

Henry VI, (1421-71), is recorded as having sought refuge from his enemies at Clitheroe after the Battle of Hexham, and was betrayed to Edward IV by the Talbots of Bashall and Salmesbury, including Thomas Talbot, son of Sir Edmund Talbot, together with his cousin John, to whom Henry surrendered his sword.

The Talbots were rewarded for their work by Edward, receiving all their costs and charges. Additionally, Sir Thomas Talbot received the sum of £100, and a yearly pension of £40, thereby identifying him as the prime mover in the capture of the deposed king.

It is recorded that the Talbot family later held the Manor of Withnell, near Chorley, when James Talbot married Mary Parke. In

1783, two of his sons were educated at the English College in Rome and were later priests in England, one becoming a Jesuit. Other Talbot family members lived in Preston.

In 1813, William Talbot founded the Talbot Schools at St Walburges, Preston. Bagganley Hall, Chorley, a one-time home of the Talbot family, was rebuilt by John Parker in 1633 and demolished in modern times to make way for the M61 Motorway.

The Tatton Family of Wythenshawe

According to recorded history, in Anglo-Saxon times a man named Tata left his home in Rostherne to set up 'Tata's tun', (Tata's town or village, hence Tatton), on the site of the present Old Hall at Tatton Park. The twin manors of Tatton passed through an heiress to Sir Richard Massy in 1286, the first record of the Tattons at Kenworthy in Northenden.

The earliest mention of the name Wythenshawe is in a charter of 1316, when Thomas de Masci of Wythenshawe granted land to his son and to his neighbour Sir William Baggilegh. The land passed to the Tattons by the marriage of heiress Alice Massy to Robert de Tatton in 1370, when the family became Lords of the Manor of Northenden and took control of the Wythenshawe and Northenden districts.

Robert de Tatton built their new house at Wythenshawe Hall around 1540 and it was to be the home over the next four centuries to fourteen generations of Tattons. They also owned Northenden Mill and had ferry rights across the Mersey. The family oversaw most of Wythenshawe from the thirteenth to the twentieth century and added to their fortunes through wise land acquisition and carefully placed marriages into other notable families.

Their home at Wythenshawe Hall withstood and survived an abortive siege by Oliver Cromwell during the Civil War. By 1926 the last member of the Tatton family had died and Wythenshawe Hall and the surrounding parkland was left to Manchester Corporation.

In 2016, Wythenshawe Hall was badly damaged by fire, requiring extensive restoration.

The Tetlow Family of Ashton

Sometimes spelled Tetlawe, or Titlow, the name is thought to have originated either in the hamlet of Tetley on Humberside, or perhaps the village of Titley in Herefordshire. The name comes from a combination of the Old English personal name 'Taeta', (or 'Titta'), and 'leah', meaning a wood clearing; hence, 'Titta's clearing'. It was recorded in the Herefordshire entry in the *Domesday Book* as Titellege, and in the Pipe Rolls of the County in 1194 as Titelea.

There is evidence of fines being levied against Robert de Tetlawe in 1410, and in 1422 Adam de Tetlow having rented properties in Ashton-under-Lyne. They held lands around Prestwich in the fourteenth century, when Joanne de Tetlawe married Richard Langley and set up Langley Hall, near Prestwich. Thus began the Langley family of Middleton and Agecroft.

Around 1320, during the reign of Edward II, Richard Tetlow, son of Adam de Tetlawe, had been granted lands around Werneth in Oldham. Adam had also apparently married Eva, daughter of William de Oldham, and obtained her lands in Werneth and Oldham.

The Tetlawes were to live at Chamber in Werneth for many generations and their name appears in numerous historical documents. Gradually, the name was changed to Tetlow, and the family line remained intact until the seventeeth century, when Jane, sole heiress of Robert Tetlow, married George Wood, who in 1646 sold it on to Henry Wrigley, a linen draper from Salford.

Some time around 1680, Wrigley's granddaughter, Martha, married Joseph Gregge and the estate passed to him. Thereafter it was in the possession of the Gregg family.

The Townley Family of Burnley

In 1200, Roger de Lacy granted lands at Tunleia, (Townley), to his son-in-law, Geoffrey, and the powerful Townley family, (sometimes Towneley, Townley or Townsley), were soon established in the Burnley area, where they adopted the surname. It derives from the Old English words 'tun' and 'leah', the settlement clearing where Burnley may have first begun.

When Cecilia of Towneley, the sole surviving heiress of the family, married John del Legh in the fourteenth century, the estate passed into his family. John died some time around 1330, and his great-grandson resumed the old name of Towneley.

The building of Towneley Hall began in about 1400, set in sixty-two acres of parkland. The Hall has a private chapel and contains the fifteenth century Whalley Abbey vestments. As Catholics, they were consequently persecuted for their faith during the reign of Elizabeth I.

In 1817, Peregrine Towneley donated an area of land at Burnley Wood on which to build a Catholic church as well as giving £1,000 towards its construction. For many years the Towneleys possessed the original scripts of the Wakefield Mystery Plays, (the Towneley Manuscript); they are now in the Huntington Library in San Marino, California and are sometimes referred to as 'the Towneley Cycle'.

Until 1826, the Townleys held land around the Stargate Pit and grew wealthy from surface coal mining in the area. Coal had to be transported across Towneley land for payment of a toll or wayleave, and this contributed significant funds to the family coffers.

Towneley Hall remained with the family until the early twentieth century, when in 1901, Lady O'Hagan, (Alice Mary Towneley), sold the Hall and its sixty-two acres to Burnley Corporation for a nominal sum of £17,500.

The Tyldesley Family of Myerscough Hall

By 1332 the Tyldesley family had established themselves as Lords of the Manor of Tyldesley. The fields and forests of the Tyldesley estates to the north, then known as Tyldesleyhurst, are nowadays called Mosley Common. The name is derived from the Old English personal name 'Tilwald' and 'leah', a clearing, and may be translated as 'Tilwald's clearing'.

An early example of the surname spelling is that of Hugo de Tildesle in the Fee Court Records of Lancashire in 1212. Later, in 1375, Thomas Tyldesley is known to have acquired lands in Chaddock hamlet by marriage to Agnes Sutherland and later, Shakerley lands were added to the family holdings.

The Tyldesley family seat was at Myerscough Hall, (known as the Lodge), where they were hosts to James I in 1617, and in 1651 the future Charles II was a guest of the family.

A devout Catholic and Royalist supporter, during the Civil War Thomas Tyldesley was killed in 1651 by Parliamentarian forces under the command of the Earl of Derby at the Battle of Wigan Lane.

By 1700, the family had ceased to be, through marriage into other noble families in the region. Documents pertaining to the Oath of Association in 1696 list all the men of Tyldesley-cum-Shakerley. The list shows only one inhabitant from the former prominent families, Thomas Chaddock. Others, including the Tyldesleys, had gone.

The Urmston Family of Urmston

William the Conqueror bequeathed substantial assets to Lord Rogier de Poitou, who had aided him in 1066. Poitou, in turn, gave part of his holdings to Albert de Greslé, (sometimes Grelley). In turn, Greslé bestowed a portion of his lands upon Orme, the son of Edward Aylward, some time during the reign of John. This area became known as Orme's Tun, meaning 'Orme's settlement' (or dwelling), which later became Orme Eston, (meaning 'Orme, his town'), then Ormeston and finally Urmston.

In 1292, Sigreda, the heiress of the neighbouring Manor of Westleigh, (in Leigh), married Richard Ormeston, and these lands also passed to the Urmston family. However, the Lordship of the Manor of Westleigh was disputed many times over the following years, and it was not until the early seventeeth century that the rights were firmly in possession of the Urmstons, where they remained until the last of the male line died in 1659. Elements of the Urmston coat of arms, (notably, the spear), are to be found included in those of the town of Leigh.

Urmston Hall, the family's county seat, was built some time around 1350 and rebuilt towards the end of the sixteenth century. Later, it became a farm and was finally demolished in 1937. The township of Urmston, in the Metropolitan Borough of Trafford, still bears the name which the family gave it.

The Venables Family of Middlewich

The Venables family, (sometimes De Venables), hail originally from the town of Venables near Evreux in Normandy, and it was Gilbert de Venables, (also known as Gilbert the Hunter), huntsman to the Dukes of Normandy, who first held the Barony of Kinderton in Cheshire for Hugh Lupus after the Norman invasion.

Venables is an Old French derivation of the Latin words 'venabulum', meaning a hunting ground, or 'venari', from the verb 'to hunt'. Hence the family were apportioned the role of hunters, or 'venables'.

Other family members became Barons of Chester and of Warrington, and over time Venables became a prominent Cheshire and Lancashire surname.

The *Domesday Book* records that Gilbert held Brereton, Davenport, Kinderton and Witton in Northwich, and that Ralph Hunter held Stapleford in Cheshire and Soughton in Wales. Later the family became Lords of the Manor of Middlewich.

Wincham Hall, recorded as Winundersham in the *Domesday Book*, was given to Gilbert de Venables following the Conquest, but it successively passed in and out of the Venables family's ownership through inheritance, marriage and sale over the following centuries. It survived until bombing in the Second World War forced its final demolition.

The family's influence throughout medieval Cheshire is evidenced by the wreath on the coat of arms of Congleton, which incorporate the heraldic colours of the Venables family, as do the arms of Northwich, where the ship shown above the shield shows on its mainsail the wyvern of the Venables family.

The family held many other lands throughout Britain, including Woodcote near Winchester, as well as Antrobus Hall in Great Budworth, where they lived for many years.

The Venables have an international website and there are regular Venables family conventions held in England and in France. The Middlewich Festival, held in September each year, also acts as a gathering of the Venables family members from around the world.

The Vernon Family of Gawsworth

The Vernon family traces its ancestry back to France before the invasion of 1066, notably in the person of Baron Roger of Vernon, (born c.1030). William de Vernon, who was alive in Normandy in 1052, is thought to have first assumed the surname from his birthplace in Vernon in Normandy. His son, Richard de Vernon, Lord of Shipbroke, was living in England by 1086.

According to the *Domesday Book*, Richard was a knight of William, a grantee of Shipbrook and of fourteen other manors in Cheshire. He was married to Adzelia, daughter of William Peverel of Nottingham, an illegitimate son of William the Conqueror.

Another Richard de Vernon, a one-time favourite of King John, was appointed High Sheriff of Lancashire from 1200-1205.

The Vernons owned much of the land around Rode, North Rode, Rode Heath and Gawsworth in Cheshire, where many of the family are buried.

William de Vernon's great-grandson, also called Richard, married Alice, daughter and co-heir to the manor of William de Avenell of Haddon Hall in Derbyshire, sometime before his death in 1546, thus adding extensive Derbyshire lands to their ownership.

Others married into the De Stokeports and influential families in Shropshire, notably in Tong, where other members of the family lie buried.

In modern times, the family is probably still best known for its ownership of Haddon Hall in Derbyshire and of Gawsworth Hall near Macclesfield.

The Honourable Joanna Elizabeth Venables-Vernon, born in 1965, is the surviving daughter of John Lawrence Venables-Vernon, the tenth Baron Vernon. Since her marriage in 1992, she took the married name of FitzAlan-Howard.

The Walmsley Family of Rishton

The Walmsley family has a long association with the Lancashire village of Rishton. In 1581 it was recorded that Sir Thomas Talbot sold the Manor of Rissheton to Thomas Walmsley. It continued in the possession of the Walmsleys until 1711, when it passed out of the family through marriage.

The surname is Anglo-Saxon and comes from the Walmersley district of Bury. It has included variations like Walmisley, Wamsley and Waumsley over time. Derived from Old English, its origins are comprised of three words: 'wald', meaning a wood, 'mere' (or 'maere'), meaning a lake, (or a boundary), and 'leah', a wood; hence, a 'lake by a woodland boundary'.

The wealth and importance of the Walmsleys continued until the nineteenth century, when they had become prosperous textile manufacturers, holding shares in the Grimshaw Bridge Mill at Eccleshill. This early water-powered carding and spinning factory was erected in 1782 by William Yates, but following its failure in 1790, it was only worked briefly by William Booth of Lower Darwen.

By the early nineteenth century, the company of Walmsley, Townsend & Green had taken over. In 1823, the surviving partner, Joseph Walmsley, was employing twenty-three hands at the mill, and the whole undertaking came into the sole possession of the Walmsley family. In 1855, the family retired from business and sold the Grimshaw Bridge plant, but their name is still well remembered in places and streets throughout Lancashire.

The Warburton Family of Tabley & Warburton

The Warburtons are one of the oldest established families in Cheshire and Staffordshire. Warburton Village in Lancashire is where the name is said to have originated. Recorded as Wareburegetune in the 1150 Cheshire Pipe Rolls, it is probably named after a seventh century woman by the name of Waerburg, with the suffix 'tun' added, indicating a settlement. Hence, 'Waerburg's settlement'. An early use of the surname was one Richard de Warberton in Cheshire in 1214.

The family once owned the Manor of Glazebrook, but in 1384 Geoffrey de Warburton ceded the manor to Hamo Massy, (Lord of the

Manor at Rixton, later of Dunham Massey). This led to the combining of the two areas and became known as Rixton-with-Glazebrook.

William Warburton, (1615-73), who lived in the district, married Jane Burgess in 1641 in Rostherne where she was born. Later, intermarriage with the Egerton family produced a substantial inheritance for Rowland Egerton, seventh son of Philip Egerton of Oulton Park. He had married Mary Brooke of Norton Priory and rebuilt Arley in the 1840s, as well as having created Budworth village.

By 1766, members of the Warburton family were prominent trustees of Cobridge School in Staffordshire, as well as being co-founders of Lymm Grammar School, where the family crest is still incorporated in the coat of arms.

The Warburtons were, like most old Cheshire families, staunch Catholics, and originally rented lands from the Biddulph family on the Grange estate in north Staffordshire. At Grange, in the early eigtheenth century, John Warburton built a pot works for the manufacture of white stoneware which he exported, most profitably by all accounts, to Holland. By the time he died in 1752, he had amassed considerable property, which included the Tabley estate in Cheshire, for which he paid a mere £1,000.

The Warren Family of Poynton

The Warrens, (or De Warrenes), make their first appearance in records in 1164, when Hamelin Plante Genest, (which was Anglicised to Plantagenet, after the broom plant – or in its Latin form, *planta genista*), a Norman baron and illegitimate half-brother of Henry II, married Isabel de Warrene. The surname may be a corruption of La Varrenne, a village in the Seine-Maritime department of Normandy.

The De Warrenes settled to live in Surrey, where they were granted the Earldom of Surrey, and by 1254 had moved to Norfolk. They also held lands in Suffolk, Somerset and Sussex. The last De Warenne Earl of Surrey died in 1347.

Some time around 1380, the family appear to have been inexplicably disinherited and a branch moved north to live in east Cheshire. On the death of the last Plantagenet of England, some descendants changed their surname to Wareing (or Waringe).

Ultimately, the Warrens were to hold significant tracts of land throughout Cheshire, which they acquired through purchase and propitious marriage of Warren daughters into other influential Cheshire families. The Manor of Adlington, adjacent to Poynton, was subsequently purchased by John de Warren from the De Stokeport family.

In 1777, Elizabeth Harriett, daughter and heiress of Sir George Warren, was married to Thomas, the seventh Viscount Bulkeley, a substantial landowner in Anglesey, and took the name of Warren-Bulkeley. Elizabeth was a local beauty, immortalised in a George Romney portrait, which was specially commissioned for the marriage; it now resides in the National Museum of Wales in Cardiff.

In 1784, Thomas was created Baron Bulkeley of Beaumaris. In 1792 Sir George Warren purchased the Worth estate from the Downes family. (It is now Davenport Golf Club). Later, in that century, Anna Dorothea Warren, Viscountess Bulkeley, left part of her estate to the second Lord de Tabley, (of Tabley House near Knutsford), on condition that the family name incorporated Warren, (ie. Leicester-Warren).

By 1811, the sixth Baronet, Sir George Leicester, had assumed the name and arms of the Warrens, and thereafter the Tabley branch were known by the name of Leicester-Warren.

By the end of the nineteenth century, the Warrens were connected to most of the county's leading aristocracy. The manor and title of Poynton itself was held by the Warren family until 1801 when the last surviving male, Sir George, died and was succeeded by his daughter, Lady Warren Bulkeley. She died childless in 1826, when it passed to Frances Maria Warren, Lady Vernon. The Vernons held the estate until the final sale in 1920.

The Whitaker Family of the Holme

The Whitaker Family, (spelled with one 't'), trace their ancestry back to 1340, when Richard de Whitacre, came to live in Cliviger at Padiham, Lancashire.

The name derives from the Old English words 'hwit', meaning 'white', (or 'hweate', meaning 'wheat'), and 'acer', referring to a cultivated field; hence, 'white field', or 'wheat field'. An early use of the surname is that of Richard de Wetacre in the 1177 Norfolk Pipe Rolls.

From 1548-95, William Whitaker was Master of St John's College, Cambridge. By 1587, he is known to have been father of seven children, six by his first wife, including Alexander, known as 'the Apostle of Virginia', who went to America as a missionary in 1611. He lived near Jamestown, had a parish in Henrico County, published *Good News from Virginia*, is said to have converted the Native American Princess Pocahontas and officiated at her wedding. In 1615, he drowned in the James River.

William Whitaker also had another son, Jabez, by his second wife Joan, (widow of Dudley Taylor), born in December 1595 in Lambeth, London. Like his half-brother, in 1619 Jabez emigrated to live in Jamestown. Both he and his only known son, William, served as Burgesses in Virginia. Consequently, there is now an extensive network of Whitaker descendants in the USA.

The forty-room manor house at Holme was the county seat of the Whitakers from the fifteenth century. Prior to their ownership, Holme belonged to the Tattersall family, and before that to Edward Legh, of the Legh family from Cheshire.

Gradually, the Whitakers strengthened their local standing through marriage with other notable families of Lancashire and Cheshire, including the Sherburnes, Stanleys, Harringtons and the Towneley family.

Mrs Cary Young Adams, a Whitaker descendant of Norfolk Virginia, in a correspondence to the author of this book, adds a variation on the account:

'Dr William Whitaker of Cambridge University married (1) Susan Culverwell, daughter of Nicholas Culverwell of London, (2) Joan Fenner, nee Taylor, widow of Dudley Fenner. He had eight children born 1583-1595, five by

Culverwell, and three by Taylor. His married life was spent at Cambridge, and all of his children were born there. Jabez Whitaker married Mary Bourchier, daughter of Sir John Bourchier of Surrey. Jabez was prominent in Virginia, serving on the Governor's Council. He left Virginia with his family in 1628, presumably to return to England. He had at least two children, but there is no record of the names of his sons. There were two William Whitakers in early Virginia. One was too old to have been Jabez's son. The other might have been, but there is no proof of this. He might have returned to Virginia, but there is no record of this. The North Carolina Whitakers claim descent from Jabez, but offer no proof.'

The Wilbraham Family of Woodhey

In the sixteenth and seventeeth centuries, the Wilbraham family, (sometimes Willbraham or Wilbram), were one of the largest landowners in Cheshire and their seat was at Woodhey.

The name appears in the *Anglo-Saxon Chronicles* as Wilburgeham, and derives from the Old English 'Wilburg', a woman's name, and the suffix 'ham', signifying an enclosure or farm, which all translates as 'Wilburg's farmstead'.

The family name is probably best associated with the castle at Mow Cop, a distinctive Cheshire landmark, which was built as a summerhouse in 1746 for Randle Wilbraham 1st of Rode Hall. The Hall had been in the family since 1669. The main house was completed in 1752, with additions in 1812 and 1927.

Dorfold Hall, which stands between Nantwich and Acton, was also built in 1616 by the Wilbraham family. It was plundered by Royalist soldiers as they fought their way through Cheshire in 1643.

The Lordship of the Manor of Longdendale had been granted in 1554 by Mary I to the Wilbraham family, their estates comprising Mottram-in-Longdendale and Tintwistle. However, as absentee landlords they had little contact with the manor throughout the period of their tenure.

The Baronetcy of Wilbraham of Woodhey was created by James I in 1621. In the seventeeth century they held around 28,000 acres of land in Cheshire, of which around 15,000 acres was located in the Longdendale valley, including Micklehurst, Mottram and a small part of Godley.

When Sir Thomas Wilbraham of Woodhey died in 1692, his Cheshire estates and titles were inherited by his son-in-law, Lyonel Tollemache, Earl of Dysart in Scotland, and thereby passed out of Wilbraham family control.

At the turn of the nineteenth century, the Wilbraham family moved to live in Lancashire and by the time they had decided to move back to Cheshire, some fifty years later, the castle was in a derelict state of disrepair.

The Winstanley Family of Wigan

The Winstanley name is thought to predate the Norman Conquest, and may be a corruption of 'Winstan's leah', a forest clearing belonging to a man called Winstan. From 1212, Roger de Winstanley held the manor under the Lord of Billinge and is noted for the benevolent grants which he made to Cockersand Abbey.

Various members of the family continued an unbroken tradition of ownership of the lands well into the early sixteenth century. In 1596, Edmund Winstanley and his wife Alice sold the Manor of Winstanley along with Winstanley Hall and several coal mines, to James Bankes, a Wigan man. Upon Bankes' death in 1617 the manor was sold on to Sir Richard Fleetwood, Baron of Newton. Others of Bankes' possessions included the Manor of Houghton in Winwick, and lands in Winstanley and adjacent townships.

A branch of the Winstanley family lived in nearby Blackley Hurst. Their lands were eventually sold to Richard or William Blackburne in 1617, and were later acquired by the Gerard family.

A number of the Winstanleys were Quakers and ironically, in 1670 they were convicted as 'Popish recusants', for which apparent 'crime' two-thirds of their properties were seized.

During the seventeeth century, Gerrard Winstanley was a writer and prominent in local politics, having been the leader of the short-lived 'left wing' political movement known as the Diggers. His political writings were widely studied in the former Soviet Union where his name is on a monument to the nation's Great Socialist Thinkers.

Winstanley Hall was occupied by the Bankes family for nearly four hundred years until 1984, although it was subsequently sold for conversion to luxury apartments.

The Worthington Family of Worthington

The Worthington family resided at Worthington in Standish from about 1150, and it is from there that they acquired the surname. The name means 'lands (or estates) belonging to a man named Woerth' and is entered in the *Domesday Book* as Werditone.

By 1215, mention is made of the Coppull Family, perhaps related to the Worthingtons, possibly the origin of the township Coppull-with-Worthington.

By 1577, their landholdings were extensive and Worthington Hall was their country seat. In 1690, Thomas Clayton bought the adjoining Manor of Adlington of Worthington from Edward Worthington and his wife Jane. These properties were, through descent, inherited by the Clayton family, most notable among whom were Richard Clayton who became Lord Chief Justice of the Common Pleas in Ireland from 1765.

In the late 1770s, in common with many other Lancashire villages, textile manufacturing was introduced to the village, on the site of the original Worthington Mill, which dated from around 1348. Initially a small dye works, it later became a paper mill, and then a textile mill, before it closed down in 1998.

The Worth Family of Tytherington

The Worth estate was owned by the family before 1208, when written history of the family records that Benedict and Jordan de Woorthe had land at Upton in Macclesfield. The name is a common placename throughout England and is descended directly from the Old English word 'worth', meaning an enclosure of land or a settlement, (as in places like Kenilworth, Rickmansworth, Butterworth, etc).

Later, some time in the fourteenth century, Robert de Worth married the heiress Anable de Tiderinton, (Tytherington), and acquired her estates and properties through this marriage. The family lived at Tytherington Hall until the end of the seventeeth century, when Jasper Worth, the heir apparent, died in 1693. Tytherington Hall had been owned by the Worths for over three hundred and fifty years. Bache Hall was also a Worth property for hundreds of years.

Over many generations, the Worth family married into the Cheshire families of the Wheelocks, the Newtons of Pownall, the Beresfords, Suttons, Draycotts, Downes, Vernons and the Davenports. The heirs of the Worth family eventually sold Worth Hall and Tytherington to the Downes family.

The Worths were eventually ruined by their allegiance to the king's cause in the Civil Wars. Their estates were confiscated by Parliament and the head of the family hanged. Most of the Worth family is buried in Prestbury Church.

Part Three

The West Midlands
Family Names in Hereford, Shropshire, Staffordshire, Warwickshire, West Midlands & Worcestershire

The Amphlett Family of Hadsor & Clent

The Amphlett Family, (sometimes Umphlett), were an important family in Worcestershire from the early seventeeth century, whose members served as High Sheriffs of Worcestershire at least six times during the eigtheenth and nineteenth centuries. The origin and meaning of the surname Amphlett is almost certainly derived from Amflete in Normandy.

The surname appears to have originated from a tenant of Salwarpe, which was held by Earl Roger. The *Domesday Book* suggests a descendant of Amfrid and Adeliza, who was sister of Hugh Grandmesnil, the son of Humphrey, was created Baron Castellan of Hastings after the Conquest. In 1069, he returned to Tilleul-en-Asuge in the Calvados region of Normandy. There are several variants of the surname, including Amflett and Amphliss.

The family first lived at Salwarpe and Astley, but in 1633 William Amphlett, (1588-1662), moved the family's principal seat to the Manor of Hadzor. His son, Richard Amphlett, (1624-1703), continued the expansion and bought the Clent House estate, where his younger son, Joseph Amphlett, (1672-1720), built a new house in about 1709. Hadzor was a semi-timbered house, known as the Old Manor.

Clent is recorded in the *Domesday Book* as being in the Worcestershire Hundred, lying just outside the Royal forests of Feckenham and Kinver.

In Medieval times the farming community of Clent was strongly influenced by Halesowen Abbey, established in the thirteenth century. From the sixteenth century scythe makers and later wheelwrights, locksmiths and nailers thrived in the area. In the eigtheenth century, Clent grew from a small hamlet into a recognisable village with its own church. At this time, John Amphlett of Clent House founded the village school.

The Arden Family of Castle Bromwich

During the reign of Edward the Confessor, before the Norman invasion, Aelfwine, (sometimes Alwin), was Sheriff of Warwickshire. After 1066, his son, Thurkill, (sometimes Thorkil), of Warwick was one of only a handful of Saxon lords whose lands were not all seized, and after a large portion was ceded to the Norman Earl of Warwick, he retained the remainder as a tenant. By the time of Domesday in 1086, Thurkill de Arden is recorded as holding estates in Arden, at Curdworth, (Credeworde) and in Minworth. The estates passed thereafter down through the family. In line with Norman tradition, Thurkill assumed the surname, Arden.

The area known as Arden is mainly in Warwickshire, and also part of Staffordshire and Worcestershire. It encompasses the land between the Rivers Avon and Tame. It was once heavily wooded, giving rise to the name 'Forest of Arden'. The name derives from the Old English word 'earn', meaning 'eagle', and 'denu', signifying a valley; hence, 'the valley of the eagles'. The name is thought to be related to the Ardennes Forest in France and Belgium.

Ralph de Arden married Isabel, daughter of Anselm of Bromwich in 1323 and over time acquired the Manor of Park Hall in Castle Bromwich. Later, Robert de Arden, (c.1412-52), acquired the Manors of Saltley, Pedmore in Stourbridge and Water Orton through his marriage to Elizabeth Clodshall. However, Robert was executed after the Wars of the Roses as a Yorkist sympathiser. Other family members fell foul of the changing religious and political climate in England; Edward Arden was executed as an unapologetic Catholic and the family estates were forfeited to the Crown. It was not until 1609 that his son Robert could recover the manor and its estate. Robert's grandson failed to produce male heirs and the Arden estates, along with Park Hall, passed through the female line, out of the family in 1643, when Goditha Arden married Herbert Price, who took up residence.

Mary Arden, mother of William Shakespeare, was a member of the family.

The Astley Family of Warwickshire

The township of Astley in North Warwickshire is the most probable origin of the Astley family name and is an old Anglo-Saxon corruption of 'est leigh', meaning 'east wood'. There are other villages of this name around the country, including in Lancashire and Shropshire, recorded in the *Domesday Book* variously as Hesleie and Estleia. Astley was held by a man called Alsi in the reign of Edward the Confessor, and after the Conquest by Robert, Count of Meulan.

The earliest known records of the surname in use are those of Philip de Estlega, who in 1166 held three pieces of land, of which Astley was one, and of Thomas de Estleye, who also held the manor before his death at the Battle of Evesham in 1265. Andrew de Astley, possibly the next Lord of the Manor, was entered in 1295 in the Hundred Rolls of Warwickshire. He was also summoned to Parliament as Lord Astley in that year. By 1400, Astley came under the lordship of the Earls of Warwick, with the Astley family remaining as tenants.

Sir William, the fourth Baron Astley, was Justice of the Peace for Warwickshire, and when he died in 1404 without male heirs, the estate and title passed through marriage of his daughter Joan, (or possibly Katherine), into the Grey family, at which time the Astley peerage fell into abeyance.

Other branches of the family were based in Reading and in Melton Constable. Of the Reading branch, Sir Jacob Astley, (1579-1652), had the peerage restored to him in 1644, when he was created Baron Astley of Reading. He was a Royalist commander during the Civil War, who was promoted by Charles I as Major General of Foot and fought at the battles of Edgehill, Newbury and Naseby. However, in 1646, his force was overwhelmed at the Battle of Stow-on-the-Wold where he surrendered to Parliamentarian forces. He was imprisoned shortly before retiring to Maidstone in Kent, where he died in 1652. In 1688 the Astley Barony of Reading became extinct, and the estates passed to the Astleys of Melton Constable.

Sir Edward Astley, (1729-1802), of Melton Constable Hall, was Member of Parliament for Norfolk, and after spending large sums improving the Melton Constable estate as well as an expensive election campaign, he was forced to sell off the Hillmorton estate in Warwickshire.

In 1814, through marriage, the family inherited the Seaton Delaval estate in Northumberland. In 1840, the House of Lords revived the Barony of Hastings in favour of the family, a title that had been in abeyance since the fourteenth century, and Sir Jacob Astley became the sixteenth Baron Hastings.

By 1948, in light of post-war debt, the Melton Constable house and estate were sold off, and Seaton Delaval was taken over by Sir Edward Delaval Astley, (1913-2007), and became his main home. Following Sir Edward's death in 2007, the current Lord Hastings sold Seaton Delaval to the National Trust and moved to live in a modest house at Barney, near Fakenham in Norfolk.

The Bagot Family of Bromley

The Bagot family name, (sometimes Baggot, Baggett or Baggott), is thought to have come from the Bethune and St Omer townships of Northern France. They held Bromley in Staffordshire for Robert de Stafford, shortly after the Conquest. It is recorded in the *Domesday Book* that one Bago of Bagod d'Artas held Bromley in 1086. He had fought with William at Hastings. In 1140, Robert Bagod was witness to a charter founding the Priory at Canwell.

The name is derived from the Old German 'bago' (or 'bacco'), meaning 'to fight'. It is recorded as a personal name in Staffordshire around 1125, and one Simon Baghot is listed in the 1198 Staffordshire Fleet of Fines.

Sir John Bagot, (1358-1437), son of Sir Ralph Bagot, lived in Blithfield and Bagots Bromley, Staffordshire, and in 1451, was High Sheriff of Staffordshire as well as its Member of Parliament. He was a distinguished knight who served with John of Gaunt in Portugal in 1386. His grandson, Richard, died at Bosworth in 1485. Another grandson, John, (c.1436-90), was Member of Parliament for Staffordshire in 1477.

Hervey Bagod IV assumed the name of Stafford and was an ancestor of the Dukes of Buckingham. In 1627, Sir Hervey Bagot was created Baron Bagot of Blithfield, and fought as a Royalist during the Civil War. He was High Sheriff of Staffordshire and a Member of Parliament. Colonel Richard Bagot was a defender of Lichfield Cathedral during that conflict. Sir Hervey's son, Sir Edward Bagot, the second Baronet, served in the Restoration Parliament after the accession of Charles II.

The present incumbent, (as of 2017), is Charles Hugh Shaun Bagot, who succeeded as the tenth Baron Bagot of Bagot's Bromley in 2001. The main ancestral seat of the Bagot family continues to be at Blithfield Hall in Staffordshire, but other branches of the family have seats in Warwickshire and Cumbria.

The Bassett Family of Drayton

The Bassett family are found in several areas of England, including Devon and Cornwall, but the main branch settled in Staffordshire. Thurstan Basset, (1050-1128), of Quilly Basset in Normandy, whose name appears on the Battle Abbey Roll in Hastings, is known to have founded the family line. He held land in Drayton, what is known today as Drayton Basset in Staffordshire.

The name originates in the Old French word 'basset' or 'bassa', meaning thickset, often referring to a man of short or low stature. The family held the posts of Constable of Dover and Lieutenants of Dover Castle during the reign of King John, (1199-1216). An early exponent of it as a family name appears in the *Domesday Book* in the person of Ralph Basset. He was titled Lord Basset of Drayton, and was summoned to Parliament as Baron Basset de Sapcote in 1264. In time he became Governor of Edinburgh Castle.

Another Sir Ralph, the third Lord Basset, fought and distinguished himself under the Black Prince at the Battle of Bordeaux in 1355, and was made a Knight of the Garter in 1368. On his death in 1389, having no male issue, his daughter Jane married Sir John Stourton, the baronetcy went into abeyance and the Drayton branch became extinct.

It was not until 1797, that Francis Bassett, Baron de Dunstanville was created Baron of Stratton. He served as Member of Parliament for Penryn in 1780. On his death in 1835, Frances Basset succeeded as second Baroness Basset of Stratton in Cornwall, and that baronetcy also became extinct on her death in 1855.

The Beauchamp Family of Worcester

Urso d'Abbetot accompanied William the Conqueror in his invasion of England in 1066. Some authorities have him as a son of Almericus, Lord of Abtot in Le Havre. Whatever his name, in gratitude the Conqueror granted Urso large tracts of land in Worcestershire and other counties, before he was made Sheriff of the county as well as a Royal Forester.

His daughter, Emmeline, married Walter de Beauchamp (of Elmley). Urso's son, Roger, offended Henry I by committing a murder while at court, and his possessions were given to his brother-in-law, Walter de Beauchamp, who was made a Knight of Worcestershire.

Early records show the name was sometimes Latinised as 'de Bello Campo' as with William de Bello Campo, who appeared in the 1161 Knights' Templars Records of London. After the Conquest, when Norman French prevailed, the two elements 'beau', meaning fair or beautiful, and 'champ', meaning a field, were common usages. Other variants include Beacham, Beachem and Beecham.

A branch of the family lived at Shrawley in Worcestershire, having previously been held by Ralph de Todeni, a standard bearer for William the Conqueror, before it passed to Guy Beauchamp, Earl of Warwick during the reign of Edward II. Another branch lived at Bengeworth where they had a castle, which was later destroyed in a dispute with William d'Anville, Abbot of Evesham.

In the fourteenth century, Richard II's 'Merciless Parliament' found Sir John Beauchamp guilty of high treason. By the authority of the Lords Appellant, Sir John was imprisoned in Dover Castle and then brought to London where he was beheaded at the Tower in May 1388. The Beauchamp Tower is supposedly named after him.

The Bermingham Family of Birmingham

The City of Birmingham in the West Midlands bears an Anglo-Saxon name which predates the Norman Conquest. The Manor of Bermingham was held in 1066 by Alwyne, son of Wigod the Dane, who married the sister of Leofric, Earl of Mercia.

The name of this once small hamlet on the edge of the Forest of Arden comes from the Old English Beornmundingaham, meaning 'homestead (or settlement) of the people of Beornmund'. It was somewhat overshadowed by the neighbouring settlement at Aston, and was rated in 1086 as being worth only 20 shillings.

Beornmund, after whom the tribe was named, could have been a head man or leader at the time of the Anglo-Saxon settlement. The *Domesday Book* identifies the placename as Bermingeham, and tenanted by Richard, who held under William FitzAnsculf. The first written record of the name is that of Peter de Bremingeham, whose name is listed in the 1170 Pipe Rolls. He purchased the manorship by a royal charter granted by Henry II in 1166. By the time Peter's son, William, had inherited the manor, Birmingham had been recognised as a town.

In the twelfth and thirteenth centuries, the grant of market town status saw the settlement grow exponentially, with the creation of a triangular market, (the Bull Ring), and alongside it the parish church of St Martin in the Bull Ring. In 1250, the town was given the right to hold a fair each summer.

The De Bermingham family retained control of the manor until 1527, when John Dudley, Duke of Northumberland, later Earl of

Warwick, gained control of the town. His family, in turn, lost it when he was executed in 1553. It was the last occasion that nobility held rights to the manor.

In 1642, during the Civil War, Royalist forces sacked Birmingham, but were defeated at Kings Norton. A year later they made another attempt on the town, assaulting it with a force of some two thousand cavalry and infantry, led by Prince Rupert, slaying inhabitants and setting nearly eighty houses on fire.

By the early eigtheenth century, a weekly stagecoach service had begun running to London via Warwick, Banbury and Aylesbury. An early commentary on the town recorded that 'Birmingham, Bromicham, or Bremicham, (as they call it), is a large town, well built and populous. The inhabitants, being mostly (black)smiths, are very ingenious in their way, and vend vast quantities of all sorts of iron wares.'

The tradition of iron work, gun-making and silversmithery still continues to this day.

The Blount Family of Sodington & Worcester

The Blount name is of Norman ancestry, and following the Conquest, was first recorded in Suffolk, where Sir Robert de Blount, (c.1029-1066), had commanded the Conqueror's fleet during the invasion of England. However, Robert appears to have died at Hastings. The surname refers originally to a person with blond hair, and is a corruption of the Anglo-French word 'blunt', simply meaning 'blond'.

In June 1544, Astley Manor was granted to Sir Ralph Sadleir and Ellen his wife but was purchased the same year by Robert Blount, who died at Astley in 1573. He was succeeded by his eldest son Thomas. Two parts of the manor were subsequently confiscated by the Crown, by reason of the recusancy of Thomas Blount, (a staunch Catholic who refused to submit to Elizabeth's strict laws of religious intolerance), and were leased for twenty-one years to John Harris. In 1620, Thomas Blount sold the manor to John Winford.

The Blount Baronetcy of Sodington was created in October 1642 for Walter Blount, who was High Sheriff of Worcestershire in 1619, and Member of Parliament for Droitwich from 1624 to 1625. He later fought as a Royalist in the Civil War. He was captured in 1645 and imprisoned in the Tower of London. In 1652 he was convicted of treason and his estates at Sodington Hall and Mawley Hall in Shropshire were sequestrated. The family only recovered their estates after the Restoration of Charles II.

A notable family member was Elizabeth Blount, (c.1498-1540). She was the daughter of Sir John Blount, a court official, and Catherine Pershall of Kinlet, Bridgnorth, Shropshire. Little is known of Elizabeth's early life, but she was deemed to have been a great beauty, who became famous for her affair with Henry VIII. As a young girl, she was brought to court as a maid of honour to Catherine of Aragon. As a teenager she caught the eye of the king and became his mistress for about eight years.

The Clifford Family of Frampton

The Clifford family trace their roots back to the eleventh century, when William the Conqueror granted lands in Frampton and Herefordshire to one of his followers, a knight named Drogo FitzPons. When Drogo died childless in 1089, he was succeeded by his brother Richard, and later by Richard's son, Walter, who was Baron of the Welsh Marches. Walter, (also known as FitzRichard de Clifford, (1113–87)), had assumed the surname de Clifford as Lord of Clifford Castle in Herefordshire. It is a locational name - the castle stands on a cliff, overlooking a ford in the river; hence 'cliff-ford'.

Robert de Clifford, (c.1274–1314), feudal Baron of Clifford, of Skipton in Yorkshire and of Appleby in Westmoreland, was created Baron Clifford by writ of Parliament in the year 1299.

The Clifford's estates remained in the family for generations, until 1684, when John Clifford left it to his grandson, William Clutterbuck, who ran a successful clothier business in Eastington. William's son, Richard, began building Frampton Court in the early eigtheenth century. He had made his fortune as Head of the Customs House in Bristol, but died a bachelor, with no heirs, and his estate passed to his sister's grandson, Nathaniel Winchcombe. In 1801, by royal consent, Nathaniel took the name and arms of Clifford.

John Edward Southwell Russell, twenty-seventh Lord de Clifford, born on 8 June 1928, succeeded to the title on 3 January 1982, and lives in Tiverton, Devon. Russell has no children and the heir presumptive is his nephew, Miles Edward Southwell Russell who was born in 1966.

The Corbet Family of Moreton Corbet

The name Corbet comes from the Old Norman French word 'corb', meaning 'crow', (the shortened form of corbeau, and 'bet', which directly translates as 'little crow'). The name of Corbet le Normand (Corbet the Norman) was first recorded in Pays de Caux in Normandy in the eleventh century. Family tradition has it that he arrived with William the Conqueror in 1066 carrying a banner displaying a raven, from his supposed name. 'Le Corbeau', usually translated as 'the crow', but 'the raven' was preferred as a bird of higher status and consequently it appears on a gold shield in the family coat of arms. Variant spellings and derivations of the name include Corbett, Corbit, Corbete and Corben.

Roger FitzCorbet is listed in the *Domesday Book* as a tenant of Lord Roger, Earl of Shrewsbury. He himself became Baron of Caus in Shropshire, a title that passed down through succeeding generations, until the Caus family line died out some time in the early fourteenth century. The family name, and its power, passed to another branch of the family at Moreton Toret, later known as Moreton Corbet.

The Corbets served as Members of Parliament and by the sixteenth century had become wealthy landowners in the County of Salop (Shropshire). Branches of the family settled in Teviotdale in Scotland and were granted the Manor of Fogo. Other Corbets moved to live in Jersey in the Channel Islands, where, by the twentieth century, they were the largest landowners in the Vale Parish once known as the Clos du Valle.

Through keen business sense and propitious marriage, the Corbets accrued significant landholdings, particularly in Shropshire.

The Acton Reynald Hall manor house and park in Shropshire was created by the family in the seventeeth century. The castle at Moreton Corbet had been acquired as early as 1235, when Sir Richard Corbet of Wettlesborough married Joan Thoreton, the daughter of Bartholomew Thoreton of Moreton Thoret.

The De Somery Family of Dudley

The De Somery Family story begins with the building of Dudley Castle. It is thought one of William the Conqueror's knights, Ansculf de Picquigny, built the first castle in or around 1070. The *Domesday Book* records that Ansculf's son, William FitzAnsculf, was in possession of the castle at the time of the survey.

After FitzAnsculf, the castle came into the possession of the Paganel family, who built the first stone castle on the site, replacing an earlier motte and bailey earthwork. In 1138, the castle withstood a siege by King Stephen, but, after Gervase Paganel joined a failed rebellion against Henry II in 1173, the castle was demolished by royal decree. Paganel was succeeded by his nephew, Ralph de Somery the First. His son, (also a Ralph de Somery), began rebuilding it in 1262, and it was almost a century later that it was completed by his descendants.

The last of the De Somery male line died in 1321 and the estate passed to his sister, Margaret, and her husband, John de Sutton, who adopted the surname Dudley.

The Devereux Family of Hereford

The Devereux family originated in Evreux in the Eure Region of Normandy. The original d'Evreux name in French simply means 'from Evreux'. They descended from Robert, Count of Evreux, the Archbishop of Rouen, and son of Duke Richard I of Normandy, who is listed in the *Domesday Book*. He married Walter Lacy of Hereford's sister, Helewysa, who bore him a son, Robert de Evrois. Before written English was formalised, many variant spellings of the name occurred, including Devereu, Deveraux and d'Eureus. For example, one William de Eureus is recorded in the 1159 Pipe Rolls of Hereford.

A large contingent of Devereux also established themselves in County Wexford, Ireland. Walter Devereux, (1541-76), who was first Earl of Essex and Viscount Hereford, established a colony in Ulster. His son Robert, the second earl, was Lord Lieutenant of Ireland in 1599.

After a failed coup d'état against Elizabeth I, Robert Devereux, second Earl of Essex, was beheaded for treason in February 1601 at the Tower of London. In 1642, the third Earl of Essex was Captain-General and Chief Commander of the Parliamentarian army during the Civil War, leading a force against Charles I at the Battle of Edgehill, the first major battle of the Civil War.

In 1645, Essex was given Somerhill House near Tonbridge in Kent, following the Battle of Naseby, and in December that year Parliament voted for him to be created a Duke. He died of a stroke on 14 September 1646 and was buried in Westminster Abbey. On 20 April 1661, Arthur Capel was created Earl of Essex, the earldom having passed from the Devereux family. It is still held by Capel descendants today.

The Dudley Family of Dudley

Before the Norman Conquest the lands of the West Midlands were in the hands of Earl Edwin of Mercia. In 1070, however, his estates were granted to Ansculf of Picquigny, who received the Manor of Sedgley, containing the estates at Dudley, where he built a motte and bailey castle. This is first mentioned in the *Domesday Book* as being held at that time by Ansculf's son, William FitzAnsculf. Later, the large stone fortress replaced it.

The name comes from two Old English words, 'Dudda', (a person's name), and 'leah', a common suffix, meaning a field or a meadow. It may therefore be interpreted as 'Dudda's meadow'.

During the twelfth century, the De Paganel family became Lords of Dudley, before the De Somery family gained the estates through the marriage of Hawyse (sometimes Helewysa) de Paganel to John de Somery. With the death of De Somery in 1322, the extensive Dudley estates entered a period of disputed ownership, but in 1327 John de Sutton inherited the castle and estates of his wife Margaret de Somery.

Lord John de Sutton VII succeeded to the estate in 1532, but soon ran into financial difficulties and was forced to sell his titles to the junior line of the family, in the person of John Dudley, the son of Edmund Dudley who was an adviser to Henry VII. His father fell out of favour and met with an untimely end. However, this did not deter John's son, also named John Dudley, from entering the service of the king. He rapidly rose to prominence and was appointed Viscount Lisle and Earl of Warwick.

When Henry VIII was succeeded by Edward VI in 1547, John Dudley became one of the Council of Regency, chief protector of the child king, with the post of Lord President of the Council and the title Duke of Northumberland.

Later, Robert Dudley, first Earl of Leicester, was a courtier and influential favourite of Elizabeth I, and reputedly her only serious English suitor. He was made Master of Horse at Elizabeth's accession. He joined the Privy Council in 1562 and was created Earl of Leicester and Baron of Denbigh in 1564. Leicester commanded the unsuccessful force against Spain in the Netherlands in 1585 and was involved in a number of scandals and intrigues. Robert Dudley died at Cornbury Park near Oxford, on 4 September 1588, on his way to Buxton in Derbyshire. His health had not been good for some time, and in all probability it was malaria or stomach cancer that caused his death. He was buried in the Beauchamp Chapel of the Collegiate Church of St Mary in Warwick, the same chapel as his ancestor, Richard Beauchamp.

The Ferrers Family of Baddesley Clinton

The family trace their ancestry back to Henry de Ferrers, (sometimes De Ferrières), who was a Norman knight who took part in the conquest of England. He became a substantial land holder and was granted two hundred and ten manors throughout England and Wales by the Conqueror for his conspicuous bravery at Hastings, including lands in Derbyshire and Leicestershire. The *Domesday Book* records him as tenant-in-chief of Tutbury in the Staffordshire Hundred of Pirehill and Chief Commissioner of the West Midlands. As a powerful local baron, administrator and overlord, his subtenants included the Baskervyles, Curzons and Levetts, all of whom were important Norman families in their own right.

A notable family member was Henry Ferrers, (1549-1633), who inherited the estate of Baddesley Clinton in Warwickshire in 1564, and carried out extensive rebuilding and remodelling.

When Marmion Edward Ferrers, the last of the male line, died in 1884, the estate passed down through his nephew to Thomas Ferrers-Walker. He subsequently sold the house to the government in 1980, since when it has been administered by the National Trust. The Ferrers Archive is kept at the Shakespeare Birthplace Trust in Stratford-upon-Avon.

The Giffard Family of Chillington

The Giffards were Norman knights who arrived in 1066 and settled in Staffordshire, with other branches, (now extinct), in Devon and Buckinghamshire. The first record of the name is that of Gautier Giffard who was the hereditary standard bearer to William the Conqueror at Hastings. One explanation of the name Giffard is that it comes from the Norman-French 'jouffle', which means 'chubby cheeks'. Another is that it comes from an even older version of the French word 'giffel', meaning 'jaw'.

Chillington Hall, near Brewood on the Staffordshire-Shropshire border, has been the home of the Giffard family for over eight hundred years, since Peter Gifford was made Lord of the Manor of Chillington. In the *Domesday Book*, Chillington is entered as Cillintone under Warwickshire, as part of the estates of William FitzCorbucion.

In the early sixteenth century, Sir Thomas Giffard was a wealthy landowner, courtier and Member of Parliament. His son, John, was a notable soldier, (said to be one of the best bowmen and horsemen in England), and is known to have studied law at the Middle Temple. He went on to become High Sheriff of Staffordshire, an office he held on five separate occasions.

At the age of about 70, Giffard gave up attending Parliament, and in 1539 his son Thomas took one of the places for Staffordshire. In

1540, however, Giffard attended the reception of Anne of Cleves at Blackheath. He spent the rest of his life in retirement at Chillington, where he died in 1556. He was buried in Brewood church where there is a monument bearing his effigy.

The Greville Family of Warwick

The Greville surname comes from the village of Greville in the La Manche Department of Normandy. It derives from the Old French person's name 'Creiz' and the word 'ville', meaning 'Creiz's settlement (or township)'. The name first appears written in its present form in the person of John de Greville, recorded in the Hundred Rolls of Wiltshire in 1273. In 1397, John's grandson, William Greville, is said to have loaned money to Richard II. His descendants include Fulke Greville, (1554-1628), a favourite of Elizabeth 1, who granted him the Earldom of Warwick. Another early recorded spelling of the family name is that of William de Greiuill, dated 1154, in the Pipe Rolls of Northumberland. Others include William Grevel, who is said to have founded the wool trade in Wiltshire in the fourteenth century.

By the seventeeth century, the Greville family were substantial Warwickshire landowners. Warwick Castle was granted to Fulke with the earldom in 1604. It had been begun as a simple motte and bailey fortress built by William in 1068 to safeguard the Midlands from northern incursions. He committed the custody of it to Henry de Beaumont, and rewarded his loyalty in 1088 by creating him Earl of Warwick.

In 1472, George Plantagenet, third surviving son of Richard, Duke of York, and husband of Isabel, Richard Neville's eldest daughter, had the Earldom of Warwick conferred upon him by reason of that marriage.

In 1547, John Dudley was created Earl of Warwick and applied for the sole possession of Warwick Castle, of which he had acquired the joint constableship in 1532. He was also created Duke of Northumberland, but was executed for treason in 1553.

Francis Greville, eighth Baron Brooke, undertook a renewed programme of improvements to the castle and its grounds in 1759, and was also bestowed with the title Earl of Warwick, a title that has remained in the Greville family ever since.

Through the twentieth century, successive earls expanded the tourist potential of Warwick Castle, in pursuit of much-needed revenue and in the face of spiralling maintenance costs, until in 1978, after three hundred and seventy-four years in the Greville family, it was sold to the Tussauds Group, who opened it as a tourist attraction after extensive restorations to the castle and grounds.

Warwick Castle has been named one of Britain's Top Ten historic houses and monuments by the British Tourist Authority.

The Harley Family of Brampton Bryan

The Harley family is of ancient lineage, possibly predating the Norman conquest, and its name may have originated in the Shropshire village of Harley. The first known bearer of the family name was Malcolm de Harley, who was chaplain to Edward I. Sir Richard Harley was the first Harley to be elected to Parliament as Knight for Shropshire in 1300.

Family members married into the Braose and Mortimer families and gained influence in the region, with Robert de Harley becoming Sheriff of Herefordshire in 1302. Further, the Harley family went on to produce the Earls of Oxford and Mortimer and gave the name to Harley Street in London.

Sir Robert de Harley of Harley settled in what is now the Parish of Brampton Bryan on the Herefordshire border, some time around 1300. Brampton Castle passed into Harley possession after the marriage of Robert de Harley and Margaret de Brampton. A century later, in 1403, at the time of the Owain Glyndwr uprising, the castle was held by Brian Harley.

From the fourteenth century, the Harleys played a leading part in the communities of Herefordshire and Radnorshire. A later Sir Robert Harley, (1579-1656), was Master of the Mint under Charles I and Member of Parliament for Radnor, and later for Evesham.

Yet another Robert Harley, (born in 1661), was elected to Parliament for the Tregony Constituency in Cornwall, and afterwards, in 1690, for the town of Radnor. In February 1701, he was elected speaker of the House of Commons and in 1704, he was appointed a member of the Privy Council. Queen Anne promoted him from the office of Chancellor of the Exchequer to that of Lord Treasurer and granted him the Earldom of Oxford, which had been vacated by the death in 1703 of Aubrey de Vere, twentieth Earl of Oxford. Needless to say, the De Vere family contested the appointment, although in vain.

In May 1711, Harley was elevated to the peerage by the titles of Baron Harley of Wigmore, County Hereford, Earl of Oxford and Earl of Mortimer, as well as being a Knight of the Bath. Unfortunately, in June 1715, shortly after the accession of George I, Harley was impeached by Parliament for high treason, and was committed to the Tower, where he suffered imprisonment until he was acquitted in July 1717, and subsequently released. His rights and titles were all restored, but disillusioned he returned to Herefordshire and played no further part in politics.

The last noble of the line was Alfred, sixth Earl of Oxford, who was born in January 1809. He was married to Eliza Nugent, but died childless in January 1853, when the peerage became extinct.

The Leveson-Gower Family of Stony Park

See: Part Six: The South-East: The Carteret Family of Sark.

The Levett Family of Staffordshire

The Levetts, (sometimes De Livet), were a prominent family in Staffordshire and Derbyshire, with ancestry going back to Norman times. The name originates in the ancient village of Livet-en-Ouche in the Eure Valley of Normandy, and derives from a Celtic word 'livet', meaning 'a swampy place'. Branches of the family held lands in Gloucestershire, Yorkshire, Worcestershire and Wiltshire, and some settled in Catsfield Levett, a few miles from the battlefield at Hastings in Sussex. Other members of the original De Livet family still live in France.

The Normandy branch records that Jean de Livet was Chevalier to Philip II of France in 1216, and builder of the first Louvre fortress in Paris. His son, Chevalier Thomas de Livet, a noted Crusader, was knighted by Philip II's successor, Louis IX of France, in 1258. In fact many early Levitts were crusaders, with both English and French members being Knights Hospitallers.

The Staffordshire Levetts included Richard Byrd Haszard Levett who was High Sheriff of Staffordshire. Another notable family member was Sir Richard Levett who was one of the first Governors of the Bank of England, a member of the original London East India Company and the Lord Mayor of London in 1699. Captain Christopher Levett, was granted some six thousand acres by the king to found the third English colony in North America, where he had been one of its earliest explorers.

Many Levetts live outside England, including South Africa, Australia, New Zealand, Canada and Ireland. The name exists in many places in England and throughout the world, including Hooton Levitt and Levitt Hagg in South Yorkshire, Fort Levitt in Maine, USA, Leavitt in California and Leavittsburg in Ohio, among many others.

The Longchamp Family of Wilton

Osbert (or Henry) de Longchamp, (sometimes Osbert de Longo Campo), was an Anglo-Norman administrator, born around 1155 in Wilton Castle, near Ross-on-Wye, Herefordshire, the son of Hugh (or Hugo) de Longchamp. The name originated in the village of Longchamps in Normandy, and in French simply means 'long field'. Hugh had received a grant of lands at Linton and the Manor of Wilton in the Wye Valley in 1156. He is believed to have erected the castle at Wilton. Osbert was appointed High Sheriff of Yorkshire and of Westmorland in 1190 by Richard I, and in 1193 he became Sheriff of Norfolk. One of Hugh's other sons, William, became Chancellor of England and Bishop of Ely, while yet another, Henry, was Sheriff of Herefordshire and Worcestershire.

The Longchamps were succeeded by the Cantilupe and Grey families, who built up a powerbase in Wales. Matilda Grey, (née

Cantilupe), asserted before a royal court in 1292 that the castle had been built by her Longchamp ancestors much earlier, in the days of Edward the Confessor, (1042-66), but evidence shows that the castle could not have been built before 1154.

Wilton Castle, which before 1308 was in the hands of the Grey Family, passed from the family when William Grey was captured by the French at the end of the defence of Guînes in 1557, and they were forced to sell it to Charles Brydges, (who was related to the Greys by marriage), in order to raise funds for his ransom.

The castle was finally destroyed in the Civil War, and much of its stone ruins may have been incorporated into a new house, constructed on the site in the nineteenth century.

In 1961, its owners, the Trustees of Guy's Hospital, sold the castle to the financier Charles Clore, and in 2002 the castle passed into the ownership of Mr and Mrs Parslow. Since then a comprehensive programme of restoration has been undertaken by English Heritage.

The Lyttelton Family of Hagley

The Lyttelton surname can be traced to about 1270, when a Thomas de Luttelton, (sometimes Littleton), married the daughter of Philip de Frankley. They originated in South Lyttleton, (or as it then was, 'South Luttelton'), near Evesham in Worcestershire, and it is from that place that the family took their surname. It is not clear how the Lytteltons gained control of Frankley Manor, but by 1410 it was securely in their ownership.

In 1564, Sir John Littelton, who had been knighted by Elizabeth I at Kenilworth, bought the Hagley estate from Sir John St Leger. However, he continued to live in the house at Frankley, as did his son Gilbert. In 1590, Gilbert's eldest son, John, married Meriel Bromley, the daughter of Sir Thomas Bromley, Lord Chancellor of England. Their son Thomas was created a baronet in 1618 and was responsible for raising the Royalist forces in Worcestershire. In turn, Charles's son, Thomas, married Christian Temple of Stowe, a lady-in-waiting to Queen Anne, and through her the Cobham title finally came to the Lytteltons.

A notable family member was Edward Lyttelton, who acquired lands in Cannock Chase and was appointed Constable of Stafford Castle and High Sheriff of Staffordshire. Later, George, first Lord Lyttelton, (1709-73), began the building of Hagley Hall, a Neo-Palladian style house, (now a Grade I Listed Building). He was secretary to the Prince of Wales and later served as Chancellor of the Exchequer.

The baronetcy became extinct in 1812 when Sir Edward Littleton, the fourth Baronet, died childless at Pillaton Hall, and his nephew, Edward John Walhouse, adopted the Littleton surname. He was a notable politician and eventually became the newly created Baron Littleton in his own right.

Hagley Hall remains the family home to Christopher Charles Lyttelton, twelfth Viscount Cobham and his wife Tessa.

The Mucklow Family of Worcestershire

The family name originated in the village of Mucklow in Worcestershire where they were Lords of the Manor and adopted it as their surname. Early spellings of Mucklow include Mucklo, Muckloe, Micklowe and Muckelo. It is thought to be from the Old English words 'mucha' and 'hlaw', probably meaning 'large (or long) hill'. The present roadway in Halesowen, known as Mucklow Hill, bears out this interpretation, for as the name implies, it is both a large and a long hill.

The first records of the name are Anne Muckloe who, according to parish records, married Richard Haull at St Helens Church in Worcester in November 1562, and Alice Mucklow, who married Gilbert Southall, at Halesowen in October 1575.

During the time of the Dissolution of the Monasteries, the lands and fishery owned by monks in the Parish of Ernleye, near Kidderminster, passed to the Lord of the Manor, Simon Mucklow, who built Areley Hall, a Grade II listed country house near Areley Kings in Stourport-on-Severn. The Mucklow family were Royalists during the English Civil Wars. Prince Rupert is reputed to have slept at Areley Hall around the time of the Battle of Worcester. The descendants of the Mucklows still live at Areley Hall.

The Mytton Family of Halston & Shrewsbury

The Mytton surname, (sometimes Mitton), came to England with the Norman Conquest, almost certainly from the town of Moutons in the Calvados Region of Normandy. Indeed, that is the origin of their family name, which is sometimes spelled Mutton or Mouton. It is not certain which came first, the surname or the placename, but in England it is closely associated with the village of Mytton, near Forton Heath, a few miles west of Shrewsbury.

One of the earliest recorded family members is Roger de Mutton, who married Ann, daughter of Richard Hussey, grandson of Thomas Hussey, who accompanied William the Conqueror in 1066.

The Myttons were one of Shrewsbury's leading families and had acquired the Lordship of Mawddwy, which included the ancient borough of Dinas Mawddwy, part of the County of Merioneth in Wales in 1536. The family at one time owned thirty-two thousand acres of land on either side of the Welsh–English border.

A notable family member was John Mytton, born in 1796 and known as 'Mad Jack' Mytton, who lived in the family seat at Halston Hall, built for the family in 1690 at Whittington, near Oswestry. Halston was known as 'Holy Stone' in medieval times, when it was one of many great estates held by the powerful Knights of St John, a brotherhood founded to protect pilgrims travelling to the Holy Land.

Jack Mytton was educated at Westminster School, and was expelled for fighting with one of his teachers. Later, at Cambridge, bored with education, he left unqualified to pursue a Grand Tour of Europe. He served as a soldier in the North Shropshire Yeomanry following the Napoleonic Wars and married twice, his second wife, Caroline Giffard, deserting him in 1830. He served as a Member of Parliament on two occasions, was High Sheriff of Shropshire and one-time Mayor of Oswestry.

Mytton was, however, a spendthrift and fell into serious debt, fleeing to Calais to avoid his creditors in 1831. He returned to England in 1833, but still unable to pay off his debts, he ended up in Southwark Prison in London, where he died penniless a year later.

There is a public house named after Mytton beside the Llangollen Canal in the village of Hindford near Halston Hall, and a hotel at Atcham near Shrewsbury is named The Mytton & Mermaid after him.

The Paget Family of Beaudesert

See: Part Nine: Wales: The Paget Family of Plas Newydd.

The Stafford Family of Stafford

The Stafford family name, (sometimes De Stafford), is first found in Staffordshire in the person of Ralph de Teoni, who was one of the standard bearers for William the Conqueror at Hastings. The name comes from two Anglo-Saxon words, 'stat', meaning town, and 'ford', signifying a ford. Hence, Statford, later corrupted to Stafford. The original settlement was built by Ethelfleda, daughter of Alfred the Great, about 910-915. This new settlement, (or burh), was fortified and produced a style of pottery, subsequently known as Stafford Ware.

Ralph's brother, Robert, built a castle in Stafford and adopted the placename as his own surname. The family grew in influence and prosperity and is recorded as holding some eighty manors in the Midlands by 1086. Stafford Castle was completed on the nearby hilltop in 1090. Initially a wooden construction, it was later rebuilt in stone. It has been rebuilt twice since, and the ruins of the nineteenth century Gothic revival castle incorporate much of the original stonework.

Later, an Edmund Stafford was engaged and married to Anne, daughter of Thomas Woodstock, son of Edward III. Thus the Staffords became associated with the royal family, and subsequent generations inherited the title of Dukes of Buckingham.

In July 1483, Henry Stafford served as Great Chamberlain at the coronation of Richard III and was given the hereditary status of Constable of England. Despite this, he changed allegiances during the Wars of the Roses and supported the future Henry VII. Richard thereafter declared Stafford to be a traitor, and he went into hiding in Shropshire. Hunted down, caught and arrested, he was tried and beheaded in the marketplace at Salisbury in November 1483. However, after Richard's death, when Henry Tudor became Henry VII, all Stafford lands and titles were restored to Edward Bagot, (sometimes 'Baggett', also known as Edward Stafford). Edward was appointed to Henry VIII's Privy Council in 1509, but in the volatile and ever-changing politics of the age, he fell foul of the king and was accused of treason against the Crown, and was beheaded in 1521.

On Edward VI's accession in 1547, at the age of nine, a later Henry Stafford was created Lord Stafford by Act of Parliament. However, following an abortive failed rebellion, his second son, Thomas, was executed for high treason, and Henry's new barony was surrendered to the king, who bestowed it in 1639 on Mary Stafford, (the only surviving heir of the family), and her husband, William Howard. Since then the Stafford estates and titles have been retained with the Howards.

The Talbot Family of Shrewsbury

Talbot family history begins in 1074, with one of William the Conqueror's counsellors, Roger de Montgomerie, (also known as Rogier de Talbot or Talbert). The family had previously been vassals of the Giffards in Normandy. This same Roger was recorded in 1086 as being a tenant of Walter Giffard at Woburn and Battledsen in Bedfordshire. However, over time he rose to become Earl of Hereford and of Chester, with powers extending from Shropshire and into Wales, as well as grants of significant other lands throughout England.

The Talbot surname is derived from a Germanic personal name Talabert, meaning 'bright valley'. It is first recorded in use in Shropshire and Staffordshire.

A notable descendant was Sir John Talbot, (1384-1453), born in Whitchurch and known as 'Old Talbot'. In time he was to become Earl of Shrewsbury, first Earl of Waterford and Lord Lieutenant of Ireland, as well as a military commander during the Hundred Years' War. Talbot was married in March 1407 to Maud Neville, sixth Baroness Furnivall, and was elected as a Member of Parliament in

1409. Maud died in May 1422 and Talbot remarried in September 1425 Lady Margaret Beauchamp, daughter of the thirteenth Earl of Warwick.

From 1404 to 1413, he and his brother Gilbert opposed the Welsh rebellion of Owain Glyndwr. In 1424, after distinguishing himself in the Battle of Verneuil, he was awarded the Order of the Garter. On the 20 May 1442, Henry VI created John Talbot as Earl of Shrewsbury. He was appointed as Constable of France in 1445, and taken hostage by the French at Rouen in 1449. Back in Bordeaux in 1452, he was killed at the Battle of Castillon.

It was this John Talbot who had the unique distinction of being portrayed in Shakespeare's *Henry VI*, before the Battle of Agincourt, as the 'valiant Lord Talbot, Earl of Shrewsbury'.

In 1801, Charles Talbot, the fifteenth Earl of Shrewsbury, began redeveloping the hunting lodge in the village of Alton in Staffordshire into a Gothic style stately home. After the fifteenth Earl of Shrewsbury died in 1827, he was succeeded by his nephew John Talbot, sixteenth Earl of Shrewsbury, who completed the gardens and house.

In 1831, the Talbots' principal residence in Heythrop burned down, and the sixteenth Earl decided to move and live at Alton permanently; he named it Alton Abbey. Over time, through poor maintenance, the house began to decay and as the grounds became neglected, the family found it increasingly difficult to sustain its upkeep. Therefore, in November 1918, the earl decided to sell off the majority of the estate by auction. The countess continued to live on the estate for another two years after the earl died in 1921.

In 1924, the remaining part of the estate and house was sold to a group of local businessmen, who formed Alton Towers Limited. Since then, Alton Towers has become one of the nation's leading, and thriving, amusement parks.

The Throckmorton Family of Coughton Court

Throckmorton comes from the Old English words 'troc', 'mere' and 'tun', meaning 'a settlement (or farmstead) near a pool with a bridge'.

The family lived at Throckmorton, (spelled Trochemerton in 1176), in Worcestershire. The surname was also recorded in 1200 in a chapelry in the Parish of Fladbury near Pershore, where John de Trockemerton was living.

The Throckmortons emerged as a family of some status in the late-fourteenth century, when Thomas Throckmorton was Constable of Elmley Castle. His son, John, was treasurer to Henry V, and an executor of the will of Richard Beauchamp, Earl of Warwick. In 1415, he is known to have held the manor from the Bishop of Worcester. Their estate at Coughton was owned by the family until 1409, when it was acquired through marriage to the De Spinney family.

The Throckmortons were devout Catholics. Sir George Throckmorton was known for his opposition to Henry VIII's divorce from Catherine of Aragon and fell out of favour with the king as a result. The family were implicated in the Throckmorton Plot of 1583, which planned to murder Elizabeth I, and also in the Gunpowder Plot of 1605, when some of the conspirators rode directly to Coughton after its discovery.

It was a later Robert Throckmorton of Coughton, near Alcester, in Warwickshire, who was first created a Baron in September 1642. Subsequent generations continued to hold the Throckmorton Baronetcy.

Coughton Court has been owned by the National Trust since 1945. It is still occupied by a family member, Claire McKaren-Throckmorton, and remains open to the public.

The Touchet Family of Staffordshire

The Touchets, (sometimes Tuchet or Touchett)), originated in Touchet in the Moratin region of Normandy, and settled in Audley, Staffordshire, shortly after the Conquest, bringing the name of their birthplace with them as a family name.

In 1313, the title Baron Audley had been created for Sir Nicholas de Audley of Heleigh Castle, but when he died without issue in 1391 the barony fell into abeyance, until 1405, when it was revived for Sir John Tuchet, a descendant through Nicholas' sister.

James Tuchet, fifth Lord Audley, was Chief Justice for South Wales in 1423, and during the Wars of the Roses he fought for Henry VI in the Battle of Blore Heath in 1459, leading a large force against the Yorkists. Another descendant, James, seventh Baron Audley, (1463-97), was a leader in the Cornish rebellion of 1497, a popular uprising against punitive taxation by Henry VII to raise money for his war in Scotland. He was sentenced for treason, beheaded and the peerage forfeited. However, the title was restored to John Tuchet in 1512, and by 1563, George Tuchet had been created Baron Audley of Orier and Earl of Castlehaven.

Mervyn Tuchet, the second Earl, was the black sheep of the family. In 1631 he was convicted of rape and sodomy and subsequently beheaded on Tower Hill in London, at which point the peerage was attainted for a second time. It was not restored again until 1678, thereafter descending through successive generations until 1777, when the male line died out and titles passed through Elizabeth Tuchet, daughter of the sixth Earl, to Captain Philip Thicknesse. Their son George assumed the surname Thicknesse-Touchet after 1837.

Thomas Percy Henry Touchet-Jesson, (1913-63), became twenty-third Baron Audley in 1942, succeeding his second cousin Mary Thicknesse-Touchet. His second wife was Sarah Spencer-Churchill, daughter of Sir Winston Churchill.

The last in the line of the barony was Rosina Lois Veronica Touchet-Jesson, styled twenty-fourth Baroness Audley of Heleigh, who from 1943 took her husband John MacNamee's surname and was thereafter known as Rosina MacNamee until she died childless in 1973. She was succeeded by her cousin, Richard Michael Thomas Souter, the twenty-fifth Baron, (1914-97), and on his death the Barony of Audley fell into abeyance between his three daughters.

Part Four

The East Midlands
Family Names in Derbyshire, Leicestershire, Lincolnshire,
Northamptonshire, Nottinghamshire & Rutland

The Annesley Family of Mansfield

A locational name, probably acquired from the village of that name in Mansfield, Nottinghamshire. It was recorded in the *Domesday Book* as Aneslei, and later, in the Nottinghamshire Pipe Rolls of 1175 as Aneslea. It was probably derived from the personal name 'An', (or Ann) and 'leah', the Old English word for a woodland clearing or grove. Hence, 'Ann's clearing'. One of the earliest records of it used as a family name occurs in around 1307 in Nottingham, in the person of Sir John de Annesley.

In the mid-thirteenth century, the family built Annesley Hall, where they lived until the family heiress, Alice Annesley, married George Chaworth in the fifteenth century and it passed to his family.

In March 1622, Sir Francis Annesley was created Viscount of Valentia, and later, in 1661, Arthur Annesley was made Earl of Anglesey, a peerage that remained in the family over many succeeding generations. In 1793, another Arthur Annesley was created Earl of Mountnorris, and yet another Arthur was created Baron Annesley of Bletchington in 1917, having served as Member of Parliament for Oxford for the previous twelve years.

Francis William Dighton Annesley, the sixteenth Viscount Valencia, was born in 1959, and is the present incumbent.

The Babington Family of Derby

The Babingtons originally came from the Parish of Babington, (earlier called Little Bavington), in Northumberland, from where they took the family name. Accounts show that they had settled there long before the Norman Conquest. It is not known exactly when they moved to live in Nottinghamshire, but a John Babington was already residing at East Bridgeford in the time of Richard II.

One branch of the family, the Babingtons of Dethick (in Derby), acquired Kingston. Their most notable member was Anthony Babington, a friend and supporter of Mary, Queen of Scots. His life was sacrificed in her cause, having fallen prey, along with other conspirators, to Elizabeth's spymaster, Francis Walsingham. Babington was imprisoned in the Tower before being dragged through the streets to be hanged and disembowelled at St Giles Field, near Holborn.

Subsequent family members held posts such as High Sheriff, Lords Lieutenant and Members of Parliament. Politically active members of the family in the twentieth century have included Sir Anthony Babington, Member of Parliament for two Belfast constituencies in Northern Ireland from 1925-1937 and Attorney General, and Robert Babington who was Member of Parliament for North Down in the Northern Ireland Parliament from 1969-72.

Several spelling derivations of the name include Babbington, Babinton and Bapinton.

The Bentinck Family of Nottinghamshire

The Bentinck family line originated in the Netherlands, where a Johan Bentinck was recorded as owning land near the village of Heerde in the Veluwe region of Holland in 1343.

The British branch of the family was founded by Hans Willem Bentinck, (also known in England as William Bentinck), who accompanied William of Orange in 1688, prior to his accession to the English throne. The family were granted the earldom of Portland, and later its dukedom. In April 1689 William was also created Baron Cirencester and Viscount Woodstock.

The name is likely to have been a corruption of the Flemish 'bontyng', the word for a small bird, (as in a common bunting, or sparrow), or possibly from the Old Germanic word 'bunz', meaning 'little barrel'. It was once a word used to describe a small rotund person. The suffix 'inck' is related to the Old English 'ing', meaning 'the people of'. Spelling variations include Bentick, and Bentink.

William was a popular name in the family line, and a succession of men of that name headed the family right up to the twentieth century. Notable among them was William Henry Cavendish-Bentinck who became Prime Minister in 1783, having previously served as Home Secretary and Lord Lieutenant of Nottingham, as were several of his subsequent descendants.

Victor Frederick William Cavendish-Bentinck, the ninth Duke of Portland, (1897-1990), was chairman of the Joint Intelligence Committee during the Second World War and Ambassador to Poland for two years following the conflict. Also in 1945, he was made a Knight Commander of the Order of St Michael and St George. When he died in 1990, he was buried, along with his ancestors, in St Winifred's churchyard in Holbeck in Nottinghamshire.

The present incumbent is Timothy Charles Robert Noel Bentinck, twelfth Earl of Portland, Count Bentinck, (born in 1953), an actor known as Tim Bentinck, probably best known for his role as David Archer in the BBC Radio 4 series, *The Archers*.

The Bertie Family of Uffington

The Berties are the English aristocratic family of the Earls of Lindsey and Abingdon. Between 1715 and 1809, the head of the family traditionally also held the title Duke of Ancaster and Kesteven.

Early written records show Bertie, (sometimes Bertin), shortly after 1066, probably of French origin, but with an indirect association with the old Germanic personal names Albert, Gilbert, or Herbert. According to other sources, the surname originates from a French diminutive name 'Bertin', which may itself have been from Bertram, which translates as 'bright raven'. The name 'Bertin' is first recorded in England in 1273, when Bertin de Burgo is listed in the Hundred Rolls of the County of Shropshire.

In 1626, the Earldom of Lindsay was created for the fourteenth Baron Willoughby de Eresby, who became First Lord of the Admiralty in 1635 and held claim to the hereditary office of Lord Great Chamberlain of England. The unfortunate Willoughby was on the Royalist side in the Civil War and was killed at Edgehill on 23 October 1642. He was succeeded by his son, the second Earl, who was also at Edgehill and surrendered to the Parliamentarians so that he could attend his mortally wounded father. Later, he fought at the first and second battles of Newbury and at Naseby.

The Uffington estate in Lincolnshire was bought for Charles Bertie, the fifth son of the second Earl of Lindsey, and the family lived at Uffington House from 1674 onwards. Unfortunately, the house burnt down in a disastrous fire of 1904, but the outbuildings, ballroom and orangery survived. Planning permission to demolish these was granted in 1979 and took place between August and September of that year, with its materials being used to repair the estate walls.

Properties in the Withington and Fallowfield districts of Manchester, formerly owned by the Egerton family of Tatton, came into the Bertie family when Anne Vernon Harcourt, who was related by marriage to the Berties, died in 1879.

The present incumbent is Richard Henry Rupert Bertie, fourteenth Earl of Lindsey and ninth Earl of Abingdon, who was born on the 28 June 1931, the second son of Montagu Bertie, seventh Earl of Abingdon, and his first wife, Aline.

The Cavendish Family of Derbyshire

The Cavendish family descends from Sir John Cavendish, who took his name from the village of Cavendish in Suffolk, where he held an estate in the fourteenth century. He served as Chief Justice of the King's Bench from 1372 to 1381, and was killed in the Peasants' Revolt in 1381.

The family became established in Derbyshire in 1547 as a result of the marriage of Sir William Cavendish, (who died in 1557), to Elizabeth Talbot, Countess of Shrewsbury, a native of Derbyshire-and better known as Bess of Hardwick. She was to become the second most powerful woman in Elizabethan England after the queen.

William Cavendish's fortunes had fared well during the sixteenth century, when he was one of Henry VIII's commissioners for the Dissolution of the Monasteries. His new wife persuaded him to sell the former monastic lands and move to live with her in Derbyshire, where in 1549 they bought the Manor of Chatsworth, and in 1552 began to build their first house on the site.

Cavendish's descendant, (also named William), was created Baron Cavendish of Hardwick in May 1605 and Earl of Devonshire in 1618. He became Member of Parliament for Newport in 1588 and was Lord Lieutenant of Derbyshire from 1619 to 1626. Later family members continued to hold positions of power, including Lords Privy Seal, Lieutenants of Ireland, and MPs for various constituencies, including Derbyshire, Lancashire and Rossendale. Spencer Compton Cavendish was Secretary of State for War in 1866, Postmaster General in 1868, Secretary of State for India in 1880 and Lord President of the Council from 1895 to 1903.

Peregrine Andrew Morny Cavendish, twelfth Duke of Devonshire, (born 27 April 1944 in Bakewell, Derbyshire), succeeded to the dukedom on 3 May 2004. Prior to this succession, he was styled Marquess of Hartington.

The Cecil Family of Burghley

Originally settling in Devon following the Conquest, the Cecil family name comes from the town of Cecile in Flanders. Maurice de Cassel, (sometimes Ciselle), was likely to have been the first recorded bearer of the name in England, and it was his son, Robert Cassel, (sometimes Kessel or Sitsilt), who assisted in the conquest of Glamorganshire in 1093.

A branch of the family moved north to St Martin's in Northamptonshire, where the local church contains their monuments. An important member was Sir William Cecil, first Baron Burghley, who was Lord High Treasurer and chief adviser to Elizabeth I from 1572.

It was he more than any other who is responsible for the establishment of a united Protestant British Isles. He founded a powerful dynasty, which included two Prime Ministers.

Robert Cecil, the Earl of Salisbury, also called Baron Cecil of Essendon, and from 1604, Viscount Cranborne, succeeded William as Elizabeth's chief minister in 1598, and continued to do so during the first nine years of the reign of James I, ensuring continuity in the change from Tudor to Stuart rule in England.

In the nineteenth century, Robert Arthur Talbot Gascoyne-Cecil, third Marquess of Salisbury, was a Conservative politician and leader, three times Prime Minister between1885 and 1902, and four times Foreign Secretary between 1878 and 1900. Salisbury was the last statesman to head a British government while serving in the House of Lords and not the elected Commons.

In the twenty-first century, William Cecil, Lord Burghley, still occupies Burghley House, which has been in the family's continuous occupation for over sixteen generations. Burghley House Preservation Trust now cares for the wellbeing of the entire estate and a board of governors maintains it as a charity.

The Clinton Family of Lincoln

The Earldom of Lincoln was first created in 1143 for William d'Aubigny, (c.1109–1176), first Earl of Arundel. It passed through several families during the reign of King Stephen, but after its investiture to Ranulph de Blondeville, it passed, unusually, to his sister, Hawise of Chester, by royal consent. Through her it passed to John de Lacy, (who died in 1240), being made Earl of Lincoln in 1232. He was son of Roger de Lacy, Justiciar of England and Constable of Chester. However, within a century, there being no further male claimants, the earldom reverted to the Crown.

Over the following two centuries it passed into the Pole and Brandon families, before in its eighth creation it went to Edward Fiennes Clinton, who became ninth Baron Clinton. Edward served as Lord High Admiral under Edward VI, Mary and Elizabeth. He was succeeded by his son, the second Earl, who represented Launceston and Lancashire in Parliament.

In 1768, Henry Clinton, (1720-94), succeeded his uncle Thomas Pelham as second Duke of Newcastle-under-Lyne, and since this date the title of Earl of Lincoln has been the courtesy title of the eldest son of the Duke of Newcastle.

On the death of Edward, the eigtheenth Earl, in July 2001, Robert Edward Fiennes-Clinton, (born in June 1972), succeeded to the Earldom of Lincoln.

The Cromwell Family of Nottinghamshire

The Cromwell family is famous for Thomas Cromwell, first Earl of Essex, who fell foul of Henry VIII's axeman and died an ignominious death after perjuring himself at the trial of Sir Thomas Moore. The family name of Oliver Cromwell, the ruthless Lord Protector of England, descended from Thomas Cromwell's sister.

Cromwell is of locational origin and comes from a village in Nottinghamshire, where the original Lord of the Manor, Ralph de Cromwella was first recorded in the County Pipe Rolls of 1177. The placename and family name translates as 'the winding stream' from the Old English word 'crumb', meaning 'winding' or 'bent', and 'waella' signifying a well or a stream.

The Curzon Family of Kedleston

The Curzon family name originated in Notre Dame de Courson in the Calvados Region of Normandy. It is derived from the Old French word 'curt', from the Latin 'curtus', meaning 'short'. Giraldine de Courson arrived with the Conqueror in 1066, and by 1086 his son Hubert had acquired lands in Berkshire. In 1223, he became Lord of Curson.

Variations on the surname include Curson, Cursone, Courson and Courzon. Early usages of it included William de Cursun in Norfolk in 1198, and Katherine la Curzoun in the court register for Essex in 1316.

Since 1297, the Curzons have lived at Kedleston Hall in Derbyshire, which was commissioned by Sir Nathaniel Curzon, first Baron Scarsdale and rebuilt in 1759 by Robert Adam with Matthew Brettingham and James Payne.

Over the years, the family established their power and influence in Derbyshire by gradually expanding the estate and serving as Members of Parliament from the mid-sixteenth century. This expansion was driven by Sir John Curzon, (1598-1686), who grew the estate to more than 10,000 acres and was created a Baronet in 1641. His son, Sir Nathaniel Curzon, the second Baronet, married Sarah Penn in 1671; she was the daughter of William Penn, who founded Pennsylvania, the American state which still bears his name.

A notable member of the family is George Nathaniel Curzon, (1859-1925), the Marquess of Kedleston, who became Viceroy of India in the early twentieth century.

Kedleston remains the home of the Curzon family, though little remains of the original village. Nathaniel, the first Baron Scarsdale, removed most of it to make way for his new house. Like many such country mansions, Kedleston proved too expensive to maintain and in recent years has been given to the National Trust, with the Curzons remaining as tenants. The Hall is nowadays a popular venue for antiques fairs and music concerts.

The Cust Family of Belton

A name found in Lincolnshire, where the Cust family were Lords of the Manor of Belton, near Grantham. It probably derives from the female given name 'Constance', meaning perseverance or constancy in Latin. In medieval times, the name was commonly known as 'Custnance', from which Cust, (sometimes Cuss), is evidently a shortened version. An early example of it as a given name exists in the 1273 Hundred Rolls of Cambridge and Huntingdonshire, where the name of Cuss Balla is recorded.

The Cust family are descended from Sir Richard Cust, (1622-1700), who was the Baron of Stamford in Lincolnshire, and a Member of Parliament for the county. His grandson, Sir John Cust, the third Baronet, became Speaker of the House of Commons in 1761.

In 1776, Sir Brownlow Cust was created Baron Brownlow; in his time he had served as Member of Parliament for Ilchester and later for Grantham. By 1815, the family titles included the Viscountcy of Alford and the Earldom of Brownlow. Several succeeding generations were Lords Lieutenant for Lincolnshire.

During the years following the First World War, the sixth Baron Brownlow, Peregrine Cust, served as a lord-in-waiting to the Prince of Wales, (who later became Edward VIII). In 1934-35, he became Mayor of Grantham and in 1939, was commissioned into the Royal Air Force, before he served as Parliamentary Private Secretary to the Minister of Aircraft Production, Lord Beaverbrook.

Edward John Peregrine Cust, (born in March 1936), is the seventh Baron Brownlow. The family seat is at Belton House, near Grantham.

The Le Despenser Family of East Midlands

Robert d'Abbetot, (known as Robert le Despenser), was granted titles, lands and high status in the court of William the Conqueror. In addition to his position as steward or butler (from about 1088 to 1098), he was also given lands in the County of Bedford and was listed in the *Domesday Book* as a land tenant-in-chief in Gloucestershire, Leicestershire, Lincolnshire, Oxfordshire and Warwickshire, as well as possessing lands in Worcestershire, which he had obtained from the Bishop of Worcester.

Robert's last name was changed to Le Despenser in England, in keeping with his position and function, (based on the Latin 'dispensa' or 'dispensator' – the word for a medieval steward or butler). There are several spelling variants of his name, including Dispensor, Despensator and Dispenser, which reflected an official position and occupation. In medieval times, a dispenser frequently carried the monarch's purse and was responsible for supplying (or 'dispensing') all his practical needs.

Upon his death, Robert le Despenser left no natural heirs and his estates passed to his brother Urse d'Abbetot, (c.1040–1108), who was Sheriff of Worcester. However, Urse did not take up the name Despenser. Urse's son, Roger d'Abbetot, having killed one of the servants of Henry I, was banished and his confiscated estates, along with the hand of his sister, Emmeline d'Abetot, given by the king to Walter de Beauchamp of Bedford.

Several variations on the family name have existed over the years, including De Spencer, De Spendure, De Spens, De la Despense and De la Spence, among many others. Of these, the Spencer family are probably the best known, for their connection to the late Diana, Princess of Wales, formerly Diana Spencer.

The Foljambe Family of Derbyshire

The Foljambes, (sometimes Fulghams or Fulghums), were descendants of Ragnar Lodbrok of Denmark. The De Folchamps, as they were known in Normandy, moved into France in about 910. A Thomas de Folchamps and his son, Robert, accompanied William the Conqueror to England in 1066, and received lands in Derby for their support and loyalty. Over time they intermarried with Saxon nobility.

The surname is first found written in Derbyshire in the eleventh century, where they had established a home at Tideswell in the Peak District. It is known that in the thirteenth century, Sir Thomas Foljambe was Bailiff of the High Peak.

The family name is derived from the Old French words 'fol', (meaning 'foolish'), and 'jambe', which means 'leg'. It was commonly used to describe persons who walked with a limp, were disabled, or who had a leg deformation of some kind.

The Baronetcy of Foljambe of Walton was created in July 1622 for Francis Foljambe of Walton Hall, near Chesterfield. He was Member of Parliament for Pontefract in 1626 and High Sheriff of Derbyshire in 1633. The baronetcy was extinct when he died, but another branch of the family became Earls of Liverpool. Many generations saw a rise to high office and influence, including Sir Godfrey Foljambe, who was a Baron of the Exchequer and senior official of the Duchy of Lancaster in the early fourteenth century.

Over time, their land holdings extended to the villages of Walton, Brimington, Whittington, Chesterfield, Brampton and Holme, as well as part of the Manors of Lowdham and Bilsthorpe in Nottinghamshire and Winkerton, Martin and Riby in Lincolnshire.

Cecil George Savile Foljambe, first Earl of Liverpool, (1846–1907), known as Lord Hawkesbury between 1893 and 1905, was a Liberal politician, and a member of the Privy Council in 1906. He remained a member of the government until his death in 1907.

In the twentieth century, Royal Artillery officer Francis Foljambe kept a detailed journal of his experience on the Western Front as it affected the English upper classes during the Great War, thereby creating an historical eyewitness document of the conflict.

As a result of many migrations, descendants live throughout the United States, particularly in Georgia, Alabama, Mississippi, New York and Utah.

The La Zouch Family of Ashby

Probably one of England's most unusual family names, La Zouch (sometimes La Zouche), derives from an Old Norman word 'souche', literally meaning a tree stump, but used as a term to describe a person of stocky or thickset stature. Variants of the surname include Souch, Sutch, Such, Zouch and Chucks.

The La Zouche family descended from Alan la Zouche, who died in 1190. He was Lord of the Manor of North Molton in Devon, and was a Breton nobleman who settled in England during the reign of Henry II. The earliest known written records of the name in the Midlands appears in 1200, when one Roger la Zuche held Ashby in Leicestershire. His surname was attached to the name of the township, which has continued to be called Ashby-de-la-Zouch since that time.

One of his descendants, Alan la Zouche, was created Baron la Zouche of Ashby in 1299. He was Governor of Rockingham Castle and Steward of Rockingham Forest. However, this barony ended when he died without male heirs in 1314. It was restored later, and through propitious marriage, in 1308, the family line inherited the titles Barons Zouche of Haryngworth and Barons St Maur.

Over succeeding generations, baronies were gained and lost in the ever-changing climate of English politics, and it was not until 1815, that Sir Cecil Bishopp, who was related to the family line, became twelfth Baron Zouche. The current eigtheenth Baron Zouche also became the twelfth Baron Frankland in 1944.

The Manners Family of Bakewell

By 1232, the Manners family was established at Etal in Northumberland, having arrived with the Norman invasion of 1066, bringing with them the placename of their descent, the village of Mesnieres-en-Bray, near Rouen in Normandy. They came from a Viking named Mainer who received the grant of land from Rollo, (c.846-c.932). There are records of Ralph and Roger de Mesnieres in 1198 and of William de Mesnieres in 1232.

In 1309, Baldwin de Manners was summoned to Parliament as Lord Manners, a peerage that fell extinct when he died in 1320.

Then in 1563, John Manners married Dorothy Vernon, heiress to Haddon Hall, near Bakewell in Derbyshire, and it came into the possession of the family. Later, as Dukes of Rutland, they moved to live in Belvoir Castle, leaving the Hall unaltered and much deteriorated, so that by the time the ninth Duke moved back to live there in 1912, it required extensive restoration.

In 1679, another John Manners was summoned to Parliament as Lord Manners de Haddon. He was created Marquess of Granby and Duke of Rutland in 1703.

In 1807, Thomas Manners-Sutton was created Baron Manners; he became Lord Chancellor of Ireland that same year.

David Charles Robert Manners, eleventh Duke of Rutland, born in May 1959 and styled as the Marquess of Granby until 1999, lives at Belvoir Castle in Leicestershire.

The Montfort Family of Leicester

The Montfort name, (sometimes De Montfort – occasionally Munford or Mountford), arrived in England after the Conquest, and the family initially lived in Warwick, though the name is most associated with Leicester. The line descended from Hugh de Montfort, son of Thurstan de Basternberg, who was granted lands in Kent, Essex, Suffolk and Norfolk. The *Domesday Book* records Hugh, (also called Hugh Beard), from Montfort-sur-Risle, in the Eure Region of France, as Regent with Odo of Bayeux and Earl William FitzOsbern.

Probably the most famous member of the family was Simon de Montfort, born in France in about 1208. He arrived in England in 1230 and inherited estates in Leicester from his father's cousin, Ranulf, Earl of Chester.

In January 1238, De Montfort married Eleanor, daughter of John and Isabella of Angoulême and sister of Henry III, and a year later he was invested with the Earldom of Leicester.

Simon de Montfort became a distinguished leader of the barons who opposed Henry III, who had reneged on rights granted earlier by Magna Carta, resulting in a bloody civil war between the barons and the monarchy. In defeat, the king agreed to the setting up of a Parliament, made up of citizens from every borough in England. However, vengeful hostilities continued, culminating in the Battle of Evesham, where Simon de Monfort was killed. Three memorials commemorate his life (and death) at Evesham Abbey, and his name is also honoured by the Simon de Montfort University of Leicester.

The Multon Family of Gillesland

The earliest known progenitor of the Multon family, (sometimes Moulton), was Sir Thomas de Multon, (1170-1240), who was born in the village of Moulton, near Spalding in Lincolnshire, from where the family name originated.

Sir Thomas was a judge as well as Sheriff of Lincolnshire, of Cumberland and Constable of Carlisle Castle in 1233. He was excommunicated by the Pope, as a witness to sealing of Magna Carta at Runnymede in 1215. A military man in his youth, he served in King John's army in the Normandy campaigns from 1202 to 1204, and against Llywelyn the Great in Wales in 1211. The Barony of

Gillesland and the patronage of Lanercost passed to Sir Thomas when he married Maud de Vaux, the daughter of Hubert and his wife Margaret de Burgh.

In 1299, Thomas de Multon was summoned to Parliament as Lord Multon de Egremont. Later, in 1307, another descendant, also named Thomas, inherited the peerage and served as a Member of Parliament. He married Eleanor de Burgh, daughter of the Earl of Ulster.

Thomas died leaving no male heir, and his daughter Margaret inherited the title and estates. His other daughter, Elizabeth, married Robert the Bruce of Scotland. Margaret married Ranulph, (sometimes Ralph), de Dacre, and upon her death in 1361, the Multon peerages became extinct, the estate passing through her husband into the Dacre Family. Ralph Dacre had already been summoned to Parliament as Lord Dacre in 1321.

The Peverel Family of Nottingham

The Norman knight, Guillaume de Peverel, (also known as Gulielmus Piperellus, and later as William Peverel), (c.1040-1115), is listed on the Rolls at Battle Abbey in Hastings, and had accompanied William in his conquest of Britain. An unproven tradition maintains that he was actually the illegitimate son of the Conqueror by Maud Ingelrica, a Saxon princess, born before his marriage to Matilda of Flanders. Whatever his true lineage, William Peverel was greatly honoured after Hastings with rewards of more than one hundred English manors. This feudal barony was known as the Honour of Peverel. By the time of Domesday in 1086, his holdings had expanded to one hundred and sixty-two manors throughout Nottinghamshire and Derbyshire, which he held as a tenant-in-chief of the king. He built both Nottingham and Peverel Castles.

An early record of the surname also appears in the *Domesday Book* in the person of Rannulus Peurellus. In 1186, Richard Peuerel is recorded in Warwickshire, as is a William Peperel in 1221.

Various alternative spellings for the surname have been recorded over time, including Peverall, Pevreal, Peperall and Pepperill. It may be a derivation of an old Latinised French name 'Puererellus', meaning 'little boy', or possibly a corruption of the word 'pepper', indicating a person of a fiery disposition.

In the twelfth century, the Manor of Sampford, near Tiverton in Devon, was granted to another William Peverell, and the family name was appended to call the place Sampford Peverell, a name which survives to the present day.

Peverel Castle, near Castleton in the Derbyshire Peak District, was begun in 1176, but was returned to the Crown in 1223. During the thirteenth century it underwent periods of building work so that by the year 1300 it was in its present form. Toward the end of the fourteenth century, the lands and its barony were granted to John of Gaunt, Duke of Lancaster.

In the nineteenth century, Sir Walter Scott featured the castle in his novel *Peveril of the Peak*. It is nowadays managed by English Heritage, protected as a scheduled monument and is designated as a Grade I Listed Building.

The Pierrepont Family of Thoresby

The Pierreponts were an old Nottinghamshire family, whose history traces back to Henry de Pierrepont, who married Annora de Manvers in the late thirteenth century. Their estate at Thorseby was purchased by Sir Robert Pierrepont in 1633, after the family had prospered as wealthy landowners and politicians over the two preceding centuries.

Sir George Pierrepont had been created Earl of Kingston-upon-Hull in 1628, a title that remained in the family until 1773, when the male line died out. In 1778, a descendant, Charles Pierrepont, was elevated to the peerage, and in 1796, he became Viscount Newark. By 1806, he had also been created Earl Manvers.

The family continued to be influential in the county until the fifth Earl fell ill, and since the 1940s the Thoresby Park estate has been in the hands of an appointed trust. Gervais Evelyn Pierrepont succeeded as the sixth Earl Manvers, but the title was extinct when he died in 1955.

The Spencer Family of Althorp

The Spencer family is an old aristocratic family, whose members have included knights, baronets, and peers. Their hereditary titles include the Dukedom of Marlborough, the Earldoms of Sunderland and Spencer, and Viscounts Churchill. They trace their direct ancestry to Henry Spencer, who died some time around 1478. They were granted a coat of arms in 1504, as direct descendants of the royal house of Stuart.

In 1469, John Spencer was made Lord of Wormleighton in Warwickshire and in 1486 he became a tenant at Althorp in Northamptonshire. Through trade, the family accumulated sufficient wealth to purchase estates in Wormleighton and Althorp, where they built a manor house in 1512.

In the late sixteenth century, Sir Robert Spencer, (1570–1627), represented Brackley in Parliament, and in 1601 he was made a Knight of the Garter. Two years later he was created Baron Spencer of Wormleighton. During the reign of James I he was reputed to be the richest man in England.

The Spencers continued to be elevated to various levels of the peerage, including Lord Lieutenants of Ireland, Lords Privy Seal, First Lords of the Treasury and Knights of the Garter, among many other honours.

In 1815, Francis Spencer, the younger son of George Spencer, fourth Duke of Marlborough, was created Baron Churchill of Wychwood, and in 1817, the fifth Duke, (now of Marlborough), added Churchill to the family name, some members preferring to be called solely by that surname. Sir Winston Spencer Churchill, grandson of the seventh Duke of Marlborough, became the celebrated British Prime Minister during the Second World War.

The other branch who chose to retain the Spencer family name had their family seat at Althorp, while the Churchills and Spencer-Churchills, the Dukes of Marlborough, had their seat in Blenheim Palace in Woodstock, Oxfordshire. The eighth Earl Spencer married the Honourable Frances Ruth Roche in 1954 and had a daughter, Diana, who later married Prince Charles to become the Princess of

Wales in 1981. The family succeeded to the earldom and estates in 1975.

The Tailbois Family of Lincolnshire

In the eleventh century, the Norman knight Ivo Taillebois, (sometimes Tallboys, Tailboys or Tailgebosch), was a powerful nobleman, a supporter of William the Conqueror and tenant-in-chief in England. In 1071, Taillebois led an army and captured the rebel leader Hereward the Wake at his base on the Isle of Ely. He probably became High Sheriff of Lincolnshire before 1068, and married Lucy, the Saxon daughter of Turold, who had been Sheriff of Lincolnshire before the 1066 Conquest.

Recorded in the *Domesday Book*, Taillebois held Bourne and many of its manors. William II (William Rufus), further endowed him with the lands of Ribblesdale and Lonsdale in Cumbria, as well as granting him the Barony of Kendal, which comprised a large area of the ancient county of Westmorland.

The surname is a reference to Taillebois, a village in Normandy, and is derived from the Old French word 'taillebosc', meaning 'cut wood', probably originally in reference to a one-time local woodcutter.

The title Baron Tailboys of Kyme was created in 1529 for Gilbert Tailboys, the stepfather of Henry FitzRoy, Duke of Richmond and Somerset, (1519–36), who was himself the only illegitimate child acknowledged by Henry VIII. Tailboys served as a Member of Parliament as well as being promoted to the House of Lords.

Despite his rise in society, Tailboys died intestate in April 1530, and the barony passed to his three children. However, when Elizabeth Lady Tailboys died some thirty years later, the family line became extinct. Gilbert's widow remarried, to Edward Fiennes, the ninth Lord Clinton.

The Villiers Family of Leicestershire

The Villiers surname, (sometimes de Villiers or Devilliers), arrived in England during the Norman Conquest, when Galderfridus de

Villiers of St Evroult accompanied William in 1066. The name refers to their place of origin, the village of Villiers Herbisse & Troyes in Normandy. The family settled in Brooksby, Leicestershire, (recorded in the *Domesday Book* as Brochesbi), where Galderfridus was made Lord of the Manor of Rokesby, while his son, Pagan de Villiers, was granted the Barony of Warrington.

The Villiers became an eminent aristocratic family; early records show that in time they became knights, baronets and peers, who included the Dukedom of Cleveland among their number.

The family included William de Viliers, who in 1185 was listed as a Knight Templar in Yorkshire and Nicholas de Vylars in Sussex in 1327. Villiers was the surname of the Dukes of Buckingham, who were also the Earls of Clarenden and Jersey; they held great power and influence under the Stuart monarchs, with no less than sixteen coats of arms being granted to family members.

George Villiers, first Duke of Buckingham, (1592–1628), was a notable favourite of James I. He was High Sheriff of Leicestershire in 1591, and a Knight of the Shire from 1604 until his murder in 1628. Barbara Villiers, Duchess of Cleveland, became Charles II's mistress, and bore him five children.

Francois Coulon de Villiers, sometimes referred to as the 'Chevalier of the Order of St Louis', was a Canadian French army officer born in 1712, whose family had emigrated from Nantes in France. He served as a soldier in Illinois and Louisiana during the Seven Years' War, and while at Fort Duquesne he accepted George Washington's surrender on 4 July 1754. He died in 1772 and is buried in New Orleans.

At the time of writing, George Edward Laurence Villiers, who was born in 1976, bears the title eighth Earl of Clarendon.

The Willoughby Family of Wollaton & Middleton

Willoughby family history can be traced back to the thirteenth century, when a Nottingham merchant by the name of Ralph Bugge bought lands in Willoughby-on-the-Wolds in Nottinghamshire. Over time, the family purchased properties and acquired land through marriage, including the Wollaton and Cossall estates some time around 1314–1319, when the Manor of Wollaton was bought from Sir Roger Morteyn. Later in the fifteenth century, they purchased the Middleton estate in Warwickshire.

The Willoughby surname is derived from the place of that name and has had various spellings including Willughby and Willubie. It was recorded in the *Domesday Book* as Wilgeby, and referred to in local church records in 1341, as Wylloughby. The township, known to the Romans as Vernometum, was located on a main arterial road from Bath to Lincoln.

Wollaton Hall, which was to become the family's county seat, was completed by Sir Francis Willoughby in 1588. Because he produced no male heirs, most of the estate passed to his son-in-law, Sir Percival Willoughby of Bore Place in Kent, a descendent of the Willoughby de Eresby family. In 1688, Thomas Willoughby was a Member of Parliament and was created Baron Middleton in December 1711, one of ten peers created by Queen Anne in one day.

Since the time of Percival Willoughby, the estate has passed in unbroken male succession for over six hundred years to the present day.

Part Five

East Anglia
Family Names in Cambridgeshire, Essex, Norfolk & Suffolk

The Beauclerk Family of Suffolk

Beauclerk, (sometimes Beauclerc or Bonclerk), is a name first found in England in the County of Suffolk, and has long been associated with the British aristocracy, with many royal associations. It is derived from the Old French, and simply means a 'good (or learned) clerk'. The correct pronunciation of the family surname is its French rendering of Beauclaire, (pronounced 'boh-clair').

In this connection, the Dukedom of St Albans was first created in 1684 for Charles Beauclerk, the Earl of Burford and Baron Hedington. He is thought likely to have been Charles II's illegitimate son by Eleanor (Nell) Gwynne. He was Lord Lieutenant of Berkshire from 1714 to 1726 and made a Knight of the Garter in 1718.

The third son of the first Duke, Vere Beauclerk, (1699-1781), was made Baron Vere of Hanworth, and his successor, Aubrey Beauclerk, the second Baron, was Member of Parliament for Thetford and for Aldborough.

William Amelius Aubrey de Vere Beauclerk, the tenth duke, was Privy Counsellor in 1869 and Lord Lieutenant of Nottingham from 1880 to 1898.

The St Albans dukedom has continued down the family line to its present incumbent, Murray de Vere Beauclerk, the fourteenth duke, (born in 1939), the eldest son of the thirteenth duke. Since 1989 he has been Governor General of the Royal Stuart Society and a Freeman of the City of London. He is also a Liveryman of the Drapers' Company, and holds the title of Hereditary Grand Falconer of England.

The Bigod Family of Thetford

The Bigod Family trace their recorded ancestry back to Roger Bigod, (sometimes Bigot), a Norman knight who arrived in England at the time of the Conquest and is thought to have fought at Hastings. He became a royal adviser to William and held great power in East Anglia. The *Domesday Book* records him as holding six lordships in Essex and his name appears as a witness to the Charter of Liberties of Henry I.

In 1122, Hugh Bigod, (1095-1177), had become Earl of Norfolk, and by the time of Magna Carta at least two of his immediate descendants were witnesses to the original document. By then the family had already begun building Framlingham Castle in Suffolk, on the site of an earlier Saxon settlement. However, disgraced for their part in a rebellion against Henry II, the castle was razed to the ground by royal command. The king also took away Hugh's earldom, a title that was lost until the reign of Richard the Lionheart, who restored both the title and what remained of the castle to the Bigod family.

Framlingham became the Bigod family seat, but they also held considerable lands in Yorkshire, with a manor at Settington near Pickering, and a home in London. However, as the line failed to produce male heirs, the estates and titles passed through marriage on the female side to the Mowbray family, with Thomas Mowbray inheriting the castle and title in 1397.

In 1483, the estate and title passed to a descendant, John Howard, who was created first Duke of Norfolk. His tenure was short, however, as he was killed and his property confiscated in 1485, following the Battle of Bosworth, where he fought alongside Richard III.

The rebuilt Framlingham Castle was eventually confiscated by Henry VIII, following his unsuccessful marriage to Catherine Howard. It was granted to Princess Mary, and it was there she declared herself queen in 1553.

The fourth duke, also called Thomas Howard, rebelled against Elizabeth I, and for a time the castle was a prison for Catholic heretics. It was finally restored to the family in 1603.

The Howard era ended in 1635, when Framlingham was sold to Sir Robert Hitcham, who died a year later, leaving a will instructing a poorhouse to be established within the castle, a function that continued until 1839. The building briefly saw military activity during the Napoleonic war and in Second World War, before in 1913 it was taken over by the Ministry of Works.

The Colville Family of Suffolk

The Colville surname is first found in Suffolk, where the family seat was located. They were descended from Gilbert de Colleville, (sometimes Colavilla), who came from Coleville-sur-Mer, a township near Caen in Normandy. Gilbert had accompanied Duke William in his conquest of England.

The name translates as 'Koli-ville', meaning 'Koli's settlement', Koli being an Old Norse personal name. An early recorded example of the surname include that of Walter de Colevile in the Hundred Rolls of Lincolnshire in 1273.

A branch of the family is also found in Scotland, where Philip de Colville was a witness to a charter to Dunfermline Monastery some time before 1159. It is here that the history of the family name best survives, and where most Colville descendants live. Later the family name changed to Colvin, and they were based in Sussex, then London and the surrounding counties, notably at Monkhams Hall near Waltham Abbey in Essex.

Charles Colville, Viscount Colville of Culross, is a member of the House of Lords, and is currently the clan chief of the Colvilles.

The D'Aubigny Family of Arundel

The D'Aubigny family, (sometimes D'Albini, De Albini, or Daubeny), were prominent emigrés from the village of St Martin d'Aubigny, north of Coutances on the Contentin Peninsula of Normandy. The most common contemporary form of the surname is 'Albini'. Lands were granted by Duke William to Roger d'Aubigny, (also known as Roger Mowbray), for his distinguished service at the Battle of Hastings.

One of Roger's sons, William, (sometimes called 'Strong Hand'), was a butler to William the Conqueror and was married to Maud Bigod. Their son, also named William, was later created Earl of Lincoln by King Stephen, and eventually became the Earl of Arundel. When Henry II ascended to the throne, he gave William possession of Arundel Castle in Sussex. In 1143, he was made Earl of Lincoln and began building Castle Rising Castle in Norfolk. William died in 1176.

The family held D'Aubigny titles and estates over succeeding generations, passing through marriage to the De Somery Family of Dudley, and then to the De Cromwells.

The earldom of Arundel is the oldest existing peerage in England. The heir apparent to the title is Edward William FitzAlan-Howard, eigtheenth Duke of Norfolk, born on 2 December 1956. He is hereditary Earl Marshal, head of the College of Arms and son of Miles FitzAlan-Howard, seventeenth Duke of Norfolk. The style Earl of Arundel is used as a courtesy title by the Duke's eldest son.

The De Bretagne Family of Essex

The De Bretagne surname (sometimes Brittany), derives from the region in France of that name, and arrived in England with the Conquest of 1066. The earliest known progenitor of the family was Judicael de Bretagne, (known as 'de Rennes'), Count of Rennes, born around 910 in Rennes, Ille-et-Vilaine in Brittany.

In England, Alan IV Fergant 'de Cornouaille', (translates as 'of Cornwall'), Duke of Brittany and Count of Rennes and Nantes, probably born around 1067 in Nantes, is considered to have been created the first Earl of Richmond. He had married Princess Constance of England in 1085. Constance outlived her husband and remarried twice more. In 1191, Richard I proclaimed his nephew, Constance's son, Arthur, (by her third husband Geoffrey, son of Henry II), as his heir. He was known as Arthur I de Bretagne, (sometimes as Arthur Plantagenet). On his death the peerage reverted to the Crown.

John of Brittany, (Jean de Bretagne c.1266-1334), became fourth Earl of Richmond and served under Edward I and Edward II. Following generations, (also named John), inherited the title until 1341, when John died without male successors and the peerage reverted to the Crown, with the Earldom of Richmond and Dukedom of Brittany falling to John of Montfort (Jean de Montfort). He contested inheritancy of the Duchy of Brittany with his niece, Joan of Penthièvre, and became thereby embroiled in the Hundred Years' War with France.

Following John de Montfort's death in 1345, the earldom of Richmond passed into the royal house of Plantagenet and thereafter on to the Tudors.

The English surname Britton has the same root, simply meaning 'from Brittany'. Other spelling variations include Britain, Brittan, Briton and Britney.

The De Clare Family of Suffolk

The De Clare family were historically associated with the Welsh Marches, Suffolk, Surrey, Kent and Ireland. They were descended from Richard FitzGilbert, Lord of Clare, (1035-90), who accompanied William during the Conquest. The family settled to live in Suffolk, where William granted them large estates, including the small village of Clare, as well as lands in Tonbridge.

They originated in the township of Clere in Normandy, and it is from there that the surname is derived; 'De Clare' simply means 'from Clare'.

Richard FitzGilbert of Tonbridge is referred to as Richard of Clare in the Suffolk return of the Domesday Survey. On his death, Richard's estates passed to his son Gilbert de Clare, second Lord of Clare, (1055-1117), who was the first formally to use the surname De Clare instead of 'Fitz', and was known by the title Baron de Clare. Gilbert's eldest son Richard de Clare, third Lord of Clare, (1090-1136), was the ancestor of the Earls of Hertford and Gloucester.

In 1176, Richard de Clare, second Earl of Pembroke, died without male heirs so that his line came to an end, and his many estates, particularly those in Wales and Ireland, passed to his daughter Isabel, who married William Marshal, who thereafter was known as first Earl of Pembroke.

Variant spellings and derivations of the name include Clair, Clere, O'Clear and O'Clair, among others.

The De Gael Family of East Anglia

Ralph De Gael, (also known as Ralph de Guader, Raoul de Gael or Radulf Waders), was born in 1042, probably at Montfort in Normandy, and in 1066 he fought alongside William at Hastings. He was appointed as Earls of East Anglia and Lord of Gaël and Montfort, and was a leading figure in the revolt of the Earls in 1075, the last serious opposition to William the Conqueror. The uprising failed and Ralph fled to Brittany where he inherited the Breton Barony of Gael.

Ralph had been married to Emma, (daughter of King William FitzOsbern, first Earl of Hereford and cousin of the now William). She was Baroness of Gael, Earl of East Anglia and Countess of Norfolk. She died in 1095, along with her husband Ralph, who had taken part in the siege of Nicaea. They met with an untimely end, on the way to Palestine during the Crusades. On his death, many of Ralph's possessions passed to the Breton aristocrat, Alan Rufus.

The De Tibetot Family

See: Part Seven: The South-West: The De Tibetot Family of Kempsford.

The De Vere Family of Essex

The De Vere family derived their surname from the township of Ver in the Manche Department near Coutances in Normandy. The family's Norman founder in England, Aubrey de Vere, (sometimes Albericus or Alberic), (c.1040-1112), is recorded in the *Domesday Book* as holding lands in Essex, Cambridgeshire, Huntingdonshire and Suffolk.

His descendant, Aubrey de Vere II, was first Lord Great Chamberlain of England, and built Hedingham Castle in 1140, on land that was previously held by a Saxon named Ulwine. His son, Aubrey III, was created Earl of Oxford by the Empress Matilda, a title which continued for many generations until finally becoming extinct with the death of the twentieth Earl in 1702.

Many honours have accompanied the family through the centuries. The seventh earl, for example, was one of Edward III's generals, and commanded a leading wing alongside the Black Prince at the Battle of Crecy, and the eleventh earl commanded English forces at Agincourt. The thirteenth earl fought for Henry VII and was substantially rewarded on the accession of the king for his loyalty. The fifteenth earl carried the crown at the coronation of the ill-fated Anne Boleyn.

In 1713, Hedingham Castle was bought by Sir William Ashhurst MP, the Lord Mayor of London.

The De Walcott Family of Norfolk

Following the Norman invasion of England, the township of Walcott was given to Robert Malet, who died some time before 1088, when it passed to Ranulf, brother of Iger and held by Humphrey, possibly his nephew. Within the century, the De Walcott family, (sometimes simply Walcot, Wolcott or Walcott), are recorded as Lords of the Manor, living at East Hall in Walcott during the reign of Henry II. It is also on record that one William de Edgefield lived with his mother, Maud de Walcott, who gave part of her land to the Monks at the nearby Bromholm Priory. By about 1280, Thomas de Walcott was also Lord of West Hall in Walcott.

Several possible explanations have been put forward as to the derivation of the place and family name. From Old English and Welsh, it has been interpreted as meaning 'the cottage by the well'. From Middle English, it may have referred to a person who originally lived there; hence, possibly, 'Wulfrige's (or Walla's) cottage'. There are several places in England with names derived from Walcot. As well as that in Norfolk, there is a Walcote in Leicestershire and in Warwickshire, which were listed in the *Domesday Book*; while Walcot in Shropshire appeared as a placename in the twelfth century and Wolcot in Devon in the thirteenth.

The Walcotts held the Manor in Norfolk from the late twelfth century until the fourteenth century. It is from this village that their family surname is derived, though it seems to have died out in Norfolk some time in the late fourteenth century. However, other early instances of the family name appear elsewhere to the north, including Stephen de Walecote who was listed in the 1199 tax rolls known as the 'Feet of Fines' for Oxford, and John Walcott of Northampton, in the poll tax rolls of 1379.

In 1320, John, son of Walter de Walcote, (1300-56), was made rector of the church at Ittering in Norfolk, and in 1322 he was appointed rector at Walcott by Sir Alexander de Walcote, (c.1265-1340). In 1378, William le Parker sold the Manor of Brumstead and the Manor of Eccles to Simon de Walcote, Rector of Walcott.

The FitzRoy Family of Suffolk

The FitzRoy Family name came to Essex and Suffolk following the Norman invasion. The term 'Fitz' is similar to the Scottish Gaelic term 'Mac', and simply means 'the son of'. It is first recorded in England about 1149 in the person of an illegitimate son of Henry I, and later, in 1245, as 'Fitz le Roy', meaning 'son of the king', an indicator that the surname is of royal origin: some have it that he was (arguably) a bastard son of King John.

Later, Henry FitzRoy was born to Henry VIII by his mistress Elizabeth Blount in 1519. The FitzRoy surname was also employed by Charles II, when he created Charles FitzRoy, also an illegitimate son, the Duke of Southampton in 1675. His brother Henry FitzRoy was created Baron Sudbury in that same year, having already been earlier created Viscount Ipswich and first Duke of Grafton. He was also Lord Lieutenant of Suffolk from 1685 to 1689.

By the eigtheenth century, the FitzRoys had risen to positions of political power with Augustus Henry FitzRoy being Member of Parliament for Bury St Edmunds, twice Lord Lieutenant of Suffolk, Secretary of State, Prime Minister and Lord Privy Seal. He was also a Knight of the Garter and a member of the Privy Council.

Thereafter, descendants tended to hold the title of the Earls (or Dukes) of Grafton. The family arms include Charles II's royal coat of arms crossed by a baton, indicating their royal lineage and illegitimate origins.

In the nineteenth century, Vice-Admiral Robert FitzRoy, (1805-65), was a Royal Navy officer and a celebrated scientist. He is remembered as the captain of HMS *Beagle* during Charles Darwin's ground breaking voyage of scientific discovery to the Galapagos Islands.

The Howard Family of Norfolk

The Howards have traditionally held the title of Dukes of Norfolk, the leading peers of England, indicating the power and prestige of this noble family. The family founder is regarded as Sir William Howard of Norfolk, who died in 1308. He became a Member of the Model Parliament in 1295, and married well, into the Mowbray family. His wife, Margaret, was heir to the Duchy of Norfolk, a title which passed to William through their marriage. It was a direct descendant, John, who in 1483 succeeded to the Mowbray estates, and was in turn created Duke of Norfolk and Earl Marshal of England. He was killed at Bosworth in 1485, fighting alongside Richard III.

During the reign of Henry VIII, Thomas Howard, second Duke of Norfolk, was a court counsellor. He was created Baron Howard of Effingham in March 1554, was Lord Privy Seal in 1572, twice Lord Lieutenant of Surrey and was made a Knight of the Garter in 1554. Unfortunately, as uncle to the ill-fated Anne Boleyn and Catherine Howard, both he and his son Henry, the Earl of Surrey, were accused of treason. Henry was executed but Norfolk survived to regain his dukedom later, during the reign of Mary.

Later, during the reign of Elizabeth I, Charles Howard, second Lord Howard of Effingham, commanded her fleet against the Spanish Armada.

In 1683, Francis Howard was Governor of Virginia, and in 1784 another family descendant by the name of Thomas was made Master of the Mint and was Governor of Jamaica from 1789 to 1791.

In 1996, David Peter Mowbray Algernon Howard, seventh Earl of Effingham, (born in 1939), succeeded to the dukedom, and the heir apparent is his son Edward Mowbray Nicholas Howard, Lord Howard of Effingham, who was born in 1971.

Arundel Castle, a Grade I Listed Building, has been the principal seat of the Dukes of Norfolk for over four hundred years. Another branch of the Howards has lived at Castle Howard in Yorkshire for more than three hundred years.

The Irby Family of Lincolnshire

The Irby surname comes from the old Parish of Irby in the Marsh in north-east Lincolnshire, now known as Irby-upon-Humber. It was recorded in the *Domesday Book* as Irebi, but has had many variations in its spelling over the years, including Irbey, Irbie and Irbye. The name is thought to be of Old Norse origin, from the word 'irabyr', meaning 'the farmstead (or village) of the Irishmen'.

One of the earliest records of the name is that of Margaret de Ireby, who was documented in Lincoln during the reign of Henry III, and William de Irreby, recorded in York in 1273.

In the seventeeth century, Sir Anthony Irby of Whapload, (c.1605-82), was a Member of Parliament for Boston on two separate occasions, including once to the 'Short Parliament' of 1640. His predesessor, also named Anthony Irby, (1577-1610), had been knighted by James I in 1603, and was a major investor in the Virginia Company in New England, where the surname is still fairly common.

The title Baron Boston was created in 1761 for Sir William Irby, (1707-75), who was a Member of Parliament for Launceston and Bodmin. The Irby family seat was at Hedsor House in Buckinghamshire, but they also owned Plas Llanidan and land in Moelfre in Anglesey. Hedsor had been owned by the De Hedsor family since before 1086, and they had taken their name from the village. The Irbys had purchased it from them in 1764, and it remains in their family to this day.

When, in 1871, Lieutenant Colonel Leonard Paul Irby married Ethel Maud Casberd-Boteler, the surnames were combined, and thereafter the family were known by the name Boteler-Irby, first adopted by Gerald, their son, the ninth Baron Boston. His grandson, George William Eustace, succeeded as the eleventh Baron Boston and as the twelfth Baronet Irby of Whapload and Boston in February 2007.

The Lestrange Family of Hunstanton

The Lestrange family name, (sometimes Le Strange), comes from the Old French word meaning, simply, 'a stranger'. Variations on the spelling of the surname include L'Estrange, Strang, Strange, Letrange and Strainge.

In England it was first recorded in Norfolk where the family held the Manor of Knockyn, (sometimes Knockin), during the reigns of Kings Henry II and Henry III.

The name of one John Lestrange appears in the tax rolls for the County of Norfolk in 1195, Ralph le Estrange, in the Curia Regis Rolls of Suffolk in 1199, and Fulco Strange in the records of the Abbey of Ely. Roger le Strange who died in 1311, is known to have fulfilled various important judicial, military and administrative posts for Edward I, (1272-1307), so that by the fifteenth century the Le Strange family were one of the most powerful in Norfolk.

In 1846, Henry Styleman Le Strange, (1815–62), a major local Hunstanton landowner, was instrumental in the development of the area south of Old Hunstanton as a sea bathing resort and invested in the building of a railway line from King's Lynn to bring tourists to the town. The Lynn & Hunstanton Railway was an instant success and in 1861, Le Strange became the railway company's chief director.

Hunstanton Hall, built in around 1490, seat of the Le Strange family from the time of Domesday until after the Second World War, was badly damaged by fire in 1951. It was subsequently split up into apartments and sold, although the family retained the park and part of the gardens. During the 1990s, extensive restoration work on the Hall was undertaken.

The North Family of Cambridgeshire

The Norths trace their family to Edward, first Baron North, (1496-1564), a successful lawyer of his day who became Lord Lieutenant of Cambridgeshire in 1559. He had been knighted in 1541 and in 1543 served as High Sheriff of the County, as did several of his descendants. He was a Privy Counsellor during the reigns of Henry VIII and Elizabeth I, and was chosen to receive Philip of Spain when he arrived at Southampton in June 1554 on his way to marry Mary I.

Dudley, third Baron North, (1581-1666), was one of the principal courtiers of James I. His family was linked by marriage with the Dudley family that had been so powerful at the Tudor court.

In 1752, Francis North was made Earl of Guilford, a peerage that fell into abeyance on the death of George Augustus North, the third Earl, in April 1802. George was the eldest son of Prime Minister Frederick North. Later, the Earldom was reinstated, and currently Piers Edward Brownlow North, born in March 1971, is the tenth Earl of Guilford.

The Pakenham Family of Suffolk

Pakenham is an Anglo-Saxon name based on the village of that name in Suffolk. Listed in the *Domesday Book* as Pachenham, it translates loosely as the 'village or settlement belonging to a man called Pacca'. The Pakenham family took their name from the village.

During the seventeeth century, the Pakenhams inherited the titles of Barons and Viscounts Longford. Francis Aungier was third Baron Aungier of Longford in 1677, and his younger brother, Ambrose, who represented Surrey in Parliament, was created Viscount Longford in the Peerage of Ireland in 1675, though that title had existed in the family since 1621.

In 1785, Elizabeth Cuffe married Thomas Pakenham, who represented Longford County in the Irish Parliament, and upon his death was created Countess of Longford in the Irish Peerage in her own right. In 1794, Thomas Pakenham was created Baron Silchester. In the nineteenth century several family members were Lords Lieutenants of Longford (in Ireland).

Francis Aungier Pakenham was Chancellor of the Duchy of Lancaster in 1947. He had served as Minister of Civil Aviation, (from 1948 to 1951), was First Lord of the Admiralty in 1951, Lord Privy Seal, (from 1964 to 1968), Secretary of State for the Colonies, (from 1965 to 1966), had been a Privy Counsellor in 1948, and was made a Knight of the Garter in 1971. In 1999, he was created Baron Pakenham of Cowley for life. A lifelong member of the Labour Party, as Lord Longford he was politically active until his death in 2001.

The Longford Prize, awarded annually, is named after him. It recognises excellence in the world of prison and social reform. Among the many he befriended and helped were individuals who had committed the most notorious crimes, including the infamous 'Moors Murderess' Myra Hindley.

Thomas Francis Dermot Pakenham, eighth Earl of Longford, the current incumbent, (born 14 August 1933), is an Anglo–Irish historian and prizewinning author. He commutes between London and County Westmeath in Ireland, where he is the chairman of the Irish Tree Society and honorary custodian of Tullynally Castle.

The Tollemache Family of East Anglia

The Tollemache family, (sometimes Talmach, Tollmarche or Tallemache), have lived in Suffolk since before the Norman Conquest, and have had a significant impact on the politics of East Anglia since the reign of Edward I. Family members have held four hereditary titles: the Baronetcy of Helmingham Hall, of Hanby Hall, of Tollemache and the Earldom of Dysart.

Helmingham Hall, the country seat of the Tollemache family, was inherited through marriage. The Hall was built on the site of Creke Hall which it replaced in the late fifteenth century. They also owned Bawdsley Hall, which was used primarily as a hunting lodge, and its stables were reputedly used for the breeding of Suffolk Punch horses. The Hall remained in family ownership well into the late nineteenth century, when according to the 1881 census, Stanhope Alfred Tollemache was its master.

The seventeenth century saw many new acquisitions, largely through marriage, including Harrington in Northamptonshire and the Dysart Estates at Ham, Petersham and Canbury, as well as other land holdings in Cheshire. Further purchases in the eighteenth and nineteenth centuries added properties in Buckminster and Sewstern in Leicestershire and Hanby Hall in Lincolnshire, as well as others in Tarporley and Beeston in Cheshire. By this time family members had been elevated to the peerage as Earls of Dysart.

Sir Lyonel, fourth Baronet Tollemache, donated Ham House to the National Trust in 1948 and sold the remaining Surrey estates in 1949.

The Townshend Family of Raynham

Records show the Townshend family first living in Norfolk in the village of Snoring Magna, but by 1379, branches of the family were in Yorkshire and Buckinghamshire. By the early seventeeth century the family lived at Raynham Hall, which was completed shortly after 1637.

The Townshend surname, (sometimes Townsend), is a topographical name indicating someone who lived at the edge of a settlement (that is, at the 'town's end').

Early family history is somewhat vague, but in April 1661 Sir Horatio Townshend was created Baron Townshend, and by 1682 had been elevated to the rank of Viscount. He was both a Member of Parliament and one-time Lord Lieutenant of Norfolk.

The family distinguished themselves in politics; Charles Townshend, (1725-67), was Chancellor of the Exchequer, and by 1787 another descendant, George Townshend, had been created a Marquess. He was also Lord Lieutenant of Ireland and later of Norfolk. In 1872, yet another George Townshend was created Earl of Leicester. Subsequent family members were Members of Parliament for Tamworth.

Major General Sir Charles Vere Ferrers Townshend, (1861-1924), led a military campaign in Mesopotamia during the First World War, as well as serving with distinction in the Sudan.

Charles George Townshend, the eighth Marquess, born in 1945, styled Viscount Raynham, succeeded to the title on the death of his father in April 2010.

The Waldegrave Family of Suffolk

The name is thought to have originated in Waldegrave, (now Walgrave), in Northamptonshire, from where the family adopted its surname. The *Domesday Book* lists the place as Waldegrave.

The earliest known progenitor of the family was Fulcher de Maloure, a Norman Baron from Saint Brieux in Brittany, who was granted estates in Rutland and Northamptonshire. The family went on to own the Manor of Smallbridge in Bures St Mary in Suffolk. Later, in 1205, John, son of Warin de Walgrave, was Sheriff of London.

Sir Richard Waldegrave was Member of Parliament for Lincolnshire in 1335 and went on to become Speaker of the House of Commons. Sir Edward Waldegrave of Borley, Essex, (c.1517-1561), was knighted by Queen Mary and granted the Manor of Chewton in Somerset, now the residence of Earl Waldegrave. He was both a Member of Parliament and Chancellor of the Duchy of Lancaster. After the queen died, his fortunes reversed, and he was imprisoned in the Tower of London, where he died in September 1561.

In 1686, Sir Henry Waldegrave was created a Baron, and a year later was Lord Lieutenant of Somerset. He died three years later, at which point James Waldegrave was created Viscount Chewton and

Earl Waldegrave. In the eigtheenth century, family members were Members of Parliament for Orford, for Bedford and for Newcastle, and John Waldegrave was Lord Lieutenant of Essex in 1781.

James Waldegrave, the present incumbent and thirteenth Earl, styled Viscount Chewton, was born in December 1940, and currently operates a cheese making estate at Chewton Mendip in Somerset.

The Warenne Family of Lewes

The De Warrens, (sometimes De la Varenne, De Garenne, De Warenne or De Warren), were an Anglo-Norman family that held extensive lands in France, England, Wales, and Ireland. The name is derived from the town and river of Varenne, a few miles from Dieppe in Normandy. Ranulf de Warenne, (c.998-1058), the earliest documented patriarch of the family, was a Norman knight and lived at Castle de Warenne in France.

William de Warenne, created first Earl of Warren and Surrey, was the maternal second cousin of William the Conqueror, and received about three hundred lordships as a reward for his service and support at Hastings. He was also appointed to be Co-Chief Justice of England while William was away in France. The third earl's daughter and heiress, Isabel de Warren, married the Conqueror's descendant, William de Blois, the son of King Stephen, and thus through Isabel's marriage into royalty, the De Warren wealth and titles passed into the House of Plantagenet.

Lewes Castle in East Sussex, (originally known as Bray Castle), is the ancestral home of the Warenne Family. They also founded a nearby religious order at Lewes Priory, where much of Warenne history is recorded and many early family members are buried, including the last of the Warrens, John, the seventh Earl, who died without heirs in 1347. He was succeeded by his nephew, Richard FitzAlan, tenth Earl of Arundel.

Part Six

The South East

Family names in Bedfordshire, Berkshire, Buckinghamshire, East & West Sussex, Greater London, Hampshire, Hertfordshire, Oxfordshire, Surrey & Kent

The Ashburnham Family of Sussex

The Ashburnham family name derives from the village of that name in Sussex, where they are first known to have lived. By the twelfth century, they had become Sheriffs of Surrey.

The township is recorded in the *Domesday Book* as 'Esseburne', derived from the Old English words 'aesc', meaning an ash tree, and 'burna', a brook or a stream. The suffix 'ham' signifies a settlement or a farmstead. Hence, possibly, 'the settlement by the stream where ash trees grow'. Spelling variants of the family name include Ashburn, Ashburham and Ashbourn. The town of Ashbourne in Derbyshire has the same name derivation.

Family tradition has it that they were there long before the Norman invasion of 1066, and that it was one Bertram de Ashburnham, (c.1036-66), who was Sheriff of Surrey, Sussex and Kent, and Constable of Dover during the reign of the Saxon King Harold, and who defended the town against the Norman invasion. He was subsequently beheaded on the orders of the Conqueror, as were his three sons. A decendant, Stephen de Ashburnham, donated land to St Martin of Battel, now known as Battle Abbey.

As recusant Catholics during the reign of Elizabeth I, their estates were seized by the throne in payment of fines, and it was not until 1592 that Sir John Ashburnham, (1571-1620), finally recovered the family estates. Even so, he was a notable spendthrift, and later obliged to sell the estate to the Relf family in order to pay off his debts, which amounted to the then astronomical sum of £8,000. Sir John's son, (also named John), became a Gentleman of the Royal Bedchamber, accrued substantial wealth and was able to buy back the family's lost Ashburnham estate.

Through marriage, the family acquired significant other land holdings throughout England, including in Sussex and Bedfordshire, as well as over seven thousand acres in Breconshire and Carmarthenshire in Wales.

John Ashburnham was present at the coronation of William and Mary (of Orange) in 1689, and was later created first Baron Ashburnham, a title which has remained in the family up to the present.

Sir James Fleetwood Ashburnham succeeded as the thirteenth Baron Ashburnham of Bromham, Sussex in 1999. He currently lives in Winchelsea, Sussex.

The Bruce Family of Aylesbury

This celebrated Scottish family came to England with James I and lived at Houghton House for seventy years. In its time it has produced a king of Ireland and three kings of Scotland. Thomas, who acquired Houghton House in 1624, was made Earl of Elgin in 1633, and his son Robert also became Earl of Ailesbury (Aylesbury) and Viscount Bruce of Ampthill. From 1660 to 1685 he was Lord Lieutenant of Bedford, and of Huntingdon from 1681 to 1685. He was also Member of Parliament for Bedfordshire, and in 1681 he was a Privy Counsellor.

Robert was a Royalist and became Lord Chamberlain after the Restoration of Charles II. He was a strong supporter of the Stuarts against William of Orange and retired into voluntary exile in Brussels, after a spell of imprisonment in the Tower in 1689, accused of plotting to restore James II to the throne. He died forty years later and never returned to Houghton House, which was sold to the Duke of Bedford in 1738.

Charles Bruce, (1682-1747), was Member of Parliament for Great Bedwyn, (1705-10), and for Marlborough, (1710-11). He was summoned to Parliament as Baron Bruce of Whorlton in 1711 and created Baron Bruce of Tottenham in 1746. On his death, the Earldom of Elgin passed to his cousin, while the Earldom of Ailesbury, the Viscountcy of Bruce and the Baronies of Bruce of Skelton and Bruce of Whorlton became extinct. The Barony of Bruce of Tottenham passed to his nephew, Thomas Brudenell-Bruce, (1729-1814), who became second Baron Bruce of Tottenham, and inherited the title Earl of Ailesbury in 1776. He was Lord Lieutenant of Wiltshire, a Privy Counsellor, and was knighted in 1786.

George William Frederick Brudenell-Bruce, Baron Bruce of Tottenham, (1804-1878), was Lord Lieutenant of Wiltshire in 1863 and succeeded to the Earldom of Cardigan and Barony of Brudenell of Stonton in 1868.

George William Thomas Brendall-Bruce, fourth Marquess of Ailsbury, (1863-94), was also a central figure in a major turf scandal in 1887; his insolvency was caused by gambling debts, which resulted in his being 'warned off' for life from all racetracks under the control of the Jockey Club.

Michael Sydney Cedric Brudenell-Bruce, eighth Marquess of Ailesbury, (born 31 March 1926), styled Viscount Savernake until 1961 and Earl Bruce between 1961 and 1974, is the son of Cedric Brudenell-Bruce, seventh Marquess of Ailesbury and Joan Houlton Salter. He succeeded his father as eighth Marquess on his death on the 15 July 1974. He is the heir apparent to the Ailesbury Marquessate and the other titles.

The Byng Family of Winchester

The Byng family name, (sometimes Bing), has two possible derivations. First, from the Old English name Binningas, which is itself derived from the Old Norse word 'bingr', meaning a stall, and may be roughly interpreted as a name given to a person who made stalls or mangers. Second, it may come from the Yiddish word 'bing', for the German town of Bingen in the Rhineland. The surname was first found in England in Middlesex, where the family had lived since Anglo-Saxon times.

Sir George Byng, (1666-1733), was made Baron Byng of Southill and Viscount Torrington in 1721, after two decades serving as Member of Parliament for Plymouth, and was appointed as a Privy Counsellor that same year. He became First Lord of the Admiralty in 1727. He had the distinction of having destroyed the Spanish fleet and capturing Gibraltar in 1704.

His son, John Byng, (1704-57), born in Southill, Bedfordshire, was made a rear admiral by the age of forty, but had to suffer the ignominy of failing to lift the French siege of the British stronghold of Fort St Philip in Menorca in 1756 during the Seven Years' War. He was summoned home, put under arrest on arrival and was executed by firing squad on the deck of his own flagship, for neglect of duty.

The family seat is at Great Hunts Place, near Winchester in Hampshire and the present incumbent is Timothy Howards St George Byng, the eleventh Viscount Torrington, who was born in 1944. He inherited the peerage on the death of his grandfather, Anthony Stanley Byng, in 1961.

The Cadogan Family

See: Part Nine: Wales: The Cadogan Family of Merionethshire.

The Camoys Family of Stoner

Opinions differ as to the origin and meaning of the Camoys family name. Three possibilities have been suggested: one is that it derives from the Old French word 'cammus' or 'camois', a nickname used to describe a person with a snub nose; another has it that it is a corruption of the French word 'chemise', a long shirt-like garment, a nightdress or a priest's under garment; a third explanation is that it is a locational name from Campeaux in the Calvados Region of Normandy. All seem equally possible.

The first recorded written evidence of the surname is that of Adam le Camhus, in the 1256 Assize Rolls of Northumberland. In 1335, Ralph de Camoys was summoned to Parliament and thought to have been the first creation of Baron Camoys. He married well, into the illustrious Despenser family, the Earls of Winchester, who were butlers to the Crown, and by 1318 he held substantial interests in the old Counties of Northamptonshire, Hampshire and Huntingdonshire.

In 1315, Sir Ralph Camoys was captured at the Battle of Bannockburn and a large ransom had to be raised for his safe return home. Despite this early setback, in later life he twice embarked on successful pilgrimages to Santiago de Compostela before becoming the Governor of Windsor Castle.

Three generations of the family fought at Crecy in 1346. Subsequently, in 1415, Thomas de Camoys fought at Agincourt, and commanded the left wing of Henry V's army which won a resounding and historic victory. He was a Knight of the Garter and had married Lady Elizabeth Mortimer, great granddaughter of Edward III. Elizabeth's first husband was Henry Percy, Earl of Northumberland, (known as Harry Hotspur, and celebrated in Shakespeare's *Henry IV*), who was killed at the Battle of Shrewsbury in 1403. Thomas Camoys died in March 1419, and his grandson, Lord Hugh de Camoys, (1413-26), inherited the title. On Hugh's death the Barony of Camoys fell into abeyance between his two sisters, Margaret Radmylde and Alianora, Lady Lewknor.

In September 1839, the abeyance ended after four hundred and thirteen years, in favour of Thomas Stonor of Stoner Park in Oxfordshire, who became third Baron Camoys. Thereafter, the Baron Camoys title has remained in the Stoner Family, with Ralph Thomas Campion Sherman Stonor, (born in 1940), being the seventh Baron Camoys. He served as Lord Chamberlain from 1998 to 2000, the first Catholic to do so since the Reformation.

The Carteret Family of Sark

The De Carterets arrived in England with the Norman invasion of 1066, having originated in Carteret, near Barneville in the Valognes region of Normandy. They were granted lands in Jersey in the

Channel Islands, where they were appointed bailiffs, as well as becoming hereditary seigneurs of the nearby Island of Sark. An Old French version of the name is 'de Chatelet', signifying one who lives near a fort.

Sir George de Carteret, (c.1609-c.1679), held high position in the Channel Islands, including as Bailiff of Jersey in 1643 and later became Lieutenant Governor of the island. He was created Baron Carteret of Metesches in 1645, became Treasurer of the British Navy in 1660, and was a Privy Counsellor and Vice-Chamberlain of the Royal Household from 1660 to 1670. He went on to become Vice-Treasurer of Ireland and Lord of the Admiralty.

In 1744, John Carteret succeeded his mother, Grace Carteret, as the second Earl Granville. When his son Robert, the third Earl Granville, died without issue in 1776, the Carteret titles became extinct and the Earldom of Granville passed to the Leveson-Gower family line and the Thynne family of Longleat, where it continues to the present day.

Vice-Admiral William Spencer Leveson-Gower, the fourth earl, (1880-1953), was a notable officer in the Royal Navy who fought in the First World War and was mentioned in despatches, as well as receiving the Order of St Anne of Russia, the Distinguished Service Order and the Order of the Redeemer of Greece, among innumerable other honours and awards for his work in the diplomatic and military services.

Granville George Fergus Leveson-Gower, born in 1959, succeeded as sixth Earl Granville of Stone Park in Staffordshire in 1996. His son and heir, George James Leveson-Gower, styled Lord Leveson, was born in 1999.

The Cobham Family of Cobham

The Cobham surname dates back to Anglo-Saxon times and is derived from the village of that name in the Graveham District of Kent. The village name was first recorded as Cobba Hammes Mearce as early as 939. By the time of the Domesday Survey, it was recorded as Covenham in the Borough of Elmbridge. The name probably comes from the name of a man called Cobba, plus the suffix 'ham', an Old English word meaning a settlement or homestead. Hence, 'the settlement of Cobba'.

Records show Henry de Cobham, who died around 1230, was the first Baron Cobham. His father, John de Cobham, had been Constable of Rochester and Sheriff of Kent. Henry purchased the Manor of Cobham near Rochester from Sir William Quartremere, and by 1200 he had become a major Kentish landowner.

Henry's son, Reginald, first Lord Cobham of Sterborough, accompanied Edward III to Amiens in France in 1329, on a visit to pay homage to King Philip. Reginald also fought alongside Edward in his wars against the Scots in the 1330s. Later, following Philip's confiscation of the Duchy of Aquitaine at the start of the Hundred Years' War, Reginald took up arms against the French. In 1337, he was appointed a counsellor to Edward, Prince of Wales, (known as the Black Prince), with whom he served at Crecy. Shortly thereafter, he was summoned to Parliament for the first time as a lord. In 1352 he was made a Knight of the Garter. Reginald died from the plague in 1361, by which time he had accrued great wealth, with estates in five counties and a peerage secured for his descendants.

His son, the second Lord Cobham, (also called Reginald), married a rich widow, daughter of the Earl of Stafford. His second wife, Eleanor, daughter of Sir John Arundel, Marshal of England, was equally wealthy. He played little part in state affairs other than being given the custody of the Duke of Orleans, who had been taken prisoner at Agincourt. In his private life, he was distinguished as a philanthropist. He founded an intercessory college of priests, which became known as Sir Reginald's College, at Lingfield in 1431, having been granted the freehold from the Bishop of Winchester.

Reginald's younger son, Thomas, succeeded to his father's lands and titles when Reginald died. He became a Justice of the Peace and was Sheriff of Surrey, Essex, Hertfordshire and Norfolk. At Thomas's death, the Sterborough line of the Cobhams became extinct, and the college suffered under Henry VIII's Dissolution of the Monasteries, being surrendered to the Crown in 1544. The college buildings were later pulled down and a manor house built on the site.

The Craven Family of Hawkwood

The Craven family name goes back well before the Norman Conquest of Britain and is derived from Craven, a district in the former West Riding of North Yorkshire. The place was listed in the *Domesday Book* as Crave, and probably comes from the old Welsh word 'craf', meaning garlic.

At a time before English spellings were formalised, there were several variants of the surname, including one John de Cravene which appeared in the Curia Regis Rolls of 1166, and Johannes de Crauen in the 1379 Yorkshire Poll Tax Rolls.

In 1664, William Craven was created first Baron Craven, the eldest son of Sir William Craven, who had been Lord Mayor of London in 1610. William became Viscount Craven of Uffington in Berkshire at the same time. He was Lord Lieutenant of Middlesex from 1670 to 1689, and in1681 he was a Privy Counsellor. On his death all peerages except the barony became extinct.

William was a popular name in the family line, as evidenced by William Craven who was Lord Lieutenant of Berkshire from 1702 to 1711, by a William who was Member of Parliament for Warwickshire from 1746 to 1764, and yet another who was created Viscount Uffington and Earl of Craven in June 1801.

Benjamin Robert Joseph Craven, ninth Earl of Craven, born in 1989, is the current incumbent of the title and the family seat is at Hawkwood House near Waldron, East Sussex. Others have included Hampstead Marshall Park and Lodge, Ashdown Park in Berkshire, and Coombe Abbey in Warwickshire.

William Craven, sixth Baron Craven, built Craven Cottage in 1780, which later became the home stadium of Fulham Football Club.

The Fettiplace Family of Oxford

The origin of the Fettiplace family name is somewhat obscure, though it is recorded that during the reign of Henry III, Torold L'Ape, the owner of Ape Hall in Oxfordshire and Mayor of Oxford, was later known by the name Adam Fetteplace, (sometimes Fettiplace). The name may derive from the Old French words 'faites place', meaning 'to make room', (or to reserve a place), a phrase traditionally shouted by ushers as the king or other nobility were passing by. It has been variously spelled as Fetyplace, Feteplace or Phetyplas.

Adam Fetteplace had significant land holdings in Oxfordshire and Berkshire, as well as the Manor of Wantage. By 1263, he had purchased the estate of North Denchworth, (previously in Berkshire, now in Oxfordshire), from Baron Ralph de Camoys, and established his home there.

In 1306, Sir Philip Fettiplace was serving as a Knight of the Shire as well as being parson of the church of Grendon. The marriage of Sir Thomas Fettiplace of East Shefford and Childrey to Beatrice, widow of Gilbert Talbot, Baron of Archenfield and Blackmere, brought greater wealth and influence into the family early in the fifteenth century, and within a few years of the marriage Thomas had become High Sheriff of Berkshire.

The Fettiplaces continued in royal service during the Tudor and Stuart periods and several family members were knighted during the reigns of Henry VII and Henry VIII. Yet another Fettiplace escorted Anne of Cleves to England. Anthony Fettiplace of Childrey and Swinbrook, (who died in 1510), married the granddaughter of Sir Geoffrey Boleyn, thereby making Elizabeth I a cousin to the family.

Many family members supported Charles I in the Civil Wars and their fortunes and influence suffered as a result.

Failing to produce male heirs, most of the main branches of the Fettiplace family died out in the early eigtheenth century, which saw the name scarcely found in England. Others had emigrated to America and Australia, where there are still significant numbers of descendants. There is a record of two Fettiplace brothers, William and Michael, arriving with Captain John Smith in Jamestown, Virginia in 1607. In the USA the name is more commonly spelled Phetteplace, and is most common around Portsmouth, Rhode Island, where many family immigrants finally settled.

The Fiennes Family of Banbury

This surname is derived from the commune of that name in the Pas-de-Calais department in the Hauts-de-France region of France.

The family arrived in England when Jean de Fiennes fought alongside William at Hastings. They settled in Kent shortly afterwards and were appointed as Lords of the Manor and of the Cinque Ports as well as Constables of Dover Castle.

The name probably comes from the Old Norse word 'finnr', meaning 'fair one', which crossed into Old French as 'fines', meaning delicate or gentle. An early use of it as a surname exists in the person of Hugo Fin, recorded in the Yorkshire Pipe Rolls of 1189, and a Richard Fine in Warwickshire in 1196. Variations of the spelling include Fines, Fynes, Finn and Fynn, and in Ireland, O'Finn is a common surname.

In October 1415, James Fiennes, first Baron Saye and Sele, fought at the Battle of Agincourt and received the Lordship of Court-le-Comte from Henry V. His fortunes fared less well when he was indicted along with the Earl of Suffolk for treason and took refuge in the Tower of London. However, he was beheaded at Newgate in 1450. Earlier, John Fiennes is recorded in 1447 as having been summoned to Parliament, and was made Lord Treasurer in 1449.

By 1624, the Fiennes peerage had been elevated to that of Viscount, with William Fiennes created Viscount Saye in that year. In 1625, James Fiennes was Member of Parliament for Banbury, in 1628 for Oxfordshire and in 1668 he became Lord Lieutenant of Oxford. On his death in 1674 the barony fell into abeyance, while the Viscountcy passed to the next generation in the person of William Fiennes.

With no surviving male heirs thereafter, the barony fell into abeyance in the early eigtheenth century, when in 1715, Cecile, wife of John Twistleton, became the sole heir and the descent fell through the Twistleton side of the family until 1788, when Gregory William Eardley-Twistleton-Fiennes, the eighth Baron, married the Honourable Maria Marowe Eardley and all three family names were combined.

A half century later, in 1849, Frederick Benjamin, the sixteenth Baron, adopted the surname Twisleton-Wykeham-Fiennes by Act of Parliament, and that elongated surname remained with the family until relatively modern times. Nowadays, family members tend to use only the Fiennes surname.

William Fiennes is a celebrated multi-award winning author, with novels including *The Snow Geese*, (2002), and *The Music Room*, (2009). He is second cousin of the explorer Sir Ranulph Fiennes, and a third cousin of the actors Ralph and Joseph Fiennes, as well as being a distant relative of the travel writer Celia Fiennes, (1662-1741).

The family home remains at Broughton Castle near Banbury in Oxfordshire, (which had been previously owned by the Duchess of Portland). They have lived there since it was bought and restored by Frederick Fiennes, the sixteenth Baron, in the nineteenth century.

The Finch Family of Kent

Finch comes from an Old English word 'fink', signifying a finch, (the bird), and was probably attached to a breeder or catcher of finches, regarded as an edible delicacy in Anglo-Saxon times. One of the earliest known bearers of the surname was a Saxon, Godric Finc, in 1049, during the reign of Edward the Confessor. Later, a Norman, Gilbert le Finch, was listed in the 1205 Curia Rolls of Norfolk.

In 1623, Elizabeth Finch was created Viscountess Maidstone, and in 1628 she added the Countess of Winchilsea to her titles. Thereafter, the Finch surname, (later Finch-Hatton), has been associated with the Earls of Winchilsea and Nottingham, and the Finch-Knightleys with the hereditary Earls of Aylesford.

Sir Thomas Finch was Member of Parliament for Winchilsea, (1621-2), and for Kent, (1628-9). His descendants continued careers in politics, becoming Lords Lieutenants for Kent and Earls of Nottingham. In 1680, Daniel Finch was First Lord of the Admiralty, and in 1714, he became Lord President of the Council.

In the mid-eigtheenth century, the Honourable Edward Finch, second Earl of Nottingham, married Anne Hatton, daughter and sole heiress of Christopher, Viscount Hatton, and their children adopted the Finch-Hatton surname.

The present incumbent is Daniel James Hatfield Finch-Hatton, the seventeeth Earl of Winchilsea and twelfth Earl of Nottingham, who was born in October 1967. He lives in Yeovil, Somerset.

The Hastings Family of Sussex

The Hastings family name originated in Sussex, where Robert de Hastings fought alongside the Conqueror and was given the township of Hastings in gratitude. Robert took it as his surname and became its first mayor. An early written account also names one Henry de Hastings, (c.1235-1269), who was created a baron by Simon de Montfort; it was he who led Londoners in the Battle of Lewes, and his son fought for Edward I in Scotland and Ireland.

Henry's son, Sir William Hastings, built the castle at Ashby-de-la-Zouch in Leicestershire, and was later beheaded for treason during the reign of Richard III. He had been a loyal follower of the House of York during the Wars of the Roses, and during the reign of Edward IV, he served as Lord Chamberlain. At the time of Edward's death he was one of the most powerful and one of the richest men in England.

During the Civil War, Ashby Castle, the Hasting's family home, was garrisoned by Royalist troops, known as 'Trained Bands', under the command of Henry Hastings. The castle withstood a siege lasting two years, and after the war it was demolished. The family moved to live at Donington Hall near Derby.

Subsequent generations became Earls of Huntingdon, until Henry Weysford Charles Plantagenet Rawdon-Hastings, fourth Marquess of Hastings, died in 1868, when the peerage fell into abeyance. In February 1921, a remote descendant, Elizabeth Frances Philipps, successfully had the abeyance terminated in her favour; the title was restored and the family has retained it ever since.

The Keppel Family of Chiltington

This surname was imported from Holland in approximately 1688, when one Arnold Joost van Keppel, Lord of Voerst, accompanied William of Orange to England. In 1697 he was created Baron Ashford, Viscount Bury and first Earl of Albemarle.

The name already existed in German as Kappel or Köppel, and originally comes from the Latin word 'cappa', referring to a hooded cloak or cape. Variations on the family name spelling include Chape, Keppler, Capello, Capel, Chapel, Capelle and Cappel.

In 1737, Sir William van Keppel was made Governor of Virginia, and over the following century, several family members retained the earldom as well as being Members of Parliament for Chichester, for Arundel, Norfolk East, Lymington, Birkenhead and for Berwick. In 1876, William Coutts Keppel became Baron Ashford.

A notable bearer of the family name is Admiral Augustus Keppel, the first Viscount Keppel, (1725-86), who fought in the American War of Independence and became First Lord of the Admiralty. Another is the television quiz show panellist, Judith Keppel, born in 1942, the granddaughter of Walter, ninth Earl of Albemarle, who appears as a panellist in the BBC2 television quiz show *Eggheads*, and who was the first person to win a million pounds in ITV's *Who Wants to be a Millionaire?*

The present incumbent is Rufus Arnold Alexis Keppel, tenth Earl of Albemarle, born in 1965, a distant cousin of Camilla Parker-Bowles, Duchess of Cornwall. He graduated from Chelsea School of Art and the St Martins School of Art & Design and has worked since then as an industrial designer. He lives in East Chiltington, Sussex.

The Lyle Family of Shirburn

The Lyle family, (sometimes Lisle), originated in Shirburn in Oxfordshire, and its earliest recorded member was Warine de l'Isle, whose descendants applied to Edward III to embattle Shirburn Castle, (that is, to add crenelations to the battlements).

John de Lisle, second Baron Lisle of Rougemont, (c.1318-1355), inherited the Manor of Campton in Bedfordshire from his father, but spent little time in residence, much of his career spent serving in the wars in France as a companion of Edward III. He was also one of the founding members of the Order of the Garter in 1348, as well as being one of its earliest known recipients.

William de Lisle, the fourth Baron, died a bachelor without issue some time in 1428, at which time any barony fell into abeyance among the daughters of Robert de Lisle, first Baron Lisle.

Another family member, Lady Alice Lisle, (1617-85), was executed for harbouring fugitives after the defeat of the Monmouth Rebellion at the Battle of Sedgemoor. She was sentenced to death by 'Hanging' Judge Jeffries at the 'Bloody Assizes' at Winchester, and was the last woman to have been executed by a judicial sentence of beheading in England.

In September 1945, the first Baronet, Sir Charles Ernest Leonard Lyle, (1882-1954), was created Baron Lyle of Westbourne. He was Member of Parliament for Stratford from 1918 to 1922, for Epping from 1922-1923 and for Bournmouth from 1940 to 1945.

Upon the death of Charles John Leonard Lyle, (born in 1905), second Baron Lyle of Westbourne, in August 1976 the peerage became extinct.

The Montagu Family of Beaulieu

Over the past five centuries, the Montagu family, (sometimes Montague), have held many titles and peerages, including Earls of Halifax, Beaulieu and Sandwich, and were also the Dukes of Manchester. The first recorded spelling of the family name appears in the entry for Somerset in the *Domesday Book* in Drogo de Montagu, (sometimes Drogo de Monte Acuto).

The name is believed to have derived from the village of Montaigu-les-Bois in Normandy, and comes from two French words: 'mont', meaning 'hill', and 'agu', meaning 'pointed' or 'needle-like'; hence 'a pointed hill'. It appears that the family moved to Buckinghamshire, where in 1273, William de Montagu was recorded in the Hundred Rolls of that county.

In February 1626, Henry Montagu, (c.1563-1642), a judge, politician and peer, was elevated as the first Earl of Manchester, and was an executor of Henry VIII's will. He had already been created Baron Montagu of Kimbolton and Viscount Mandeville in 1620. He had an illustrious career, being Member of Parliament for Higham Ferrers, (1591-1603), and for London, (1604-11). Like his grandfather before him, he became Chief Justice of the King's Bench, Lord High Treasurer, President of the Council, Lord Privy Seal and Lord Lieutenant of Huntingdon.

These high ranking positions continued through succeeding generations until modern times, when shortly after 1999, the third Baron Montagu of Beaulieu was one of the ninety elected hereditary peers to the House of Lords.

The present Lord Montagu, Ralph Douglas-Scott-Montagu, (born in March 1961), still lives at the ancestral country seat on the Beaulieu Estate in the New Forest of Hampshire, which is home to the National Motor Museum. His father, Edward Douglas-Scott-Montagu, third Baron, founded the museum in 1952 as a tribute to his own father, who had been one of the great pioneers of motoring in the United Kingdom. Nowadays, Ralph Montagu works as a graphic designer and is head of Heritage Radio.

The Mordaunt Family of Turvey

Mordaunt became a distinguished family name in Bedfordshire, and descended from a Norman knight named Osbert le Mordaunt, who arrived in England some time around 1199. He was granted lands, with his brother, and became Lord of the Manor of Radwell. Another early mention is in the fourteenth century, when Edmund Mordaunt was Lord of the Manor of Turvey, a few miles west of Bedford, where the main branch of the family eventually settled.

The name has been variously recorded as Mordant, Mordagne, and Mordanti, and may be derived from the Old French 'mort d'entaille', literally (and curiously) meaning 'death by cuts'. Alternative explanations suggest the derivation of the name Mordaunt comes from the French verb 'mordre', meaning 'to bite', of which the present participle, 'biting', is 'mordant' in modern French, possibly referring to a sarcastic or biting sense of humour.

Sir John Mordaunt was appointed Chancellor of the Duchy of Lancaster during the reign of Henry VII. He had been wounded in 1471 at the Battle of Barnet and at Bosworth in 1485, fighting alongside the Earl of Warwick. He commanded Lancastrian troops at the Battle of Stoke in 1487. In that same year he was speaker of the House of Commons.

Later in 1540, another family member, John, second Baron Mordaunt of Turvey, (1508-71), was Sheriff of Essex, Bailiff of the Duchy of Cornwall in 1543 and Constable of Hereford Castle in 1558.

In 1659, yet another John was created Baron Mordaunt of Ryegate and Viscount Mordaunt of Avalon. He was Constable of Windsor Castle and was Lord Lieutenant of Surrey from 1660 to 1675. His son, Charles Mordaunt, (c.1658-1735), became third Earl of Peterborough and was a noted general during the War of Spanish Succession in 1701.

Charles was also the first Earl of Monmouth, titles inherited from his uncle and cousin respectively. He died in 1735, and thereafter the aristocratic side of the family seems to have died out.

Some Mordaunts fared less well than their illustrious ancestors. Patrick Mordaunt of the Ship Inn, Shadwell, for example, was indicted at the Middlesex Sessions in September 1709 for an unspecified crime; he died some time around 1759, and in 1723, Elizabeth Mordaunt was sentenced at the Old Bailey to seven years transportation for stealing ten pence.

Many of the people with the surname Mordaunt emigrated to Ireland during the seventeeth century, and a number are known to have arrived in Auckland, New Zealand in 1865.

The Nevill Family

See: Part Nine: Wales: The Nevill Family of Monmouthshire.

The Pelham Family of Laughton

The Pelham family originally derived their surname from the township of Pelham in Hertfordshire, which was entered as Perleham in the *Domesday Book*. The name may translate as 'the settlement of Peola', a Saxon who may have first owned the land. Alternatively, some have it derived from the Old English word 'peol', (a pool), in which case the meaning might be 'the settlement by the pool'. Spelling variations include Pellam and Pulham.

There is also a place known as Pelhams Land near Boston in Lincolnshire, though this may be entirely unrelated. Other places of this name include Brent Pelham in Hertfordshire, Pulham in Dorset and Pulham in Norfolk, the latter recorded in the year 1050, before the Norman Conquest.

The Pelhams settled in Laughton in East Sussex in the fourteenth century, and built a mansion, Laughton Place, in 1534, from where they were to become the Earls of Chichester. Over the next two centuries, they acquired extensive lands around Lewes, Bishopstone and Laughton, as well as the castles at Pevensey and Hastings.

In 1545, Sir Nicholas Pelham was instrumental in repelling the French during their abortive attempt to invade the south coast.

By 1768, Charles Anderson-Pelham was Member of Parliament for Beverley and by 1774, for Lincolnshire. In 1794 he was created Baron Yarborough. Forty years later, a descendant, also called Charles, was elevated as Earl of Yarborough and created Baron Worsley. Successive generations were Members of Parliament for Lincolnshire and for Grimsby, and were Lords Lieutenants of Lincolnshire up to the twentieth century. In 1926, Sackville George Perlham became fourteenth Lord Conyers.

The family also owned Stanmer House, which had to be sold to Brighton Corporation in 1947 in lieu of exorbitant death duties. The official residence of the Yarborough Earls is now at Brocklesby in Lincolnshire, and the present incumbent is George John Sackville Pelham, styled Lord Worsley, who was born in August 1990 and lives in Chelsea, London.

There is also a township called Pelham in Massachusetts in the USA and another in Hillsborough County, New Hampshire. The township of Pelham in Westchester County, New York State claims to be the oldest of that name in America, as Thomas Pell signed a treaty in 1654 with the Siwanoy Indians to buy the land which was to become the town of Pelham.

The Playz Family of Knapton

An Anglo-Norman name, found chiefly in South-East England and East Anglia, which some believe comes from the township of Plaise in Normandy. Others cite the Old French word 'plais', meaning an enclosure or fenced woodland as most likely. An early reference to its use as a family name is that of William de la Place, as listed in the Hundred Rolls Census of England in 1273. Hugh de Playz, who died in 1244, is also listed among the barons who stood against King John and forced his sealing of the Magna Carta.

Giles de Playz, (c.1270-1302), is known to have been made first Lord Playz, and later his son, Richard de Playz, (sometimes De Plais), (1296-1327), was knighted in 1316, and became second Lord Playz. He is known to have held Knapton, and in 1317 he was summoned as a Member of Parliament. In 1327 he was Commissioner of the Peace for Cambridgeshire. He died later that year.

Richard's grandson, Sir John, fourth Lord Playz, died on an expedition to Spain under the Black Prince, and the title became extinct. He left no male heirs, but had a daughter, Margaret, (1367-91). Through her marriage to Sir John Howard, first Duke of Norfolk, Platz lands and estates passed into the Howard family. Sir John's and Margaret's daughter, Elizabeth, (c.1410-75), married John de Vere, (1408-62), and their son, also named John, became Earl of Oxford in 1470. On the death of the fifth Earl of Oxford, (also named John de Vere), in 1526, the peerage fell into abeyance.

The Pocock Family of Chieveley

Pocock is a name derived from the Old English 'pecoc', 'peacoc' or 'pecok', and is simply an Anglo-Saxon word which translates as 'peacock'. It was used as early as the seventh century as a nickname for a person who dressed gaudily or outlandishly. It seems likely to have originated in Durham, but is found widely spread across English counties, especially in North Yorkshire, Lincolnshire and East Anglia.

Other variations on the spelling include Pocok and Pacok. The name Pecoc also appears in the *Domesday Book*, and later one Pecoc de Briminton is recorded in the Cheshire Assize Rolls of 1285. Geoffrey Pokoc also appears in the 1273 Hundred Rolls for Cambridgeshire. The name is found in the parish register of Dunfermline, as Paycok in 1564, and as Paicok in 1572.

Abingdon Abbey and Bradley Court, east of the village of Chieveley near Newbury in Berkshire, came into the hands of the Pocock family in the late sixteenth century.

Notable bearers of this surname include Sir George Pocock, (1706-92), who was Chaplain to the Royal Navy at Greenwich Hospital. In 1755, he was promoted to the rank of Rear Admiral aboard HMS *Cumberland* and fought the French off Tranquebar. Sir George died at his house in Curzon Street on 3 April 1792, and was buried at Twickenham. There is a monument to his memory in Westminster Abbey.

There are approximately 114,000 people with the surname Pocock living in Great Britain, of which the greatest density is in Leicestershire. There is a Pocock family tomb in the Church of St Peter and St Paul in the Parish of North Curry in Taunton Deane, Somerset; it dates from the late eigtheenth or early nineteenth century, and is designated as a Grade II Listed monument.

A contemporary bearer of the Pocock family name is the celebrated astronomer and space scientist, Maggie Aderin-Pocock MBE, who frequently appears on television and currently lives in Guildford, Surrey.

The Sackville Family of Knole

The Sackville surname first appears in Sussex after the Conquest of 1066, when Herbrand and Jourdain de Sachevilla accompanied William the Conqueror. The name is derived from the Norman French town of Saqueneville near Dieppe, and is thought to be a corruption of the Latin words 'sicca villa', meaning 'dry town'. Variations on the family name include Sackfield, Shackfield and Zacksfield.

The family were granted extensive lands in the south east of England, where early records of the name mention John de Sakewyle in 1273 in Suffolk. One Andrew de Sakevile was also documented in the County of Norfolk during the reign of Edward I.

The family held the earldom and dukedom of Dorset, rising to prominence when John Sackville, (who died in 1557), married into the powerful Boleyn family. The first Earl, Thomas Sackville, (1536-1608), was second cousin to Elizabeth I.

Sackville was the family name of the Earls of Dorset, and it is linked to Knole in Kent, and Withyham and Buckhurst in Sussex. Descendants became Barons Buckhurst, Earls de la Warr, Earls of Middlesex and Barons Cranfield. The author Vita (Victoria) Sackville-West, daughter of the third Baron Sackville, who was born at Knole House in 1892, is associated with this family.

The St John Family of Oxfordshire

St John, (or St Jean), is a popular placename in Normandy, and following the Conquest it is recorded that one William, son of Adam de Port, adopted the family name of St John when he married an heiress of a powerful Norman family of that line in the twelfth century.

The surname is generally pronounced 'Sin-gen' and is first found in England in the village of Stanton St John, where the family settled to live during the reign of Edward III. They had several other residences over the years, including in Lincolnshire, Surrey, Middlesex and Wiltshire.

It is recorded that John St John was summoned to Parliament as Lord St John de Lageham in 1299.

In 1559, Oliver St John was created Baron St John of Bletso. But it was not until 1624 that the family became an important, powerful and pivotal influence in the unfolding history of England, when the fourth Baron, another Oliver St John, became first Earl of Bolingbroke. He had already served several terms as Member of Parliament for Bedfordshire, and been made a Knight of the Order of the Bath in 1610.

The Bolingbroke title was immortalised by Shakespeare, especially in his play *Henry IV*, when Henry Bolingbroke, Duke of Hereford and later Duke of Lancaster, became king.

In 1712, Henry St John was created Baron St John and Viscount Bolingbroke. His descendants held a variety of political roles, with St Andrew St John becoming Member of Parliament for Bedfordshire in 1780 and a Privy Counsellor in 1806. Later in 1905, Beauchamp Mowbray St John was Lord Lieutenant of Bedford.

The present incumbent is Anthony Tudor St John, twenty-second Baron St John of Bletso, (born in 1957), who is an hereditary peer in the House of Lords, a solicitor and director of several commercial enterprises in the City of London.

The Wyndham Family of Petworth

The Manor of Petworth in West Sussex was first held by the Percy family, whose descendants became the Earls of Northumberland, the most powerful family in northern England. (See: Part One: The North-East: The Percy Family).

The Percy's family seat was at Alnwick Castle in Northumberland, bordering Scotland. Through marriage into the Seymour family, they also inherited the title Dukes of Somerset.

In around 1749, the sixth Duke, who had taken a dislike to his son-in-law, the heir presumptive, decided to make his grandson, Sir Charles Wyndham, his sole heir instead. Charles served as Secretary of State for the Southern Department from 1761 to 1763.

Wyndham's family originated at Felbrigg Hall in Norfolk and had married into the nobility, when Sir John Wyndham wed Lady Margaret Howard, fourth daughter of John Howard, first Duke of Norfolk, and Earl Marshal of England. Thereafter, the Wyndhams became Earls of Egremont.

George Wyndham, third Earl of Egremont, (1751-1837), bequeathed Petworth and Cockermouth Castle to his illegitimate son and adopted heir, Colonel George Wyndham, (1787-1869), who was created Baron Leconfield in 1859 by Victoria. He held estates at Orchard Wyndham, which are still owned by the family today.

The family name is recorded over time in several variants, including Windham, Wyndham, and Wymondham, and originates from places called Wymondham in the counties of Leicestershire, Norfolk, or Wiltshire. All were recorded in the *Domesday Book* and appear as Wimundesham in the Oxford Dictionary of English Placenames, which suggests 'Wigmund's farm' as the most likely derivation, probably of fifth century Anglo-Saxon origin.

The house and deer park at Petworth were given to the nation in 1947 by Edward Wyndham, fifth Baron Leconfield, (1883-1967), and they continue to be managed by the National Trust.

Part Seven

The South West
Family Names in Avon, Cornwall, Devon, Dorset,
Gloucestershire, Somerset & Wiltshire

The Ashley Cooper Family of Dorset

The forebears of the Ashley Coopers appeared around 1260, when Benedict Ashley, born in Tetbury, Wiltshire, was known to be living in Ashley Place during the reigns of Henry II and Edward I. The name is thought to be of Anglo-Saxon origin and comes from two Old English words, 'aesc', an ash tree, and 'leah', meaning a woodland clearing. Hence, 'a clearing in a wood of ash trees'. There is also another village called Ashley in Staffordshire. Spelling variations on the surname include Esselega, Asly and Astley.

An early use of the spelling was that of Robert le Cupere, listed in the 1176 Pipe Rolls of Sussex, and later in 1273, in the person of Robert de Aslegh, recorded in the Hundred Rolls of Devon.

Cooper, or Cowper, is a corruption of the word 'copper', derived from the Old English 'coper'. Ashley Cooper, (which is occasionally seen hyphenated), has been the family name of the Earls of Shaftsbury since the early seventeeth century.

In 1661, Sir Anthony Ashley Cooper, (1621-83), was created Baron Ashley, and a year later was made the Earl of Shaftsbury. During his lifetime he was Lord Chancellor and Lord Lieutenant of Dorset.

Anthony was a popular given name among the Ashley Coopers, with at least nine heads of the family being called by that name up to the present, many continuing in the tradition of political, social and philanthropic reform.

Of particular note was the seventh Earl of Shaftsbury. In 1845, he supported two Lunacy Acts to improve treatment of people in mental asylums, but he is probably best remembered for the introduction of the Ten Hours Act in 1833, a ground-breaking law enacted to protect and regulate child labourers. Shaftsbury's Mines and Collieries Act of 1842 outlawed the employment of women and children underground in coal mines. In 1864, he succeeded in passing the Chimney Sweepers Regulation Act, preventing small boys being forced to climb up inside chimneys to clean them, and in 1844, as president of the Ragged School Union, he promoted education for children of the poor.

Nicholas Edmund Anthony Ashley-Cooper, the twelfth Earl, (born in June 1979), is the present incumbent of the title. He graduated from the London Business School with a Masters Degree in Business Administration. Popularly known as Nick Ashley-Cooper, in a long-established family tradition, he supports many charitable organisations, particularly those concerned with helping children with disabilities.

The seat of the Ashley-Coopers is the Georgian mansion of St Giles House in Dorset, where the present Earl continues to live with his family.

The Beaumont Family of Dorset

The Beaumont surname arrived in England with the Normans, when Robert de Belmont, (more commonly Beaumont, and sometimes Ballomonte, Beamont or Beaumond), Count of Meulan, is known to have settled his family in Dorset and Gloucestershire. Robert had taken his name from the estate of Beaumont-le-Roger, owned by his grandfather in France. His father, Roger, had been Lord of Belmont, but the first mention of the family name in English history is in the Battle Abbey Roll of 1066, in which Robert de Bellomonte is listed as one of the knights who fought alongside Duke William.

Nicknamed 'Prudhomme', Robert, Earl of Mellent and Lord of Norton, was knighted on the battlefield at Hastings on the 14 October 1066. He was the first member of the Norman Beaumonts to be seated in England, and became Earl of Leicester, while his brother, Henri, was made Earl of Warwick. Later, a descendant, Galeran de Beaumont, was created Earl of Worcester.

Over the past seven hundred years there have been two main families of Beaumonts: the Carlton Towers and the Whitley branches, both apparently from the same Norman ancestry, while numerous and important other offshoots exist.

Beaumont family history can be traced back well before the Normans, to Bernard the Dane, some time in the middle of the ninth century. He was descended from one of the kings of Denmark and possibly a brother (or son) of Rollo, an outlaw from the west coast of Norway, who settled and built a castle at Brienne in Normandy.

Over time the Beaumonts achieved great wealth, extensive land holdings and power in England, being friends of several royal dynasties. In March 1309, Henry Beaumont was summoned to Parliament as Lord Beaumont, and by 1369, Sir John Beaumont had been made Warden of the Cinque Ports. In 1440, another John Beaumont was created Viscount Beaumont, although just over a century later, the Viscountcy became extinct on the death of William Beaumont, and fell into abeyance.

In modern times, Miles Francis FitzAlan-Howard, (1915-2002), succeeded as fourth Baron Howard of Glossop in 1972 and as seventeeth Duke of Norfolk in 1975. Timothy Wentworth Beaumont, styled as Baron Beaumont of Whitley, was a politician, philanthropist and publisher, as well as being an Anglican clergyman. He was politically active in the Liberal Party, later the Liberal Democrats and the Green Party. A life peer from 1967, he became the second Green Party member of either of the British Houses of Parliament in 1999. He died in 2008 and the peerage became extinct.

The Berkeley Family of Gloucestershire

The Berkeleys are an ancient aristocratic family, who have lived at Berkeley Castle in Gloucestershire since the reign of Henry II.

Earl Godwin, father of Harold, the last Saxon King of England, had originally owned Berkeley Manor. The castle itself is one of the so-called 'Marcher Castles', built to keep out the Welsh, and was the oldest building in the country to be inhabited by the family who built it. It was there that Edward II was cruelly murdered by his captors in 1327. The owner of the castle at that time, Lord Berkeley, Edward's official gaoler, had a convenient and dubious alibi for the time of the murder, and was cleared of all charges.

The family traces its lineage to Robert FitzHarding, a Viking of royal blood who fought with William at Hastings. They were given lands by the Conqueror and had seats in Slimbridge in Gloucestershire and Wooton Under Edge in Somerset.

The surname derives from the Old English 'beorc', signifying a birch tree, and 'leah', a clearing in a wood; hence, a 'birch wood clearing'.

William de Berkeley, (1463-92), known as 'William the Wasteall', gave the entire Berkeley estate to Henry VII in exchange for being made Earl Marshal of England. He had also been created Viscount Berkeley in 1481, became Earl of Nottingham in 1483 and was elevated as Marquess of Berkeley in 1489. On his death the Marquessate and Viscountcy became extinct, but the Barony passed to Maurice Berkeley.

In 1679, a descendant, George Berkeley, was created Viscount Dursley and Earl of Berkeley; he was Lord Lieutenant of Gloucester from 1660 to 1689, and of Surrey from 1689 until his death in 1698. These Lordships passed on through several generations until 1705, when Sir James Berkely became First Lord of the Admiralty. He was also a Privy Counsellor and a Knight of the Garter.

When Randal Thomas Mowbray Berkeley, eighth Earl of Berkeley, died in January 1942, the Earldom of Berkeley and Viscountcy of Dursley became extinct. Berkeley Castle passed to a junior line, the Berkeleys of Spetchley in Worcestershire, who descend from a younger son of the first Baron Berkeley. The new owner of Berkeley Castle, Captain Robert George Wilmot Berkeley, was the thirteenth cousin in the male line of the last Earl of Berkeley. He died in 1969 and the peerage became extinct.

Other members of the family line include Michael FitzHardinge Berkeley, who was created Baron Berkeley of Knighton for life in March 2013.

Berkeley Square in Mayfair, London, still bears the family name. It was sold by John Berkeley, third Baron Berkeley of Stratton, to William Cavendish, first Duke of Devonshire around 1730. As part of the purchase, he agreed not to build on any part of the land that might obscure the Duke's view. Therefore, shortly thereafter, Berkeley Square emerged from that undeveloped strip, where it remains to this day, a celebrated island of tranquillity in the teeming metropolis of the capital. The gardens in the centre are open to the public, and their very large plane trees, planted in 1789, are among the oldest in central London.

The Brydges Family of Gloucester

Brydges, (sometimes Bridges or Brugges), as the name implies, is related to people who lived near, or on a bridge. It is held to be of Flemish origin, reflected in the Belgian town of Bruges, which simply means 'bridges'. The Old English word 'brycg' has a similar connotation.

Its use as a family name in England is first recorded in Somerset, Gloucestershire and the surrounding West Country, where Robert atte Brugge is known to have lived in Gloucester during the reign of Edward III.

Sir Giles Brydges, (1396-1467), is also known to have held the Manor of Archer-Stoke in Gloucestershire. He was the fourth Lord Chandos and held the office of Sheriff of the county.

Sir John Brydges, (1491-1557), was first Baron Chandos of Sudeley, was granted the Castle and Manor of Sudeley by Queen Anne, and held the office of Lieutenant of the Tower of London in 1553. A year later he was given the dubious honour of leading Lady Jane Grey to the scaffold on the day of her execution.

Successive generations held high office in the West Country, including several who were Lords Lieutenants and Members of Parliament for Gloucester.

Sir James Brydges, first Duke of Chandos, (1673-1744), was created Viscount Wilton and Earl of Carnarvon in 1714 and raised to Marquess of Carnarvon in 1719. He was also Member of Parliament for Hereford and Lord Lieutenant of the county. When James Brydges died in 1789 without children, the peerage became extinct.

In 1796, Richard Temple-Nugent-Brydges-Chandos-Genville, the second Marquess of Buckingham, (1776-1839), married Lady Anne Eliza Brydges and the Brydges peerage passed into his family. He became the Marquess of Chandos in 1822. It passed down through the family line until the third Duke failed to produce male heirs, and it passed through marriage to the Lyttelton family.

Oliver Lyttelton, (1893-1972), was created Viscount Chandos in 1954. He served as Member of Parliament for Aldershot, was President of the Board of Trade and Minister of War Production from 1940 to 1941. He was also Secretary of State for the Colonies, (1951-4), became a Privy Counsellor and was made a Knight of the Garter in 1970.

Thomas Orlando Lyttelton, (born in February 1953), succeeded his father as third Viscount Chandos of Aldershot in 1980, and from 1995 to 1997 was opposition spokesman on Treasury matters in Parliament. He was created Baron Lyttelton in April 2000 and lives in London.

The Carew Family

See: Part Ten: Ireland: The Carew family of Wexford.

The Cary Family of Somerset

Early historical records indicate that as a name Cary, (sometimes De Kari or Carey), evolved in part in Brittany from the Celtic word 'cari' or 'kari', meaning 'pleasant stream'. The earliest known example of the surname is a Norman knight named Adam de Kari, (c.1170-1180), who occupied Castle Cary in the Tamar Valley, a few miles south of Wells in Somerset. There is evidence that the site of Castle Cary was occupied, and probably fortified, well before this date.

It is presumed that the family took its name from the River Cary which is overlooked by the castle, and that the adoption of its name naturally followed. It appears in various documents under the spelling Cari, Cary, Castra Cary, Castell Cairoc and Caricastel.

Alternatively, the name may have come from 'caer' meaning 'rock', 'crag' or sometimes 'castle' in various Celtic languages. The castle existed by 1138, when it was besieged by King Stephen in the course of the struggle with his cousin Matilda for the throne of England.

By the sixteenth century, the family had gained rank and position, when a descendant, William Cary, married Mary, the sister of Henry VIII's ill-fated wife, Anne Boleyn.

Sir Henry Cary, (c.1575-1633), was created Lord Carye and Viscount of Falkland in 1620. By 1681, Anthony Cary had become Treasurer of the Navy, and was made First Lord of the Admiralty just over a decade later. In 1832, Lucius Bentinck Cary was created Baron Hundson and in 1840 he was Governor of Nova Scotia.

Lucius Edward William Plantagenet Cary, fifteenth Viscount Falkland, is an active member of the British Humane Society and lives in Clapham, London.

Many Careys moved to live in Ireland, a migration that began around the sixteenth century. Then, during the eigtheenth, nineteenth and early twentieth centuries, many more migrated from England and south-west Ireland to the Americas.

The Courtenay Family of Powderham

The Courtenay family had two distinct branches, both descended from Athon, Seigneur de Courtenay, the first Lord of Courtenay, who was descended from the Counts of Sens; tradition has it that they were founders of the French monarchy in 420. Athon established his own lordship, taking his surname from the town of Courtenay, where he settled and which he fortified.

Renaud de Courtenay went on the crusade to the Holy Land with Louis VII of France in 1147, but following a quarrel with the monarch he moved to live in England.

Robert de Courtenay, who died some time around 1242, was feudal Baron of Oakhampton in Devon, a right he inherited through his mother, Hawise de Curci. Robert married Mary de Redvers, daughter and heiress of William de Redvers, fifth Earl of Devon. His great-grandson, Hugh de Courtenay, inherited the ninth Earldom of Devon in 1335, on the extinction of the male line of the De Redvers family. Over succeeding centuries the Courtenays distinguished themselves in battle at Crecy and Agincourt.

The title of Earl of Devon was created for Edward Courtenay in September 1553. It was supposed to become extinct following his death in 1559, but as he had died without issue, the title was granted to the Blount and then the Cavendish family for the next three hundred years. However, in 1831 the third Viscount, William Courtenay, successfully petitioned for it to be restored to the head of the Courtenay family of Powderham.

William was a popular given name in the family and several distinguished themselves in politics and government, with one becoming Member of Parliament for Devon in 1679, and another being Lord Lieutenant of the county from 1715. In 1762, yet another William Courtenay was created Viscount Courtenay. William Reginald Courtenay was Member of Parliament for South Devon in 1841, Chancellor of the Duchy of Lancaster from 1866 to 1867, a Privy Counsellor in 1866, and President of the Poor Law Board in 1867.

Powderham Castle, near Exeter, has been the home to the Courtenay family since it was built by Sir Philip Courtenay in 1391. In the 1940s, the Castle opened a domestic science school and in 1957, after heavy maintenance costs on roof repairs, it was thrown open to the public.

As of 2015, Charles Peregrine Courtenay, nineteenth Earl of Devon, (born 14 August 1975), and his family, continue to live at Powderham Castle.

The Eliot Family of Cornwall

Originally known as Craggs-Eliot, the Eliot surname was adopted in 1789 by Edward Eliot, who had been created Baron Eliot of St

Germans in January 1748, taking the title from the village of St Germans in Cornwall. He was Member of Parliament for Liskeard and for St Germans on several occasions.

Eliot, (sometimes Elliot, Elyot or Elliott), may come from the Old English personal name Athelgeat, which is comprised of two elements: 'athel', meaning 'noble', and 'gyth, meaning 'battle'. Alternatively, it may derive from the Gaelic 'Elloch' or 'Eloth', referring to a person who lived on or near a hill or mound.

Cragg is thought to have originated as a surname in the Yorkshire Pennines, where several places like Hardcastle Craggs, or Cragg Vale are to be found, and bearers of the name probably adopted it as a locational surname. It comes possibly from the Old Norse 'cragges', of which the Scottish version is 'craig'.

Edward Eliot, (1727-1804), combined his father Richard's surname, with that of his mother, Harriot Craggs to become Edward Craggs-Eliot, though later generations reverted to the Eliot name. Male descendants followed careers as politicians and administrators, retaining parliamentary seats in Liskeard and Cornwall. Edward Granville Eliot was Chief Secretary for Ireland in 1841, Postmaster General in 1845 and became Lord Lieutenant of Ireland in 1853.

The present holder of the peerage is Albert Charger Eliot, the eleventh Earl of St Germans, (born in 2004), whose family seat is at Port Eliot, near Saltash in Cornwall.

The De Courcy Family of Somerset

The De Courcy family, (sometimes simply Courcy), gets its name from the village of Courcy, near Reims in the Champagne Region of France. The location is associated with royalty, through Charles III's third son, Charles de Courcy. His elder brother would eventually ascend to the French throne as Louis IV.

Baldric de Courcy, who was known as 'the Teuton' on account of his German birth, had six sons, all of whom achieved notable influence in Normandy. As his first son took on the title of Lord Baqueville en

Caux, the De Courcy name and estates went to the third son, Robert, who established a home at Courcy-sur-Dives in the Normandy area.

Robert's son, Richard, was a childhood friend of William the Conqueror and was one of his generals at Hastings. Richard was rewarded for his services with a number of lordships in England including estates in Oxford and Somerset, where he settled with his English wife. John de Courcy, one of his sons, set out to make his fortune in Dublin.

Kinsale, (known then as Kingsale), south west of Cork, became the De Courcy home after 1223. Miles de Courcy was created Baron Kingsale in May that year, a title and status that is still considered the premier barony of Ireland, and its oldest recognised royal line. There has been an unbroken line of Barons Kingsdale de Courcy ever since. As of 2005, it was held by Nevinson Mark de Courcy, thirty-fifth Baron Kingsale.

The De Redvers Family of Plympton

In the mid-twelfth century, the feudal Baron of Plympton in Devon was Baldwin de Redvers, (c.1095–1155), the son of Richard de Redvers and his wife Adeline Peverel. Richard had been granted the Isle of Wight and extensive lands in Devon by Henry I. His son Baldwin, (d.1155), was one of the first of the barons to rebel against Stephen, in favour of the Empress Matilda's claim to the throne. Baldwin captured Exeter Castle, which he held briefly, but when resistance failed, he was soon forced to flee to Anjou in France. There he joined Matilda, who after she established herself in England in early 1141, made him first Earl of Devon

Baldwin founded several monasteries, which included Quarr Abbey in the Isle of Wight, as well as a priory at Breamore in Hampshire, and the Priory of St James, at Exeter.

The Redvers family name also appears as 'de Reviers' or 'Revières' and comes from a Norman ancestor, Duke Baudouin de Vernon de Reviers. Their main seat was at Carisbrooke Castle.

The seventh Earl of Devon died in 1262, leaving no male heir, therefore, his sister, Isabella de Forz, widow of William de Forz, fourth Earl of Albemarle, became Countess of Devon. Her children all predeceased her and she had no surviving direct heirs. Therefore, her lands were inherited by her second cousin once removed, Hugh de Courtenay, (1276–1340), feudal Baron of Oakhampton, the great-grandson of Mary de Redvers and Robert de Courtenay. Thereafter, from 1292, all the Redvers estates passed to the Courtneys.

During the Wars of the Roses, the fifth earl's son, Thomas Courtenay, fought on the losing Lancastrian side at Towton in 1461, where he was captured and beheaded, all his honours including Tiverton Castle and other Courtenay lands being forfeited to the Crown. In 1471, the Lancastrian forces under the Earl of Warwick prevailed, and Henry VI was restored to the throne. The Courtney fortunes were restored, and the Earldom of Devon was restored to John Courtenay, seventh Earl of Devon.

Hugh Rupert Courtenay, the eigtheenth Earl of Devon, (1942–2015), was styled as Lord Courtenay of Powderham Castle in Devon until 1998.

The De Tibetot Family of Kempsford

One of the oldest known progenitors of the De Tibetot family lived in Freteval, near Le Mans in the Maine Department of France, where Payne de Freteval was born in 1012. Records are vague, but a branch of the family, probably from Tibelot in Normandy, (from where the surname is derived), seem to have initially settled in Shropshire in the late eleventh century. However, branches of the family clearly spread far and wide across England.

Robert Tibetot, (sometimes Tybotot, Tiptaft or Tiploft), was born some time around 1247 in Melton Mowbray, Leicestershire. He was a crusader with Edward I to the Holy Land in 1270. He had inherited lands at Chaworth, near Kempsford in Gloucestershire, through his wife Eva, (de Chaworth), which passed to her son, Sir

Payne de Tibetot, (sometimes Pain de Tibetot); he was summoned to Parliament as Lord Tibetot in 1308.

Robert, the third Lord Tibetot, (c.1341-1372), who was born in Nettlestead in Suffolk, was summoned to Parliament in 1368 and became Lord of Nettlestead Manor. He left his estates to his son John de Tiptoft, who became Earl of Worcester. His son, also named Robert, died in 1372 without leaving male heirs. The peerage thereby went into abeyance and the estates went to his three daughters, one of whom, Elizabeth, (c.1371-1478), married into the powerful Despenser family. Recent research names Elizabeth as the seventeeth great-grandmother of Elizabeth II. Her sisters Margaret and Millicent, both married into the Scrope family, Lords of Bolton, effectively bringing the main branch of Tibetot family to an abrupt end.

The Edgcumbe Family of Cornwall

The Edgcumbe family name, (sometimes Edgecumbe or Edgecombe), comes from the Old English 'egg combe', literally meaning 'at the edge of a valley', and thereby probably a locational name that the family adopted for itself. The name is found in Devon, around Tavistock, with a record of Richard Edgcumbe in 1292.

In 1353, William Edgcumbe is known to have married Hillaria Cotehele, orphaned ward of the Earl of Cornwall, which brought extensive Cotehele lands, near Saltash, into Edgcumbe family ownership. William's brother John also founded a family at Tregeare near Launceston in Cornwall.

For the following five centuries, the main branch of the family lived at Cotehele, but in the late fifteenth century, a descendant, Sir Piers Edgcumbe, acquired lands around Plymouth through his marriage to Joan, heiress to the Dumford estates, and began work building his own estate and deer park at what became known as Mount Edgcumbe, overlooking the River Tamar.

Like many Cornish gentry, the Edgcumbes were fervent Royalists during the Civil War, and Mount Edgcumbe came under attack from

Parliamentarian forces in 1644. Colonel Piers Edgcumbe was forced to abandon Mount Edgcumbe and retreat to the house at Cotehele.

Richard Edgcumbe was created first Baron Edgcumbe in 1742, and was Chancellor of the Duchy of Lancaster. His son, George, was Lord of the Admiralty and elevated later as Viscount Edgcumbe and Valletort.

During the nineteenth century, family members distinguished themselves in politics, with several Lords Lieutenancies of Cornwall among their number, as well as Members of Parliament for Lostwithiel, Fowey and Plymouth.

During the Second World War, in 1941, the Mount Edgcumbe house was seriously damaged by incendiary bombs, but was rebuilt for the sixth earl, and was occupied by the Earls of Mount Edgcumbe until 1987. In 1971, parts of the estate were purchased by Plymouth City Council, and opened to the public as a country park.

Robert Charles Edgcumbe, the eighth earl, was born in June 1939 in New Zealand, and succeeded to the Edgcumbe titles in 1982. He currently lives in Empacombe House in Cornwall.

The Fortescue Family of Devon

The earliest surviving record of the Fortescue family relates to its holding of the Manor of Whympstone, (sometimes Whimpston), in Devon, granted to them by John in 1209. Whympston, in the Parish of Modbury, became the first English seat of the family, though other sources claim an even earlier possession, and maintain that they were already in the district in about 1140, when Ralph, (sometimes Rudulfus), Fortescue is recorded as donating land to Modbury Priory. His name also appears as such in the *Domesday Book*.

A notable early family member was John Fortescue, who was born about 1394 at Norris, (sometimes Norreys), in Devon, the second son of the Captain of the Castle of Meaux, north east of Paris. He was Chief Justice of the King's Bench and was the author of the work *De Laudibus Legum Angliae* ('The Commendation of the Laws of England'), an influential treatise on English law, published in Latin around 1537, over sixty years after his death. He also served as a

Member of Parliament from 1421 to 1437. John also wrote a number of topical works that addressed the political conflict during the Wars of the Roses, as well as several treatises and pamphlets. His eldest brother, Henry Fortescue, was Lord Chief Justice of the Common Pleas in Ireland.

The family name is of Old French origin, introduced at the time of the Norman Conquest in Richard le Fort, whose name is derived from the Old French word 'fort', (meaning strong), from the original Latin 'fortis', with 'escu', (meaning a shield), from the Latin 'scutum', which together signify 'a strong shield'. Richard le Fort is traditionally thought to have carried a heavy shield at Hastings.

Variations on the surname include Fortescue, Foskew and Fortesquieu. The title of Earl Fortescue was created in 1789 for Hugh Fortescue, third Baron Fortescue. His descendants became Earls of Clinton and later Barons Fortescue. Members also served as Lords Lieutenant of Devon, were created Viscounts Ebrington in the County of Gloucester, and Earls Fortescue.

The present incumbent is the eight earl, Charles Hugh Richard Fortescue, who was born in 1951, and the heir apparent to the family name and estates is Thomas Edmund Horatio Fortescue, who was born in 1993.

The Grandison Family of Wiltshire

Grandison is a locational surname of Swiss-French origin, derived from Granson on Lake Neuchatel in Switzerland, near the French border. The first known bearer of the surname was Rigaldus de Grancione, (born c.1040), and was brought to England by Otho de Grandison, a French Savoyard who settled in England some time around 1280.

The surname takes various forms including Grandisson and Graundisson. There is a place called Stretton Grandison in Herefordshire which was held by William de Grande in 1303.

Family members distinguished themselves in religion, the military and in politics. For example, John Grandison was Bishop of Exeter in

1327; Sir Oliver St John, first Viscount Grandison, (1559–1630), became Lord Deputy of Ireland; George Villiers, fourth Viscount Grandison, was knighted in 1644, was promoted to captain of a Troop of Horse in 1660, and was a captain of the Yeomen of the Guard from 1662 to 1688.

John FitzGerald-Villiers, fifth Viscount Villiers, was created first Earl Grandison in 1721. When he died in 1766, the earldom became extinct and the viscountcy passed to his second cousin once removed, William Villiers, third Earl of Jersey.

In the late eigtheenth century, George Bussy Villiers, (later known as Child-Villiers), fourth Earl of Jersey, was a Member of Parliament for Tamworth, Lord of the Admiralty, a Privy Councillor, Vice-Chamberlain of the Household, Lord of the Bedchamber and Master of the Horse to the Prince of Wales.

The Viscountcy of Grandison is still held by the Earls of Jersey.

The Pomeroy Family of Berry Pomeroy

According to the *Domesday Book*, the De la Pomeroy family held the large feudal Barony of Berry Pomeroy from the time of the Norman Conquest. The family were prominent landowners in Devon and began building Berry Pomeroy Castle, one of the last fortresses to be built in Britain by a non-royal founder.

The Pomeroys had already owned the 'Manoir of Berri' for over four hundred years, it having been originally granted by William the Conqueror to Ralf de Pomaria, a Norman knight from La Pommeraye near Falaise. It is from here that the family name derives.

In December 1547, the castle of Berry Pomeroy was bought from the impoverished Sir Thomas Pomeroy by the wealthy and powerful Edward Seymour. Edward was the Duke of Somerset and Lord Protector, (known commonly as 'Protector Somerset'), and grandfather to Henry VIII's son, Edward, by Jane Seymour, as well as the castle's most famous owner.

The castle underwent a chequered history thereafter, and the fine manor house which was built in its place remained the property of the Seymour baronets. By the eighteenth century, they were permanently settled at Maiden Bradley in Wiltshire, and in 1750 succeeded to the family title of Duke of Somerset. It is still owned by the present duke, a direct descendant of the Berry Pomeroy Seymours.

The Poulett Family of Hinton

The Poulett family name, (pronounced 'Paulett'), seems to have originated in the village of Pawlett in Somerset, from where the family took its surname. An early example of its use occurs in Somerset in 1203, in the person of Walter de Poeleth. Also around that time, a Robert de Polet is recorded living in Buckinghamshire.

Other variations on the name exist, including Pollett, Powlett, Poulet and Pollit. The Pawlett placename is listed in the *Domesday Book* as Pavelet, and is derived from the Old English 'pal', a pole, and 'floet' meaning a stream, though the significance is somewhat obscure.

In 1627, John Poulett was created Baron Poulett. He had been Member of Parliament for Somerset from 1610 to 1614 and for Lyme Regis from 1621 to 1622. John proved to be a popular name within the family as at least four generations of that name followed. The family seat and estate was in Hinton, Somerset.

John Poulett was Lord Lieutenant of Devon in 1701, also being created Viscount Hinton of Hinton St George and Earl Poulet, and in 1706 he was appointed a Privy Counsellor and a Knight of the Garter, before becoming Prime Minister in 1710. Subsequent generations were Members of Parliament for various south-west constituencies, as well as serving as Lords Lieutenant of Somerset and of Devon. In 1904, Henry William Montagu Paulet was Lord Lieutenant of Hampshire.

When George Amias FitzWarrine Poulett, the eighth Earl Poulett, (who was born in 1909), died in March 1973, the peerage became extinct. He had already sold the Hinton estate in 1968 and moved to live with his last wife in Jersey in the Channel Islands.

In another branch of the family, Nigel Paulet, the eigtheenth Marquess of Winchester, born in 1941, succeeded to the title in 1968. He currently lives in South Africa.

The Russell Family of Dorset

This family name derives from one Hughe de Roussel, (or Hugh de Rosel), a companion of William the Conqueror who became Marshal of England. He had been a benefactor of the Abbey at Caen in Normandy, and was rewarded by William with lands in Kingston in Dorset. His surname, Roussel, is most likely to be a variation of the Norman French word 'rous', meaning red, and the suffix 'el', meaning little. Hence, 'little red', the kind of appellation often referring to a person's hair colour.

An early example of its use as a surname is in 1115, when Robert Rousel is listed in the Winton Rolls of Hampshire. A significant contingent of the Russell family also moved to settle in Scotland. One of the earlier recorded family members in Dorset was Stephen Russell, who was Member of Parliament for Weymouth in 1394. He served Henry VII as a Gentleman of the Privy Chamber. He was sent on several diplomatic missions by Henry VIII, was created Baron Russell in 1539 and subsequently made first Earl of Bedford in 1550.

In 1669, the fifth earl, William Russell, married the widowed Lady Rachel Vaughan and thereby her Bloomsbury estate came into the Russell family's ownership.

Over the following two centuries, family members were active in politics, so that by the mid-nineteenth century John Russell had been variously elected Member of Parliament for Tavistock, for Huntingdonshire, for Devonshire, for Stroud and for London. He went on to become Home Secretary in 1834, Colonial Secretary in 1839 and was Prime Minister from 1846 to 1852. In 1862, Victoria made him a Knight of the Garter.

Another illustrious family member was the author and philosopher Bertrand Russell, (1872-1970), who was awarded the Nobel Prize for Literature in 1950 and the Order of Merit in 1949.

The incumbent peer of the family is John Francis Russell, seventh Earl Russell, a Liberal Democrat politician, who was born in 1971. He was a councillor on Lewisham Borough Council from 2006 to 2010 and the party candidate for the Greenwich and Lewisham Greater

London Assembly in 2012. He is currently chairman of trustees for the adventure learning charity Wide Horizon. Russell Square in London is named after the family.

The Stourton Family of Wiltshire

The Manor of Stourton can be traced back to Bartholomew of Stourton, who was living in south-west England before the Norman Conquest. The medieval manor house at Stourton was built by Robert, (or possibly John), Stourton in the twelfth century and remained in the family's possession until 1714, when Edward, the thirteenth Baron Stourton, fell into debt and sold the estate to Sir Thomas Meres.

The Stourton name means the 'farmstead on the River Stour'. Spelling variations include Storeton, Sterton and Storton. Several places of that name exist elsewhere, as in Cheshire, (recorded in the *Domesday Book* as Stortone), in Yorkshire, as well as the village of Sturton in Lincolnshire.

In May 1448, Sir John Stourton was created Baron Stourton, and the title descended unbroken through the family line until the twentieth Baron, Alfred Joseph Stourton, (1820-93), also became twenty-fourth Baron Segrave and Baron Mowbray in 1872.

The incumbent, Edward William Stephen Stourton, (born in 1953), is the twenty-seventh Baron Mowbray, twenty-eighth Baron Segrave and twenty-fourth Baron Stourton, titles he inherited on the death of his father in December 2006.

The Thynne Family of Longleat

The Thynne family lived in Stretton in Shropshire, where they became Lords of the Manor following their arrival in England after the Norman Conquest. Some opinions have it that the surname is a corruption of the phrase 'of the inn', believing an early family member to have been an innkeeper. Others think it is derived from one John Boteville, a legal counsellor at the Inns of Court, Lincoln's Inn. Hence, 'John of th' Inn'. Spelling variants of the name have included Tyne,

Thinn and Thine.

Sir John Thynne, (c.1515-80), built Longleat House and founded a dynasty that were to become the Marquesses of Bath. He had served as a steward to the first Duke of Somerset, Edward Seymour, until the Duke's execution for treason in 1552. The original family name had been Boteville, (sometimes Botfield, Botfelde or Botville), and was often referred to as Thynne-Boteville.

In July 1641, Sir Henry Frederick Thynne, of Caus Castle in Shropshire, was created first Baronet Thynne of Kempsford in the County of Gloucester. Thomas Thynne, first Marquess of Bath, was born in 1734, and succeeded as third Baron Thynne of Warminster in Wiltshire in 1750. He was Lord of the Bedchamber and Master of the Horse to the queen from 1763, and later was made Lord Lieutenant of Ireland, a Knight of the Garter and a Privy Counsellor. His descendants included Lords Lieutenants for Somerset and for Wiltshire.

The present incumbent, Alexander George Thynne, the seventh Marquess of Bath, inherited the title on the death of his father, Henry Frederick Thynne, in 1992, and is commonly known as the peer who introduced lions to the country seat of Longleat House, which has subsequently been extended into a popular safari park. He is commonly accepted to be an accomplished artist and eccentric.

Part Eight

Scotland
Family Names in the Scottish Highlands, Lowlands,
Borders & Islands

A note about the Act of Union

Wales and Cornwall had already been absorbed by England by
1543, and when in 1603 James VI of Scotland ascended the
English throne as James I, it became his avowed intention
to unify both countries.

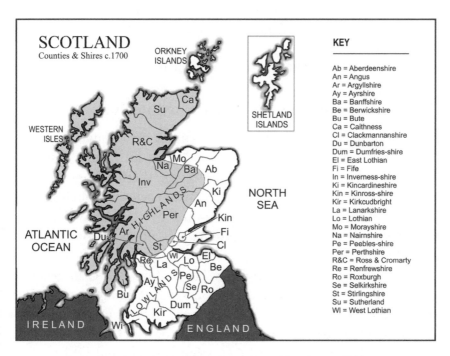

SCOTLAND
Counties & Shires c.1700

ORKNEY
ISLANDS

SHETLAND
ISLANDS

WESTERN
ISLES

ATLANTIC
OCEAN

NORTH
SEA

IRELAND

ENGLAND

KEY

Ab = Aberdeenshire
An = Angus
Ar = Argyllshire
Ay = Ayrshire
Ba = Banffshire
Be = Berwickshire
Bu = Bute
Ca = Caithness
Cl = Clackmannanshire
Du = Dunbarton
Dum = Dumfries-shire
El = East Lothian
Fi = Fife
In = Inverness-shire
Ki = Kincardineshire
Kin = Kinross-shire
Kir = Kirkcudbright
La = Lanarkshire
Lo = Lothian
Mo = Morayshire
Na = Nairnshire
Pe = Peebles-shire
Per = Perthshire
R&C = Ross & Cromarty
Re = Renfrewshire
Ro = Roxburgh
Se = Selkirkshire
St = Stirlingshire
Su = Sutherland
Wl = West Lothian

A map depicting shires and counties of Scotland c.1700.

Since the time of Edward I, relations between the two countries had been volatile. Edward was eager to annex Scotland to England, despite fierce opposition from the Scots. The death of the Scottish King Malcolm II in 1287, saw various rival claimants coming forward to fill the political vacuum. Then, when Scottish lairds signed a treaty with France, the infuriated Edward marched ahead of an army to subjugate Scotland. However, he had understimated the determination and power of Robert the Bruce, and the English finally suffered defeat at his hands at Bannockburn in 1314.

With opposition on both sides, the English Parliament threw out early attempts at unification, but in 1707 the Act of Union was passed by English and Scottish governments, which led to the creation of the United Kingdom of Great Britain.

The event was not a happy one for the Scots; Scotland effectively became a vanquished nation, where the wearing of the kilt and playing the bagpipes was prohibited, as English landlords took steps to Anglicise the native population. The highlands were also cleared, driving Scottish crofters from their traditional lands and forcing many to emigrate.

Scottish independence remains an issue today.

The Arbuthnott Family of Kincardineshire

The Arbuthnott family name, (sometimes Arbuthnot with one 't'), derives from the place of the same name in the old county of Kincardineshire. Old documents refer to Aberbothenoth, which roughly translates as 'the mouth of the stream below the noble house'. The Arbuthnott lands have been owned by the family for more than twenty-four generations, up to its present owner, the Viscount Arbuthnott.

An early family progenitor was Hugh, from the Clan Swinton family, who probably acquired lands in Arbuthnott through his marriage to Margaret Olifard, heiress of Arbuthnott, sister of Osbert Olifard - known as 'The Crusader'. Another Hugh, known as 'Hugh le Blond' on account of his fair hair, was Laird of Arbuthnott in about 1282.

In 1507, James Arbuthnott possessed a Crown Charter of the feudal Barony of Arbuthnott. Later that century, Alexander Arbuthnot, a descendant of the family, was a leading figure in the Church of Scotland and Moderator of the General Assembly of the Church of Scotland in 1577. In the next century, Sir Robert Arbuthnott, a direct descendant of the Laird of Arbuthnott, was elevated to the peerage as Viscount of Arbuthnott and Baron Inverbervie by Charles I.

In 1705, Doctor John Arbuthnot was attending Epsom races when the husband of Queen Anne, Prince George of Denmark, was taken ill. Arbuthnot rushed to his side and treated the Prince, who recovered. As a result, Arbuthnot was appointed a royal physician, and was much praised for his skill by Doctor Samuel Johnson.

In 1945, the Arbuthnott clan chief was awarded the Distinguished Service Cross and appointed Knight of the Thistle and Commander of the Order of the British Empire and was head of the Venerable Order of St John in Scotland. The present Viscount of Arbuthnott and Chief of Clan Arbuthnott succeeded to the position on his father's death in 2012.

The Borthwick Family of Roxburghshire

The Borthwick family and clan name arrived in the lowland borders of Scotland when Vikings settled near Borthwick Water in the Parish of Roberton in the old county of Roxburghshire. The first recorded use of the surname is in 1368, when Thomas de Borthwic and his son William, jointly signed a charter transferring lands at Middleton in Midlothian.

There are several variants on the spelling, including Borthwic, Borthwicke, Barthwicke and Borthock, among others. The family name derives from the place of the same name, which comes from the Old English 'bord', meaning board or table, and 'wic', which together suggest an outlying village, though the precise interpretation is uncertain.

Some authorities have the originator of Clan Borthwick as Andreas, who accompanied the Saxon, Edgar the Ætheling and his sister, Margaret, to Scotland in 1067; she was destined to become a queen and a saint. A family of this name have held Borthwick Castle since the fourteenth century.

In 1450, Sir William III of Borthwick was created first Lord Borthwick in the Peerage of Scotland, and was Lord of the Parliament from 1455 to 1457. A succession of his descendants inherited the peerage until the death of John Borthwick some time around 1675, when it became dormant.

Later, in 1762, the House of Lords granted the peerage to William Borthwick and the succession descended through his line until modern times, when John Hugh Borthwick, twenty-fourth Lord Borthwick, (born 14 November 1940), inherited the title in 1996 and became Chief of the Clan Borthwick.

The Boyle Family

See: Part Ten: Ireland: The Boyle Family of Cork.

The Bruce Family of Galloway

The Bruce Family is best known on account of its most celebrated family member, Robert the Bruce, (sometimes De Brus), who became king of Scotland. The Earldom of Galloway emerged in 1186, when it was still a separate kingdom with its own laws. Its first known Lord was Fergus, who died in 1161, leaving two sons, Uchtred and Gilbert, sometimes known as Gille Brigte. The two brothers soon went their separate ways, with Uchtred remaining loyal to the Scottish kings, while in 1176, Gilbert swore allegiance to Henry II of England. After his death, his son, Duncan, on account of his father's perceived betrayal of the Scots, renounced all claim to the Lordship of Galloway, settling instead for the title, Earl of Carrick.

Duncan's granddaughter, Margorie, was widowed, and became Countess of Carrick in her own right, after her first husband, Adam de Kilconquhar, died of disease on a crusade to Acre in 1270. She met Robert de Brus while he was out hunting on her land, formed a romantic attachment and they were married soon after at Turnberry Castle.

Robert the Bruce was the principal candidate for the throne as the great grandson thrice removed of David I, and was crowned at Scone in 1306 as Robert I of Scotland. At this point the titles Earl of Carrick, Lord of Annandale and Baron Bruce were merged into the Crown.

On the death of Robert in 1332, his son David acceded to the Scottish throne. However, he died unexpectedly and childless in 1371 and was succeeded in turn by his nephew, Robert Stewart.

In 1404, his descendant, James Stewart, (1394-1437), was created Earl of Carrick, and in April 1406, he became James I of Scotland, at which point that peerage was also merged with the Crown.

By Act of Parliament in 1469 it was decreed that the Earldom of Carrick should be granted in perpetuity to the firstborn princes of the kings of Scotland. Then, after the Union of the Crowns of Scotland and England in 1603, the dukedom and earldom have been held by the eldest son and heir of the British monarch. Thus, Charles, Prince of Wales, is also the current Duke of Rothesay and Earl of Carrick.

The Campbell Family of Argyll

Some opinions have the family name derived from a Norman knight known as De Campo Bello, (meaning 'of the beautiful field'), whom some believe came to England with William the Conqueror – but as his name is absent from the Roll at Battle Abbey, this seems unlikely. Most probably he arrived shortly after Hastings, as a second or later generation of Norman immigrants. Contemporary documents record the name spelled as Cambel or Kambel. In the Parliament of Robert the Bruce held in 1320, the name of the head of the family was listed as Sir Nigel de Campo Bello.

In 1280, Sir Colin Campbell of Lochow, considered to be the legitimate founder of the family, had been knighted by Alexander III. He gained substantial land holdings, and his great prowess in battle earned him the surname of Mohr or More, meaning 'great'. During the Anglo-Scottish conflict, the Campbells initially sided with

Edward I of England, but afterwards turned to join Robert the Bruce. Following their victory at Bannockburn, the Bruce rewarded Sir Beil Campbell with the hand of his sister, Mary, and conferred upon him the lands forfeited by the Earl of Athol. His son, Colin, was made hereditary governor of Dunoon Castle. By the mid-sixteenth century, the Campbells had become Chancellors of Scotland.

Archibald Campbell, (1597-1661), was created Marquess of Argyll in November 1641, but was tried for high treason and executed in 1661, at which time all his honours and titles were forfeited. They were restored to the family in 1681, but when another Archibald Campbell was executed in 1685, the honours were lost again. In June 1701 yet another Archibald, clearly a popular name in the family, was made Lord of Inverary, Mull, Morvern and Tirie, Viscount of Lochow and Glenyla, Earl of Campbell and Cowall, Marquess of Kintyre and Lorn and Duke of Argyll.

Since the eigtheenth century, family members have been Secretary of State for India, Lords Lieutenants of Argyll and Bute, and Lords Privy Seal. At the time of writing, Chief of Clan Campbell is Torquhil Ian Campbell, thirteenth and sixth Duke of Argyll, (born 29 May 1968), styled as Earl of Campbell before 1973, and as Marquess of Lorne between 1973 and 2001. The family's main seat is Inverary Castle, although the duke and duchess spend time at other residences, including one in London.

The Cathcart Family of Auchencruive

The first written record of the Cathcart Clan appears in 1178, when Rainaldus, sometimes Ranulfus, de Kethcart was witness to a charter by Walter FitzAlan at the Church of Kethcart for the monastery of Paisley. His son, William de Kethcart, was witness to another charter a few years later. The family name comes from the River Cart which runs south of Glasgow through the old county of Renfrewshire.

Sir Alan de Cathcart is known to have supported Robert the Bruce, and fought alongside the king's brother, Edward, at the Battle of Loudoun Hill, as well as taking part in many other attacks on the English in Galloway during the Wars of Independence. He had married the sister of Sir Duncan Wallace of Sundrum, who was himself married to Eleanor Bruce, Countess of Carrick.

His grandson, another Alan de Cathcart, obtained estates in Carrick and in 1447, he was made Lord Cathcart, with the estate of Auchencruive in Ayrshire. This became the principal family seat and remained so until the early eigtheenth century.

A later Alan Cathcart, son of the second Lord Cathcart, was killed with his two half brothers, Robert and John, when the Clan Cathcart fought against the English at Flodden Field in 1513. The third Lord Cathcart led the clan against the English at the Battle of Pinkie Cleugh, where he died in 1547. The fourth Lord Cathcart led the clan at the Battle of Langside in 1568 alongside James Stewart, first Earl of Moray, against the army of Mary Queen of Scots.

The eighth Lord, Charles Cathcart, was a colonel when the first Jacobite uprising broke out in 1715 and he commanded troops in support of the British government at the Battle of Sheriffmuir. When the second uprising broke out in 1745, Charles, ninth Lord Cathcart, commanded the Royal Scots 1st Regiment of Foot in support of British troops at the Battle of Culloden in 1746.

The tenth Lord, William Schaw Cathcart, was created Knight of the Thistle after distinguishing himself as a Lieutenant General and Commander-in-Chief of forces in Ireland, and after capturing the Danish fleet at Copenhagen in 1807, during the Napoleonic Wars. He was granted the titles Viscount Cathcart and Baron of Greenock. Later, he was made Earl Cathcart.

In 1801, the remnants of the derelict Cathcart Castle, together with Cathcart House and the surrounding sixty acres of land were restored to Cathcart family ownership when they also acquired the contiguous lands of Symeshill. Cathcart Castle today remains the seat of the Earl Cathcart, Chief of Clan Cathcart.

The Colquhoun Family of Dunbartonshire

The first person recorded using the Colquhoun surname was Ingelram de Colquhoun, who lived in the reign of Alexander III. In the thirteenth century, his father, Humphrey, sometimes Humphredus, de Kilpatrick, had been granted the lands of Colquhoun, on the shores of Loch Lomond in the Scottish Lowlands, by Maol Domhnaich, Earl of Lennox.

The family and clan name is thought to be derived from the Gaelic 'coil' or 'cuil', meaning a nook or a corner, and 'cumhann', meaning narrow. The usual Scottish pronunciation is 'ka-hoon'. Variants on the spelling and derivation of the name include Calhoun, Calhoon, Colhoon, Colhoun, Hoon, Cahoun, and Cahoon.

In 1368, Sir Robert of Colquhoun married the heiress of the Lord of Luss, after which the title Barony of Luss came to the family. The clan's early stronghold was at Dunglass Castle on the River Clyde, close to Dumbarton Castle, where clan chiefs were later appointed governors and keepers.

Sir John Colquhoun was appointed governor of Dumbarton Castle during the minority of James II of Scotland, but was murdered in 1439 during a raid at Inchmurrin. His son, also Sir John Colquhoun of Luss, succeeded him to the lands and title and in time rose to be Comptroller of the Royal Household. He grew in power, influence and wealth as, in 1457, he was granted leave to combine all of his lands into the Barony of Luss, and within a year he also received the forests of Rossdhu and Glenmachome together with the lands of Kilmardinny.

In the seventeeth century, feuding between Clan Colquhoun and Clan MacGregor came to a head, and 1603 saw Luss invaded by the MacGregors, resulting in the massacre of five hundred Colquhoun men at the Battle of Glen Fruin. It was the best part of a century before peace was made, and the chiefs of both clans met and shook hands at Glen Fruin.

The fifth Baronet, Sir Humphrey Colquhoun, represented Dunbartonshire in the last Scottish Parliament in 1703, and was strongly opposed to the Treaty of Union with England. On the 30 March 1704, having no male heir, he resigned his baronetcy to the Crown, the title passing to the male issue of his daughter's husband, James Grant of Pluscardine.

Sir Ivar Colquhoun, thirtieth Laird of Luss and thirty-second Chief of Colquhoun, succeeded as chief of the clan in 1948. He was the longest serving clan chief, having done so for almost sixty years until his death in 2008. He was succeeded by his son, Sir Malcolm Rory Colquhoun, ninth Baronet of Luss.

The Colville Family

See: Part Five: East Anglia: The Colville Family of Suffolk.

The Crichton Family of Midlothian

Crichton is an ancient family name of the Scottish borders, whose surname may be derived from the old barony of Crichton near Edinburgh, or from Kreiton in Lothian. Early written examples of the placename have it as Crectone in 1166, and as Creiton in 1222. Other variants have included Crechtune, Creighton and Crectune. The name probably comes from the Gaelic word 'crioche', meaning a border, and the Old English 'tun', signifying a settlement. Hence, 'the settlement on the border'.

Around 1128, during the reign of David I, Turstan (or Thurstan) de Crectune witnessed a great charter at Holyrood. Some time around 1200, Thomas de Kreytton, possibly Turstan's son, was a Burgess of Berwick. His other son, William, married Isabel de Ross, the heiress to the Barony of Sanquhar in Dumfriesshire. In 1464, Sir Robert Crichton of Sanquhar was Sheriff of Dumfries, and in 1468 he became Coroner of Nithsdale. His son, also named Robert, was created Lord Crichton of Sanquhar by James III in 1487.

The Lowland Clan Crichton had their seat at Crichton Castle, as well as owning other castles at Sanquhar and Blackness.

In the year 1440, Sir William Crichton was Chancellor of Scotland and Governor of Edinburgh Castle. He took part in the infamous 'Black Dinner' at the castle, when, following a feud with the Douglas Clan, two of their family, including the Earl of Douglas, were dragged forcibly out of the dining hall and summarily executed. Later, Clan Douglas laid siege to the castle which was surrendered to the king, followed by a truce.

When Frederick Lewis Maitland, sixth Earl of Lauderdale, a Royal Navy captain, married Margaret, heiress to Clan Makgill and direct descendant of James Crichton, first Viscount Frendraught, their surnames were conjoined as Maitland-Makgill-Crichton.

David Maitland-Makgill-Crichton, born in 1972, is the current clan chief and lives at Monzie Castle in the market town of Crieff, in Perth and Kinross.

The Cunningham Family of Glencairn

The ancient family of Cunynghame of Kilmaurs, in Ayrshire, (sometimes Cuninghame or Cunningham), became the Earls of Glencairn in the mid-fifteenth century, during the reign of James III of Scotland. Cunninghame is an area in the northern part of Ayrshire, though a sixth century map of the region shows it as Canowan.

It is also recorded that in 1059, Malcolm, the Saxon son of Friskin, was granted the Thegndom of Cunninghame. The family name thereby comes directly from the place, and is probably derived from the Celtic 'cuinneag', which means 'a milk pail' and the Saxon suffix 'ham', signifying a village or early settlement. Another possibility is that it derives from 'cunny' or 'coney', meaning a rabbit. There is some suggestion that the early Cunninghams kept or harvested rabbits.

The first known use of it as a surname was one Warnebald Cunningham, who was granted the lands of Cunninghame by Hugh de Morville in around 1115. The extended family, Clan Cunningham, had settled in the parish of Kilmaurs by the late thirteenth century. In 1263, they fought alongside Alexander III of Scotland at the Battle of Largs, and in gratitude, Hervy de Cunningham received a charter from the king confirming the family's right to these lands.

Some time around 1459, Alexander de Cunynghame, the son of Sir Robert de Cunynghame, was created Lord Kilmars and was Lord of the Parliament in 1463. He supported James III during a rebellion of noblemen led by Prince James at Blackness, and was probably created Earl of Glencairn in May 1488 on the back of that victory.

Clan Cunningham supported Robert the Bruce during the wars for Scottish Independence, and he gave them the lands of Lamburgton. Later, through marriage, the family acquired other substantial lands at Finlaystone in Refrewshire and Glencairn in Dumfriesshire.

During the late sixteenth century, a bitter feud existed between the Cunninghams and the Montgomery Earls of Eglinton, following the fourth Earl of Eglinton's murder by the Cunninghams in 1586.

By the mid-seventeeth century, the family had grown in power and influence, as evidenced by William Cunningham, who had risen to become Lord Chancellor of Scotland by 1664, despite the fact that in 1653, the eighth Earl of Glencairn led an uprising in support of Charles II and against General Monck, the Governor of Scotland. It was during the Restoration of Charles II to the English throne that he was appointed Lord Chancellor.

On the death of the fifteenth Earl of Glencairn, John Cunningham, who had been ordained in the Anglican Church, the earldom became extinct and the estates at Finlaystoun passed to his son, Robert Graham of Gartmore.

In about 1610, as part of the Plantation of Ulster, Sir James Cunningham was among many other Cunningham families to be granted land in Ireland, which had been ceded after the flight of the Irish Earls. A significant influx of tenant farmers of the Protestant faith arrived in Ulster from the Cunningham lands in Ayrshire. Sir James was awarded five thousand acres on the south-eastern shore of Lough Swilly, a tidal river in County Donegal, ten miles west of Londonderry. By 1622, he had fifty tenant families on his land, and by 1720, the Cunningham name had spread throughout Ireland.

There are a few Irish variants on the spelling of the surname, including O'Cuinneagain, MacCuinneagain, O'Connagain, Counihan and Conaghan. During the days of the Irish potato famine in the mid-nineteenth century, the Great Depression in 1873-90 and the Depression of the 1920s and 1930s, many Cunninghams emigrated to Canada and America.

The Dalzell Family of Motherwell

The Dalzell surname originated in the Clyde valley of the Scottish Lowlands. It was recorded in 1200 as Dalyell or Daliel and in 1352 as Daleel. It is probably derived from the Gaelic 'dail', meaning 'field', and 'gheal', meaning 'white'; hence, 'white meadow (or dale)'. The spelling would seem to bear little relationship to the actual pronunciation, which is normally 'dee-ell' or 'die-ell'.

In the seventeeth century the name was common in the Counties Louth and Down in Ireland, where the normal spelling is Dalzell. However, the more common spelling in Scotland is Dalziel.

The family name is thought to have come to England originally in 1066, and migrated to Scotland around 1150, when a Norman knight was granted lands in Dalyell in Lanarkshire, (an old county in the Strathclyde Region), by King David of Scotland. Later, the Barony of Dalziel was granted by Kenneth II.

Early usage of the name includes a Thomas de Dalzell in 1259, who it is thought may have fought at Bannockburn in 1314, and one Hugo de Dalzell, who was Sheriff of Lanark at the time of William Wallace.

Dalzell House in Motherwell, North Lanarkshire, was built in the late fifteenth or early sixteenth century by the Dalzell Family. Another Sir Robert Dalzell was created Lord Dalzell in 1628, and his son was further elevated as Earl of Carnwath in 1639.

During the nineteenth century, the family's fortunes grew exponentially, through their involvement in Lanarkshire coal mining.

The Irish branch of the family fared less well, and at the time of the Irish potato famine, the Northern Irish Dalzells of Counties Antrim, Armagh and Down saw large migrations to America, spreading west into Indiana, Illinois, Missouri and Tennessee. Numbers of Scottish Dalzells also went to America during the Revolutionary War, 1775-83.

Brigadier-General, Arthur Dalzell, thirteenth Earl of Carnwath, served on the Western Front during the First World War. Upon the death of his nephew, Ronald Arthur Dalzell, twelfth Earl of Carnwath, in 1931, he succeeded to the peerage as Earl of Carnwath and was subsequently elected a Scottish Representative Peer in 1935. He died in March 1941 at his country residence, Sand House in Wedmore, Somerset, at which point the peerage became extinct.

The Douglas Family Name of Lanarkshire

The Douglas family and clan name comes from the Gaelic, 'dubh', meaning 'black' or 'dark', and 'glas' which means 'grey', these being the main shades used in the Clan Douglas tartan. The first known head of the clan was probably Theobaldus Flammatius, known as Theobald the Fleming, who in 1147 received a gift of lands near Douglas Water in return for services for the Abbot of Kelso.

The earliest recorded member to use the family name is William of Douglas, also known as William de Dufglas, who appears as a witness to charters between 1175 and 1211 around Lanarkshire in the Scottish Lowlands. His grandson, Sir James Douglas, fought as a captain under Robert the Bruce in the War of Independence against England, and is commonly held as the third of Scotland's great patriots, after the Bruce and William Wallace. He was commissioned with carrying the Bruce's heart to the Holy Land after his death, in atonement for the murder of John Comyn III. However, Douglas was killed en route in 1330; the casket containing the heart was returned to Scotland and interred at Melrose Abbey.

James' youngest brother, who had been elected Regent of Scotland in late March 1333, led the ill-fated Scottish army in the Battle of Halidon Hill in 1333. James Douglas, second Earl of Douglas, married a Stuart princess, which greatly enhanced family prestige. Later, in 1388, at the Battle of Otterburn he was instrumental in the Scots' victory, but was killed on the battlefield.

The Douglases were one of the most powerful families in the Scottish Lowlands during the late Middle Ages. The heads of the house of Douglas held the titles of the Earl of Douglas, known as 'Black Douglas', and later the Earl of Angus, known as 'Red Douglas'. Their family seat was at Douglas Castle. The church at St Brides at Douglas and Melrose Abbey hold the remains of many Earls of Douglas and Angus.

Seen as having accrued too much power, in 1440 William, sixth Earl of Douglas and his younger brother, were arrested and beheaded at what came to be known as the 'Black Dinner' at Edinburgh Castle.

Clan Douglas then laid siege to the castle, which was governed by Lord Crichton. It was surrendered to the king and the clan was rewarded with the title of Lords Crichton.

The Douglases had a long feud with Sir Richard Colville, who had killed the Laird of Auchinleck, one of their trusted allies. To avenge this murder, the Douglases attacked the Colvilles in their castle, where many were killed. The castle was razed to the ground and its defenders put to the sword. William Douglas, the eighth Earl, personally executed Richard Colville. In 1513, at Flodden, it is said that over two hundred Douglas men were slaughtered.

Archibald Douglas, the sixth Earl, held the post of Lord Chancellor and was guardian to James V of Scotland, and married his widowed mother, Margaret Tudor. The sixth Earl of Angus, a bitter enemy of Mary, Queen of Scots, was one of the murderers of the queen's secretary, David Rizzio, and was implicated in the murder of her second husband, Lord Darnley. He was executed in 1581.

Members of Clan Douglas maintained a high status over subsequent centuries, with Aretas Akers-Douglas being created Baron Douglas of Baads and Viscount Chilston in July 1911, Sir Francis Campbell Ross Douglas being created Baron Douglas of Barloch in 1950, Member of Parliament for Battersea from 1940 to 1946, and Governor of Malta from 1946 to 1949. Sir Harry Douglas was made Baron Douglas of Cleveland in September 1967 and on his death in April 1978, the peerage became extinct.

The Duff Family of Wemyss

The Duff family and clan, (sometimes MacDuff), originated from the kings of Scotland and the Mormaerdom of Fife, who settled around East Wemyss, near Buckhaven, where Gruoch was the senior representative of the line. She and her second husband, MacBeth, would be immortalised by Shakespeare in his tragic play of that name. Many claim that the Clan MacDuff was the premier clan among the Scottish Gaels. The early chiefs of Clan MacDuff were the earls of Fife and the contemporary earls of Wemyss are thought to be the direct descendants in the male line of Gille Micheil, Earl of Fife, one of the first Clan MacDuff chiefs.

An early record of the family line was Beth, Earl of Fife, who was witness to the Charter of Scone in 1115.

When the Earl of Mormaer was taken prisoner by Edward I in 1398, the title fell to Robert Stewart, the son of Robert II of Scotland, first Duke of Albany and Regent of Scotland.

In May 1420, Murdock Stewart, Duke of Albany was executed, and his peerages forfeited. By 1425, the titles had been absorbed by the Crown, and would not be resurrected until 1567, when James Hepburn, Earl of Bothwell, was created Marquess of Fife and Duke of Orkney.

It was two centuries before the earldom of Fife returned to the family, when in 1759 William Duff was created first Earl Fife, Baron Braco of Kilbryde and Viscount MacDuff.

James Duff was created Baron Fife in 1790, having served as Member of Parliament for Banffshire, (1754-84), and for Elgin, (1784-90). On his death in 1809, the barony became extinct, while the earldom passed to Alexander Duff. Several peerages accrued over the following years, including the Baronetcy of Skene in 1857.

Later, the sixth earl, Alexander William George Duff, Marquess MacDuff and Duke of Fife, married the Princess Royal, Louise, daughter of Edward VII. On Alexander's death, the earldom of 1759 became dormant, the earldom of 1885 and the marquessate and the dukedom of 1889 became extinct, while the earldom and dukedom of 1899 passed to Princess Alexandra Victoria Alberta Edwina Louise of Connaught.

Thereafter, the titles passed to James George Alexander Bannerman Carnegie, third Duke of Fife and eleventh Earl of Southesk, the grandson of Princess Louise. Before he died, in 2005, aged 85, he lived at Elsick House, near Stonehaven in Kincardineshire and farmed the family estate around Kinnaird Castle in Brechin.

The Erskine Family of Strathclyde

The earliest recorded use of the name was by Henry of Erskine, owner of the Barony of Erskine, during the reign of Alexander II in the early thirteenth century. The name comes from the Old English for 'green rising ground'.

The Erskine family were supporters of Robert the Bruce, and related to him through the marriage of John Erskine's eldest daughter and Thomas Bruce, Robert's brother. The Bruce's son and successor, David II, made Sir Robert of Erskine the Constable and Keeper of the Castle of Stirling. This royal office is still held by the clan chief, whose duties include greeting the monarch at the castle gates.

In 1435, Sir Robert Erskine claimed the earldom, but it was withdrawn in 1457, and it was another decade before he was created the first Lord Erskine. Later, Mary, Queen of Scots gave the Earldom of Mar to John Erskine, sixth Lord Erskine. He was keeper of Edinburgh Castle until after the murder of Queen Mary's husband, Lord Darnley.

The Earldom of Buchan came into the family, when its hereditary holder, Lady Mary Douglas, Countess Buchan, died in 1628, and the title passed to her nearest male relative, James Erskine.

In 1695, David Erskine, fourth Lord Cardross, (1672-1745), was Lord Lieutenant of Stirling and Clackmannan, and in 1697 was a Privy Counsellor.

By the early eighteenth century, the family were staunch Jacobites and raised a large army in support of James VIII, which failed to win a victory at Sheriffmuir in 1715. The Earl fled to France, where he betrayed his Jacobite associates, losing the Erskine and Mar estates for his pains. They would not be restored until 1824.

In 1960, Donald Cardross Flower Erskine was seventh Baron Erskine of Restormel Castle, (in Cornwall), and later became the sixteenth Earl of Buchan. The current clan chief, at the time of writing, is Malcolm Harry Erskine, seventeeth Earl of Buchan, (born in 1930), who is a stockbroker and lives in Basingstoke, Hampshire.

The Falconer Family of Angus

The Falconer surname is derived from the Old French word 'faulconnier', meaning a person who hunts with, tends, or breeds falcons. It appears in the early thirteenth century in Angus, where Gulielmus Auceps, known as William the Falconer, gave lands to the church at Maryton some time around 1200. Later, Matheus the Falconer was one of the witnesses to a charter by Earl David in 1202 or 1203. In 1296 it is recorded that Robert Fauconer of Kincarydn paid homage at Aberdeen to Edward I of England.

In 1646, Sir Alexander Falconer was created Lord Falconer and by 1778, the Falconers were the Earls of Kintore, and held the title until 1966, when the earldom became extinct on the death of the tenth earl. In 1997, Charles Leslie Falconer was created Baron Falconer of Thoroton for life. He was Solicitor General from 1997 to 1998, Chancellor from 2003 to 2007, a Labour Minister sitting in the House of Lords, and was a Privy Counsellor in 2003.

The Scottish Clan Falconer holds lands in Kincardineshire, and its seat is at Laurencekirk, midway between Aberdeen and Montrose.

The Fife Family of Dunfermline

This is a regional name from the former Kingdom of Fife in East Scotland. Tradition has it that the name is derived from Fib, (recorded as such in 1150, and as Fif in 1165), one of the seven sons of Cruithne, the legendary founding father of the Picts.

The earls of Fife were considered the principal peers of Scotland until the fifteenth century, and held the sole right of crowning the Scottish monarchs. The earldom belonged to the MacDuff family until it passed to the Stewarts, with the forfeiture and execution of Murdoch, Duke of Albany, ordered by James I of Scotland in 1425.

The MacDuff family male line had ended, and Isabella, the only child of Duncan IV, Earl of Fife, and his wife Mary de Monthermer, had succeeded her father as Countess of Fife on his death in 1358. Isabel married four times, but all her husbands died within a few years of their marriage. In 1371, she named Robert Stewart, Earl of Menteith, later Duke of Albany, as her heir. He was her brother-in-law by her second marriage to Walter Stewart.

The earldom was revived in 1759 with William Duff, a descendant of the MacDuffs. The name Macduff, (or MacDuib), derives from Cinaed III Mac Duib, his father, who died in 966.

Alexander William George Duff was created Earl of Fife in July 1885, as Marquess of Macduff and Duke of Albany in July 1889 and Earl of Macduff and Duke of Fife in October 1899. He was Member of Parliament for Elgin and Nairnshires from 1874 to 1879, and Lord Lieutenant Elgin from 1872 to 1902. On his death the earldom became dormant and the marquessate became extinct. In 1912, the earldom and dukedom were revived and passed to Princess Alexandra Victoria Alberta Edwina Louise of Connaught. As of 2015, David Charles Carnegie, (born in March 1961 in London), was the fourth Duke of Fife.

The Forbes Family of Aberdeenshire

The Forbes surname comes from the Gaelic term 'forb-ais', which means 'at the land'. The Forbes family went on to become the premier lordship of Scotland and were elevated to a barony in 1271 by King Alexander III. Duncan de Forboys paid homage to John Balliol, whom Edward I had decided should be king at Berwick in 1292. Edward removed Balliol from power within four years of his installation, and in 1296 John Forbes signed the Ragman Roll. The family line was established in the fourteenth century, when Sir John de Forbes, known as 'Forbes of the Black Lip', was a member of the justiciary in Aberdeenshire. His eldest son fought alongside the Earl of Mar against Donald, Lord of the Isles at the Battle of Harlaw in 1411.

Sir Alexander Forbes was created Lord Forbes in 1445, and there followed a long line of succession until William Forbes became Lord Lieutenant of Aberdeenshire and Kincardine in 1715.

Sir William Forbes, the first Baronet of Craigievar, built Craigievar Castle in 1626, and in 1633, Alexander Forbes was created Lord Forbes of Pitsligo.

Robert Forbes, the Episcopalian Bishop of Ross and Caithness was arrested for being a Jacobite in 1745. Fortunately he survived, although the family's involvement in the uprising resulted in forfeiture of their lands and title.

In 1815, the seventeeth Lord Forbes built Castle Forbes near Alford which remains the home of his descendants to this day. Nigel

Ivan Forbes, twenty-second Lord Forbes, (1918-2013), known as the Master of Forbes until 1953, was a Scottish soldier, businessman and Conservative politician. The present incumbent, Malcolm Nigel Forbes, twenty-third Lord Forbes, holds appointments in various commercial companies, resides at Forbes Castle and is currently director of Castle Forbes Collection Limited.

The Gordon Family of Aberdeen

The earliest record of the Gordon family name is that of Richard de Gordon, Lord of the Barony of Gordon in the Merse (c.1130-c.1200). Between 1150 and 1160 he granted land from his estate to the Monks of St Mary at Kelso.

Some authorities maintain that the family is of Norman descent, one of many welcomed into his kingdom by David I of Scotland. By the early twelfth century, they had settled in the village and estates of Gordon, near Kelso in the Scottish Borders.

During the Wars of Scottish Independence, Sir Adam Gordon, (1273-1333), a supporter of William Wallace, renounced all allegiance to Edward I of England, and became a staunch supporter of Robert the Bruce. He died on the battlefield at Halidon Hill leading the Gordon Clan ahead of a Scottish army.

Clan Chief Sir John Gordon was killed at the Battle of Otterburn, where the English were defeated in 1388. In 1449, Alexander, the eldest son of Elizabeth Gordon and Alexander Seton, was made Lord of Gordon and Huntly. During the same Anglo-Scottish Wars, in 1542, the Clan Gordon, under George Gordon, fourth Earl of Huntly, defeated an English army at the Battle of Haddon Rig.

During the Jacobite uprisings of early to mid-eigtheenth century, Gordons were on both sides of the conflict. The second Duke followed the Jacobites in 1715, but Cosmo Gordon, the third Duke, supported the British government by the time of the 1745 uprising. His brother, Lord Lewis Gordon, raised two regiments against him at the Battle of Inverurie that year, and at the Battles of Falkirk and Culloden in 1746.

The Clan Gordon has possessed many great houses and castles over the centuries, including Huntley Castle, which was the clan seat from the fourteenth to the seventeenth centuries, as well as Balmoral in the fifteenth century, and Auchindoun Castle in 1535. The fourth Duke built Gordon Castle in 1789.

John Campbell Hamilton-Gordon (1847-1934), was Governor General of Canada from 1893 to 1898, Lord Lieutenant of Aberdeen from 1880 till his death, was twice Lord Lieutenant of Ireland, and in May 1915 was created Earl of Haddo and Marquess of Aberdeen and Temair. He had been a member of the Privy Council in 1886 and was knighted in 1906.

As of 2002, Alexander George Gordon, a celebrated descendant, was Marquess of Aberdeen, an industrialist and CEO of Gordon Land Limited.

The Graham Family of Stirlingshire

The first Graham known in Scotland was Sir William de Graham, a knight who founded the Graham Clan. He accompanied David I when he travelled north to claim the Scottish crown. His surname can be traced back to the Manor of Grey Home, which is recorded in the *Domesday Book*. Spellings variations of the family name include Grahame and Graeme.

William, third Lord Graham, who died fighting at Flodden in 1513, had been created Earl of Montrose in 1504. His grandson, John Graham, was High Treasurer of Scotland in 1584 and Chancellor in 1599. In 1644, James Graham was created Lord Graham and Mugdock, Earl of Kincardine and Marquess of Montrose. He also became a Knight of the Garter in 1650.

By 1707 the family marquessate had become a dukedom. In 1782, James Graham, third Duke of Montrose, was instrumental in persuading Parliament to remove the law forbidding Scots to wear tartan. Mugdock Castle in Stirlingshire was the traditional seat of Clan Graham from the mid-thirteenth century, but the current seat is at Buchanan Castle.

Over succeeding centuries, family members achieved high office, including a Chancellor of the Duchy of Lancaster, Lords Lieutenants of Stirling and of Buteshire.

In 1999, James Angus Graham, eighth Duke of Montrose, also known as then Earl of Kincardine and Marquess of Graham, was elected an hereditary peer. He is currently Montrose clan chief. Until the 2010 General Election he served as Shadow Minister for the Scotland Office.

The Hay Family of Perth

The Hay Family name comes directly from the Norman family of De la Haye, (sometimes De Haya), and is derived from the village of La Haye, (or La Haye-Hue), in the Cotentin Peninsula of Normandy. The word, 'haye' comes from the Old Norman 'haia', meaning a hedge, (or 'haie' in modern French). It can also signify a stockade.

This old Norman family already held high rank as early as 823, when they possessed the Barony of La Hai-du-Puits in Coutances. Eldoun de la Haie, son of the Count of Mortain, accompanied William the Conqueror in his invasion of England and fought at the Battle of Hastings. He is recorded in the *Domesday Book* as holding extensive lands in East Anglia

One of the earliest known users of the name in England was William II de Haya, confidante of Malcolm IV. His father was William I de Haya and his mother was Juliana de Soulis, sister to Ranulf de Soules. William II was later created Baron of Erroll by King William I in 1178. He was the first recorded Hay in Scotland, and known to have been in the Scottish court, and cup bearer to William I of Scotland, known as William the Lion.

Sir Gilbert Hay, the fifth Lord Erroll, fought alongside Robert the Bruce during the Wars of Scottish Independence and was active at Bannockburn in 1314. For his service, he was made the Lord High Constable of Scotland, a title the Clan Hay still hold.

In 1452, Sir William Hay, the second lord, was created Lord Slains and Earl of Erroll. By this time, the clan held land in Perthshire, along with possessions in the north-east of Scotland, particularly in Aberdeenshire, Banffshire, Morayshire and Nairnshire, as well as in the Scottish Borders and in the Shetland Islands.

As Royalists in the English Civil Wars and Jacobite supporters of Bonnie Prince Charlie during the rebellion, the family found itself repeatedly on the losing side, and consequently fortunes fluctuated during the eigtheenth century. However, by the mid-nineteenth century they prospered, so that by 1836, William George Hay, (1801-46), was Lord Lieutenant of Aberdeen, a position he held for the next ten years. He was also created Baron Kilmarnock on the 17 June 1831, was a Privy Counsellor and in 1834 had been made a Knight of the Garter.

At the time of writing, Merlin Sereld Victor Gilbert Hay, twenty-fourth Earl of Erroll, (born 20 April 1948), is a crossbench member of the House of Lords, Chief of the Clan Hay and hereditary Lord High Constable of Scotland.

The Home Family of Berwickshire

There are two opposing views as to the origin of the Home family and clan name. Sometimes spelled, and always pronounced, 'Hume', what is known for certain is that they were powerful and influential in the Scottish Borders region from the earliest recorded times. One view is that they are descended from the Saxon princes of Northumberland, in particular Cospatrick, who was Earl of Dunbar. His descendant, Aldan, at some time around 1172, was first recorded as adopting the name of the village of Home in Berwickshire, when he became known as Aldan de Home. Another view is that it was William, the grandson of Aldan de Home, who first officially took on the name.

In 1266, William de Home is recorded at Coldstream Monastery with grants of land. Geoffrey de Home's name also appears on the Ragman Roll as submitting to Edward I of England. Geoffrey's son, Sir Thomas, received the Pepdie estate of Dunglass through marriage to its heiress.

By 1473, Alexander Home, (1460-1506), had been created Lord Home, but the peerage was forfeited in October 1516, when a descendant, (also named Alexander), was convicted of treason. Yet another Alexander was restored to the peerage in 1578 when he was created Lord Dunglass and Earl of Home.

Several descendants of the family subsequently distinguished themselves: in 1757, the eighth Earl, William Home was made Lieutenant General and Governor of Gibraltar, despite his father, the seventh Earl, spending the last years of his life imprisoned in Edinburgh Castle for his part in the Jacobite uprising of 1715.

In 1806, yet another Alexander was Lord Lieutenant of Berwick. In June 1875, the family were created Baron Douglas of Douglas.

Possibly the most distinguished family member in living memory is Sir Alec Douglas-Home, who was Prime Minister in 1963 and 1964. He had been Member of Parliament for Lanark, (1931-45), and for Kinross, (1963-74), as well as Minister of State for Scotland, (1951-5), among several other parliamentary and government posts. Sir Alec Douglas-Home died in October 1995.

The current clan chief is David Douglas-Home, CBE, fifteenth Earl of Home. He was appointed Knight Companion of the Order of the Thistle in the 2014 New Year Honours.

The Keith Family of Dunnottar

Keith Clan tradition has it that at the Battle of Barrie in 1010, a man from the Chatti tribe, known as Marbhachair Chamuis, (which translates as 'the Camus Slayer'), killed a Viking leader named Camus, and in 1018 was given the lands of Keth by Malcolm II as a reward. It is from this place that his descendants took their name. The word 'keth' comes from an old form of Welsh 'coed', meaning 'wood'.

In 1150, Hervey de Keith, (sometimes Herveus de Keth), a Norman knight, was granted the remaining lands of Keth by David I. It was his son William who was made Great Marischal of the Scots, a title which the family retained thereafter, and that Robert the Bruce confirmed by a charter in 1324.

The Bruce later gave the land of Halforest in Aberdeenshire to Sir Robert de Keth in 1308. Robert proved himself at Bannockburn. Later his family acquired estates in Inverugie, Buchan and Kincardine.

Some time around 1458, William, third Lord Keith, was created Earl Marischal, and a century and a half later, George Keith succeeded as Lord Altrie. By 1660, another William of the family was appointed Lord Privy Seal of Scotland.

The tenth Earl Marischal, George Keith, (some sources name him as the ninth Earl), and his brother took part in the failed Jacobite rising of 1715 and fled to Europe, forfeiting their lands and titles.

In 1801, the Lord Lyon of Arms recognised Keith of Ravelston and Dunnotter as rightful holder of the Marischal Keith title and in 1822 it was restored to him. His nephew was dubbed Knight Marischal for George IV's visit to Edinburgh that year.

The present Chief of Clan Keith is James William Falconer Keith, fourteenth Earl of Kintore, who lives at Keith Hall in Aberdeenshire

The Kerr Family of Cessford

The Kerr family and clan name, (sometimes Ker), comes from the Old Norse 'kjarr', (or 'kjrr'), suggesting a 'marsh dweller', or possibly from the Gaelic 'ciar', meaning 'dusky'. Yet another explanation is that the name came from the Gaelic word 'cearr', meaning 'left-handed'. It arrived in Scotland after the Norman invasion.

Tradition has it that around 1330 the name was brought over the border by two Norman knights, the brothers Ralph and Robert, (the latter possibly called John – opinions vary), who came from Lancashire. Ralph's descendants became the Kerrs of Ferniehurst, the senior branch, whilst Robert/John was progenitor of the Kerrs of Cessford.

The name appears in various forms, including Kerr, Ker, Carr, Carre and Cares. There are two main branches of the Clan Kerr, (in Gaelic, 'Cearr MacGhillechearr'): the Kerrs of Ferniehurst and the Kerrs of Cessford. They were often embroiled in feud with each other, but despite this, both Andrew Kerr of Ferniehurst and Andrew Kerr of Cessford were made Wardens of the Middle Marches in

1502. This office was taken by another Sir Andrew Kerr of Cessford, whose grandson, Mark Kerr, became the first Earl of Lothian in 1606. However, when the male line ended abruptly with his son's death in 1624, the peerage became extinct.

Further earldoms came later, with Sir Robert of Ferniehirst becoming Earl of Ancram and Sir Robert of Cessford. By 1616, he was created Earl of Roxburgh and had begun spelling his surname as Ker.

In 1631, William Kerr was created Lord Newbottle, and in 1690, Robert Kerr succeeded as third Earl Ancram. By 1701, he had been elevated as Viscount Briene and Marquess of Lothian. By 1812, another descendant, also named William, had been created Baron Ker of Kersheugh and was Lord Lieutenant of Midlothian. In 1887, Scomberg Henry Kerr was Secretary of State for Scotland.

The present incumbent is Michael Andrew Foster Jude Kerr, Marquess of Lothian. He was Member of Parliament for Berwick and East Lothian in 1974, for Edinburgh South in 1979 and for Devises in 1992. He was created Baron Kerr of Montevoit for life in November 2010. Ferniehirst Castle, in the Scottish Border region of Roxburghshire, is the family seat of the Clan Kerr.

The Lennox Family of Dunbartonshire

The ancient Earldom of Lennox consisted of Dunbartonshire and parts of Renfrewshire, Stirlingshire and Perthshire, and by the end of the thirteenth century, they were among the most powerful nobles in the area. The name comes from the village of Lennoxtown, and has various spellings, including Levanax, Leven-achs and Lenox.

Malcolm McArkill, the fifth Earl, was at the forefront of the struggle for Scottish independence, and he supported Robert the Bruce in his claim to the crown of Scotland. In 1296, he led troops into England and besieged Carlisle. Malcolm died in 1333, but his son was present when in 1371, the Bruce was crowned King of Scotland at Scone.

Malcolm died with no direct male issue in 1373, and the earldom passed through the marriage of his only daughter Margaret to Walter of Farlane, (sometimes De Fasselane), who assumed the title Earl of Lennox on their marriage, and his family, also by now Dukes of Albany, acted as Regents of Scotland during the imprisonment of James I in England.

When James returned, Lennox fell victim to his hatred of all those associated with Duke of Albany, who had overseen Scotland's decline into disorder, and in retribution, the Earl, Murdock Stewart, was beheaded in May 1425. He was seventy-nine.

In the ever-changing and volatile politics of the day, fortune smiled, and Esme Stuart, (1542-83), was recalled to Scotland in 1579 by James V1, and in 1581 was created the first Duke of Lennox, Lord Darnley, Aubigny and Dalkeith as well as High Chamberlain of Scotland.

The line was in abeyance for many years thereafter due to lack of male heirs, but in the late eigtheenth or early nineteenth century, a female descendant, Margaret Lennox, moved to acquire the ancient title of Countess of Lennox, and petitioned the House of Lords to resurrect the title. She won her appeal and was recognised as the 'keeper' of the estates until her death in 1833. Margaret was succeeded by her nephew, John Lennox Kincaid. His son, also named John, was obliged to assume the name Lennox, making him, (rather confusingly), John Lennox Kincaid Lennox.

Lennox Castle, the old family seat, was eventually sold to Glasgow Parish Council by William George Peareth Kincaid Lennox in 1927, and the Lennox family moved to live in the restored Woodhead House near Clachan. Also there, in the Clachan of Campsie churchyard, is the eigtheenth century burial vault of the Kincaid-Lennox family.

The Leslie-Melville Family of Midlothian

The Melvilles are thought to be originally descended from Galfridus de Melville, (sometimes Guillaume or Galfrid de Maleville), a Norman knight who fought at the Battle of Hastings and settled in Fife in eastern Scotland, some time during the reign of Malcolm IV in the twelfth century. The surname probably derives from Malleville, a manor in the Pays de Caux in Higher Normandy, France. This township's name comes from the Latin words 'mala', meaning 'bad', and 'ville', signifying a township or settlement. It translates literally as 'bad town'.

Galfridus was made warden of Edinburgh Castle and became Justiciar of Scotland under William the Lion. Later, Agnes, his granddaughter and sole heir, inherited the Barony of Melville, a peerage that the family retained until the early eigtheenth century.

Sir Robert Melville of Murdocairnie served under Mary, Queen of Scots as the Keeper of the Palace of Linlithgow and was later ambassador in the court of Elizabeth. He became Vice-Chancellor of Scotland, taking the title Lord Murdocairnie. In 1616, he was made Baron Melville of Monymail, and his son became Lord Monymail in 1627.

In 1641, Alexander Leslie was created Lord Balgonie and Earl of Leven and the main branch of the family, the Leslie-Melvilles, have retained the titles ever since. The family gained its surname from the 1655 marriage of George Melville, fourth Lord Melville to Catherine Leslie, a descendant of Alexander Leslie, first Earl of Leven. Through his wife he also inherited the title of the Earldom of Leven and the Castle of Balgonie in Fife. Subsequent heirs have held the courtesy title of Lord Balgonie.

Several descendants have been Lords Lieutenant of Nairnshire. The current incumbent is the fourteenth Earl Melville, Alexander Ian Leslie-Melville, Lord Balgonie, (born in 1984).

The Liddell Family of Roxburghshire

The name Liddell is thought to derive from the river of that name in Roxburghshire, and is found around the Scottish Borders as well as in the northern English county of Northumberland, especially in Newcastle-upon-Tyne, where a branch of the family settled. It may also possibly have come from the township of Liddel in Cumbria.

An early example of the use of it as a family name is that of Richard de Liddal, (or Lidel), recorded in 1202 as witness to a charter in Largs. John Lydel was a merchant in Aberdeen in 1358, and William de Lyudell, is known to have been Sheriff of Aberdeen, in that same year.

An Anglo-Saxon name, composed of two Old English elements: 'hlyde', meaning loud, and 'dael', (or 'doel'), meaning a valley or dale. Spelling variations include Liddall, Liddle, Lidale and Lidel.

Clan Liddell is considered to be a sept or subdivision of the Clan Dalziel. The Liddells were border reivers, (from the Old English word for 'robbers'), and were traditionally based in Liddell Strength Castle, recognised as an Ancient Monument near Carwinley in Cumbria. It was destroyed by the Scots in 1346. A contemporary assessment of the site value was recorded in 1349 thus: 'the manor of Liddel was valued at £70 16s. 2d., whereof the site of the castle and manor destroyed is worth six pence'. It was never rebuilt and remains today as little more than a ruined mound among the trees.

Centuries later, with family fortunes significantly recovered, in 1747 Sir Henry Liddell was created Baron Ravensworth and became Member of Parliament for Morpeth. The barony continued through successive generations, and in 1874 the earldom was added, as was the Barony of Eslington. Family members have been Members of Parliament for Northumberland and for Durham.

The main family seat was originally at Ravensworth Castle in Gateshead, but later moved to Eslington Park near Alnwick in Northumberland.

There were several family migrations to America, including Thomas Liddell who arrived in Virginia in 1657, John Liddell, who settled in Mississippi in 1841 and many others who reached California in the 1850s.

The Lindsay Family of Angus

Lindsay family history began way back before the ninth century, when Baldric of Lindsay was a tenant of a manor held by the Earl of Chester. In 1120, Sir Walter de Lindeseva, (also known as Lindsay), was a member of the council of David, Earl of Huntingdon in England, and brother of Alexander I, who in 1124, went on to become king of Scotland. He settled in Lothian and Upper Clydeside. Another branch of the family lived over the border in Northumberland and further south in Lincolnshire, where Ealdric de Lindsay held estates.

In 1180, William de Lindsay was Baron of Luffness and Laird of Crawford in Lanarkshire, and by 1256, Sir David Lindsay had become High Chamberlain of Scotland, before he met his death on a crusade with Louis of France in 1268.

Over time the Lindsays spread throughout Scotland, though the main concentration was in Angus, Nairn and Lanarkshire. It is estimated that at one time there were over a hundred Lindsay families holding land in Scotland.

George Lindsay-Crawford, (1758-1808), was Lord Lieutenant of Fife from 1798 to 1808, and in 1768, Alexander Lindsay was Earl of Balcarres and Governor of Jamaica. By 1913, David Alexander Edward Lindsay, tenth Earl of Balcarres was Member of Parliament for the Lancashire North constituency, was President of the Board of Agriculture, Lord Privy Seal, and by 1922, was Chancellor of the Duchy of Lancaster and Minister for Transport.

Sir Robert Alexander Lindsay, twenty-ninth Earl of Crawford and twelfth Earl of Balcarres, born in March 1927, styled Lord Balniel between 1940 and 1975, was Member of Parliament for Hertford from 1955 to 1974 and for Welwyn Hatfield in 1974. He was Minister of State for Defence from 1970 to 1972-and Minister of State for Foreign and Commonwealth Affairs from 1972 to 1974. He is the Premier Earl of Scotland and Chief of Clan Lindsay.

The Lovat Family of Inverness-shire

The Lovat Family name was probably derived from the Anglo-French word 'louvet', meaning 'wolf cub'. Although its precise origin is somewhat obscure, there is a record of Baron William Louvet in the *Domesday Book*, but whether he inherited the family name from the village of Lovat near Beauly in Inverness, or vice-versa, is uncertain. It is known that the title, Lord Lovat, (sometimes Lovatt), was created in 1458 for Hugh Fraser, Chief of Clan Fraser of Lovat.

The first Lord Lovat was one of the hostages for James I on his return to Scotland in 1424, and in 1431 he was appointed High Sheriff of the County of Inverness. The title continued in the family for nine generations until the ninth Lord died in 1696.

Simon Fraser, eleventh Lord Lovat, (c.1667–1747), was a Scottish Jacobite, and the Chief of Clan Fraser, noted for his violent feuds and changes of allegiance. Fraser forcibly married the dowager Lady Lovat and brought about a prolonged and bitter feud with her kinsmen, the Murrays of Athol. As a consequence, in 1698 he was tried and sentenced to death, but through the intercession of the Earl of Argyll he won a pardon from William III.

After a time in London he went to France, made contact with the court of the exiled Stuarts and was converted to Catholicism. In 1703, he returned to Scotland on a Jacobite mission, during which he betrayed the Duke of Queensberry, head of the Scottish ministry.

The truth concerning Fraser's treachery leaked out, and on his return to Paris he was incarcerated in the Bastille for the next ten years. He seems to have procured his liberty by taking priests' orders, and became a Jesuit in the College of St Omer. In 1715, he returned to Scotland, where he made amends and saw good service to the government, joined the king's troops, and assisted them in seizing Inverness from the rebels, for which service he was pardoned and many other belated favours were conferred upon him.

Despite this, he changed sides again and joined the Pretender, but was captured and arrested. On 9 March 1747, he was taken from the Tower to Westminster Hall for trial, convicted and sentenced to death. He became the last person to be executed by beheading in Britain.

In the twentieth century, Brigadier Simon Christopher Joseph Fraser, fifteenth Lord Lovat and fourth Baron Lovat, DSO, MC, (born 9 July 1911 in Beaufort Castle, Inverness and died 16 March 1995 in Beauly, Inverness), was the twenty-fifth Chief of the Clan Fraser of Lovat and a prominent British Commando during the Second World War. He played a pivotal role in the taking of the distinctive bridge at Benouville in 1944, later renamed and thereafter known as Pegasus Bridge. His descendant, Simon Fraser, sixteenth Lord Lovat, was born in February 1977, and has been Colonel-in-Chief of the 78th Fraser Highlanders since 1997.

The Marshall Family

See: Part Eight: Scotland: The Marshal Family of Pembroke.

The Menzies Family

See: Part Two: North-West England: The Manners Family of Etal.

The Montgomery Family

See: Part Nine: Wales: The Montgomery Family of Montgomeryshire.

The Murray Family of Moray

There is an opinion that the Murrays took their family name from Moray in north-east Scotland; another has them related to MacAngus de Moravia who was related to King Duncan of Scotland, and was the first Earl of Murray. The descendants of this family were designated 'de Moravia', which in Lowland Scots became 'Murray'.

In 1100, the founder of the Murray Clan, known as Freskin, was granted lands in Strathbrock, West Lothian, while his sons became chiefs of the Murrays of Tullibardine and acquired the title Dukes of Atholl. It is thought that Freskin, or his son William, married into the royal house of Moray, took the surname of Sutherland and by 1235 had become Earls of Sutherland.

A branch of the family, descended from Muireadhach Muilleathan, (who was known as Murray the long-headed), and migrated to Ireland, where they founded the Irish Clan Murray, (or Siol Muiredhaigh in Gaelic), in Ulster, some time in the twelfth century.

In 1279, Andrew Moray, (sometimes Andrew de Moray or Andrew Murray), led resistance against Edward I, and was mortally wounded at the Battle of Stirling.

In 1756, William Murray was created Baron Mansfield, and later became an earl. In a long legal and political career, he was Member of Parliament for Boroughbridge, Solicitor General and Lord Chief Justice. By 1778, David Murray was Lord Justice General of

Scotland, and over the years his successors held parliamentary seats for Aldeburgh, Woodstock, Norwich and for Perth.

In 1979, William David Mungo James Murray was Minister of State at the Scottish Office, and in 1983 held the same post for Northern Ireland.

The Murrays had been Lords of Scone and Viscounts Stormont since they were granted the estate and title by James VI of Scotland in 1604.

The present incumbent is Alexander David Mungo Murray, ninth Earl of Mansfield and Viscount Stormont, who was born in October 1956.

The Ogilvy Family of Angus

Ogilvy, (sometimes Ogilvie), is a Scottish location near Glamis in the old county of Angus. The surname has several spellings, including Ogilvie, Ogilvy, Ogilby and De Oggiluill. The name also appears as Ogelbe in 1531, as Ogglebie in 1665 and Oglevie in 1661. It may derive from the Old Welsh 'ugl' meaning 'high' and 'ma', signifying a place; hence: 'a high place', or possibly 'ocel-fa', which is Old English for 'high plain'.

The first person known to use the surname was Gilbert Ogilvie, son of Gillebride, first Earl of Angus, who was granted the Manor of Ogilvy in 1172.

In the fourteenth and fifteenth centuries the Ogilvys became hereditary Sheriffs of Angus, and in 1425, Sir Walter de Ogilby was appointed High Treasurer of Scotland, the same year that David of Ogilby was hostage for the king of Scotland. He was also an ambassador to England in 1430 and four years later he attended Princess Margaret on her marriage to the Dauphin, heir to the throne of France. His son, also named Walter, became the ancestor of the Earls of Seafield and Deskford. In 1639, the seventh Lord Ogilvy was created Earl of Airlie.

The Ogilvy family suffered greatly in their service to the Stuart monarchs. The Earl and his sons joined James Graham, first Marquess of Montrose to oppose enemies of Charles I. Sir Thomas Ogilvy, the

Earl's second son, raised his own regiment to fight for the Royalist cause, but he was killed at the Battle of Inverlochy in 1645.

Successive generations of the Ogilvys retained the Earldom, at least two of their number becoming Lord Lieutenants of Angus, including the last, Sir David George Coke Patrick Ogilvy, who died in 2001.

David Ogilvy, thirteenth Earl of Airlie, is the present Chief of the Ogilvie Clan and served as lord chamberlain to the queen. Royal links were also reinforced when Angus Ogilvy, the brother of the chief, married Her Royal Highness Princess Alexandra of Kent in 1963.

The Rollo Family of Duncrub

The name Rollo, common in early medieval documents, comes from a Latinised version of the Old Norse personal name Rolfr, of which the usual French Norman form is Rolf, (sometimes Raoul or Roul). The Germanic form of the name is Hrodwulf, from two elements – 'hrod', meaning renowned or famed, and 'wulf', meaning wolf.

Sigurd Rollo was a Viking settler who became the first ruler of Normandy. He is known to have seized the city of Rouen in 876 and laid siege to Paris in 885. He was the great-great-great-grandfather of William the Conqueror, and thereby recognised as the very first Duke of Normandy.

The Norman version of the name appears in the *Domesday Book*, and, in 1142, there is a record of Robertus filius Rouli, (Robert, son of Rollo), in the Early Northamptonshire Charters. In Scotland, as a surname, it is often found as Rollo or Rollow, and is a common name in Perthshire, (present day Perth and Kinross).

The name first appears on record in a charter of around 1141, which had been granted by Robert the Bruce, and by the early fourteenth century the Scottish Clan Rollo had been firmly established.

William Rollo of Duncrub led the Rollo Clan at Flodden in 1513. During the Civil Wars, clan loyalties were with the monarchy, which were rewarded in 1651, when Charles II created Sir Andrew, Lord Rollo of Duncrub. Despite this, Andrew was fined a thousand pounds by Oliver Cromwell for his monarchist leanings.

Another Andrew, the third Lord Rollo, supported the Glorious Revolution of 1688 that brought Mary II and William of Orange to the throne of England.

The peerage remained in the family and in 1869, John Rogerson Rollo was created Baron Dunning, an honour that remains in the family to this day. The present clan chief, David Eric Howard Rollo, the thirteenth Lord Rollo of Duncrub and fourth Baron Dunning of Dunning and Pitcairns, still lives in Perthshire.

The Ross Family of Balnagown

An Anglo-Scottish name of several possible derivations, Ross, (sometimes De Ros, Rose, Rosse or Ros), is first found in Scotland, on the Hebridean Islands, and is also a common surname in Yorkshire. One possibility is that it originated from the village of Rots, near Caen in Normandy. Another is that it derives from various places called Ross in Northumberland and Scotland. Others cite the township of Roos in the East Riding of Yorkshire as a likely starting point for the name. In Scotland, some maintain a simpler explanation – that it derives from the Old English 'rouse', which refers to red hair.

An early example of the surname is that of Bernard de Ross in the Yorkshire entry of the *Domesday Book*, and of Sir Godfrey de Rose in Irvine, Scotland in 1205.

In 1295, Robert Ros was summoned to Parliament as Lord Ros de Werke, and in 1332, John de Ros was also summoned as Lord Ros.

The Highland Clan Ross was thought to have been first instituted by Malcolm IV in 1160, and its first clan chief was Fearchar O'Beolain of Applecross, who was created Earl of Ross in about 1234. He was known as 'the son of the priest', after the monastery which St Maelrubha had founded at Applecross some time after 671.

During the Wars of Scottish Independence in 1296 the clan fought against the English at the Battle of Dunbar, at which the Earl of Ross was captured. Later freed, he fought alongside Robert the Bruce when Fearchar's grandson William led the clan against the English at Bannockburn. After the fifth Earl, Aodh, was killed in 1333 at Halidon

Hill, his successor William died without male issue, at which point the earldom of Ross and the chiefship of Clan Ross were separated.

During the Anglo-Scottish Wars, John Ross, Lord of Halkhead, died leading his forces against the English at Flodden, an encounter that ended disastrously for the Scots.

In 1651, during the English Civil War, David Ross, twelfth Duke of Balnagown, led the clan at the Battle of Worcester. He was taken prisoner and imprisoned at the Tower, where he is said to have died in 1653 and was buried in Westminster.

The 1745 Jacobite uprising saw clan loyalties divided. Alexander Ross, the Pitcalnie clan chief, raised a company of militia to garrison Inverness Castle against the Jacobites.

Following Culloden, John Ross escaped to Sutherland and was listed as a rebel fugitive. Despite this, Clan Ross generally supported the government. Following the outcome of the conflict, David Ross of Pitcairne, last of the line of Balnagown, became the Chief of Clan Ross.

The current clan chief at the time of writing is David Campbell Ross, who lives in Perthshire. The Balnagown estate is currently owned by the millionaire Egyptian proprietor Mohammed Al-Fayed of the Harrods department store in London.

The Ruthven Family of Perthshire

The Ruthven family, (pronounced 'Ri-ven'), came from Norse stock and were granted the lands of Ruthven and Tibbermore during the twelfth century in the reign of David I. They were descended from Thor, (known as 'Thor the Long'), son of Sweyn, (sometimes 'Swaine'), the Viking chief, who founded the Ruthven Clan. Its name is from the lands north of Loch Rannoch in Perthshire, (the Gaelic 'Ruadhainn', meaning 'a red place'). Walter de Ruthven, son of Alan, and grandson of Sweyn, was the first known to have taken the Ruthven surname.

Some time in the mid-thirteenth century, Sir William of Ruthven witnessed two charters and paid homage to Edward I in 1291, whereupon he was dubbed 'William of Ruthven, Lord of that Ilk'. He fought with William Wallace at the siege of Perth in 1297. It was recorded that Sir William fought with 'determined energy'. For his conduct on the battlefield, Wallace appointed him Sheriff of Perth, a position that was to be hereditary in the Ruthven family thereafter.

William, fourth Lord of Ruthven, received the abdication of Mary, Queen of Scots at Loch Leven Castle and was present at the coronation of her son, James VI, at Stirling. It was about that time that he was given the Earldom of Scone. William was a man of significant political power in his day, and became Treasurer of Scotland. In 1581 he was created the first Earl of Gowrie.

Ruthven Castle was the family seat from the twelfth century, and it was there that Mary, Queen of Scots stayed on her honeymoon in 1565. In 1584, William was beheaded for his part in the raid of Ruthven when the young James VI was held prisoner, an event known as the 'Gowrie Conspiracy'. The Ruthven brothers were all declared by Parliament to be traitors, and it was not until the twentieth century that family honour was restored and the Earldom of Gowrie reinstated.

Alexander Gore Arkwright Hore-Ruthven, (1872-1955), was created Baron Gowrie of Canberra in December 1935 and in 1945, as a captain in the 3rd Battalion, Highland Light Infantry, he was awarded the Victoria Cross for his gallant action in rescuing fallen comrades under heavy fire at Gedarif in Egypt on 22 September 1898.

He also won the Distinguished Service Order twice, was a Commander of the British Empire and served as a Privy Counsellor. From 1928 to 1934 he had been Governor of South Australia, later of New South Wales, and then from 1936 to 1944 as Governor General of Australia. On his death in May 1955, he was succeeded by his son, Alexander Patrick Greystell Ruthven, the second Baron Ruthven of Gowrie, (usually known as Grey Gowrie), who was Chancellor of the Duchy of Lancaster in 1984 and 1985. He went on to serve in a number of senior political offices, including Minister of State for Employment, Minister of State for Northern Ireland and Minister for the Arts. After leaving government, he became Chairman of Sotheby's, (1985–94), and later of the Arts Council of England. Lord

Gowrie inherited Castlemartin House and estate at Kilcullen, County Kildare, Ireland in 1967, and later sold it.

The Scrymgeour Family of Dundee

By tradition, the Scrymgeours are believed to have descended from MacDuff, Earl of Fife, and claim their office as standard bearer from the early Celts, whose armies bore holy relics into battle before them. As such, it is thought that the Clan Scrymgeour may have carried the pastoral staff of St Columba on such occasions, before it was replaced later by a consecrated heraldic banner.

One interpretation of the meaning of the Scrymgeour family and clan name has it derived from the Old English word 'skrymsher', meaning 'swordsman'. Another has it signifying 'a fencer', from the Old French 'eskirmir', or 'escarmouche', signifying a skirmish, hence the English word 'scrimmage', and 'scrimgeour', one who mingled in a scrimmage.

During the Wars of Scottish Independence, Clan Scrymgeour were supporters of William Wallace, and were confirmed as banner bearers by him at the Scottish Parliament in March 1298, when the clan chief was Alexander Scrymgeour. He was captured by the English and hanged in Newcastle in 1306 on the direct orders of Edward I. He was succeeded by another Alexander Scrymgeour who, in 1314, was royal banner bearer at Bannockburn.

It was no coincidence that at the coronation of Edward VII, Henry Scrymgeour-Wedderburn carried the standard of Scotland. Also in the twentieth century, his grandson succeeded in regaining the Scrymgeour's Dundee estates along with the title of eleventh Earl of Dundee. In 1954, he was also created Baron Glassary to enable him to take up Government office, where he became Deputy Leader of the House of Lords.

The current Chief of Clan Scrymgeour is the twelfth Earl, Alexander Henry Scrymgeour of Dundee, who followed his father into politics and sits in the House of Lords. The present Scrymgeour family seat is at Birkhill, north of Cupar in Fife. It was formerly at Dudhope

Castle before the family sold it to John Graham of Claverhouse in 1668.

The Wemyss Family of Fife

Wemyss comes from a Gaelic word 'uaimh', meaning a cave, which is the kind of rocky landscape around the Firth of Forth where the Wemyss family settled in the twelfth century. They are believed to have descended from the MacDuff Earls of Fife.

Although Sir Michael Wemyss initially swore fealty to Edward I in 1296, he changed allegiances and went over to support Robert the Bruce during the Wars of Scottish Independence and was a witness at his coronation.

Sir David Wemyss was slain at Flodden. In 1559, Mary, Queen of Scots created Sir John Wemyss Lieutenant of Fife and Kinross. He was knighted later in 1618 and made Baron of Nova Scotia in 1628. He was also made Lord Elcho and Methell and elevated to an Earldom of Wemyss and of March in 1633. He later supported the Scottish Parliament against Charles I, and died in 1649. His son, the second earl, died childless in 1679, at which time the baronetcy became extinct, and the family name and estates passed through the marriage of its sole heiress, Margaret to a third cousin, James, Lord Burntisland, from another branch of the family.

The Wemyss family were implicated in the Jacobite rising of 1745, and their titles were attainted and the peerage forfeited as a result. It was not until 1826 that Francis Charteris-Wemyss-Douglas, fourth Earl of March, obtained a reversal of the forfeiture and the Baronetcy of Wemyss was reinstated.

Thereafter, political honours continued in the family as several descendants were Members of Parliament, for Gloucestershire, for Haddingtonshire, and for Ipswitch. Several were also Lords Lieutenants: of Peebles in 1821 and 1853, of Haddington in 1918, and of East Lothian in 1967.

Rosslyn Erskine Wemyss, of the Wester Wemyss branch, was created Baron Wester Wemyss in 1919 and was Admiral of the Fleet until his death in 1919.

The present Chief of Clan Wemyss is David Wemyss, who married Lady Jean Bruce, daughter of the Earl of Elgin. Wemyss Castle in Fife is still the principal seat of the chief of Clan Wemyss and he also owns Elcho Castle.

Part Nine

Wales
Family Names in Clwyd, Dyfed, Glamorgan, Gwent, Gwynedd & Powys

A note about Welsh unification

The 'Act of Union' between England and Wales took place in 1536. The term was not used until the twentieth century, although the formerly independent Principality of Wales had

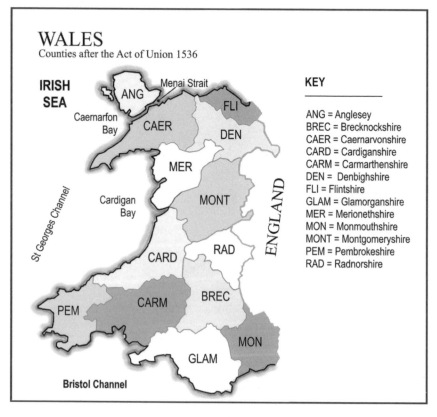

WALES
Counties after the Act of Union 1536

IRISH SEA

Menai Strait

ANG

Caernarfon Bay

FLI

CAER

DEN

MER

St Georges Channel

Cardigan Bay

MONT

ENGLAND

CARD

RAD

PEM

CARM

BREC

MON

GLAM

Bristol Channel

KEY

ANG = Anglesey
BREC = Brecknockshire
CAER = Caernarvonshire
CARD = Cardiganshire
CARM = Carmarthenshire
DEN = Denbighshire
FLI = Flintshire
GLAM = Glamorganshire
MER = Merionethshire
MON = Monmouthshire
MONT = Montgomeryshire
PEM = Pembrokeshire
RAD = Radnorshire

A map depicting counties of Wales c.1500.

come under English control in 1284, following Edward I's Statute of Rhuddlan, which imposed English common law on Wales. He created Marcher Lords to oversee the various counties and to act on his behalf. Edward's son was declared Prince of Wales, and later became Edward II.

Unification was not equally beneficial, as English was declared to be the only official language, and those using the Welsh language were not allowed in public office. Little wonder there were various rebellions; most notable was that of Owain Glyndwr in 1404, who declared himself to be Prince of Wales against Henry IV. However, his dominance was short-lived and in 1412 he was forced into hiding.

The power of the Marcher Lords came to an end in 1535 with the passing of the Laws in Wales Act which made English and Welsh law common to both united countries. According to the latest figures it is estimated that almost three million people claim to be fluent Welsh speakers, and just over ten per cent count it their first language.

The Blayney Family

See: Part Ten: Ireland: The Blayney Family of Fermanagh.

The Braose Family of the Welsh Marches

The Braose were a prominent family of Anglo-Normans who came from Briouze, near Argentan in Normandy, and who played an important role in the Norman Conquest. The surname has several variations and spellings, including Breuse, Brewes, Brehuse, Briouze, Brewose and Braiosa; the surname was derived directly from the placename.

The *Domesday Book* shows William de Braose as the holder of the feudal Barony of Bramber in Sussex, which had been granted him by the Conqueror, and it is known that he also inherited the Barony of Barnstaple. His grandson, William III, acquired the Barony of Kington, the Lordship of Gower and the Barony of Totnes.

In 1173, William de Braose, third Lord of Bamber, was appointed as Sheriff of Herefordshire. He died within two years and was succeeded by his son, William, who found favour with both Richard I and

King John to become a powerful force in Wales. He rose to high status and was granted the Lordships of Gower, Abergavenny, Brecknock, Builth, Radnor, Kington and Glamorgan. He was effectively Lord of all the Welsh Marcher lands of modern day Monmouthshire.

However, he eventually fell out of the king's favour, and the lands were confiscated by the Crown. De Braose fled to Ireland where King John mounted a manhunt, forcing him to return to Wales, where he allied himself to the Welsh Prince, Llywelyn the Great, and helped him in his rebellion against John.

A descendant, Giles de Braose, exiled in France until 1213, was Bishop of Hereford from 1200 until his death in 1215. He made peace with John and agreed terms for the restitution of De Braose lands, and also made alliances with the Llywelyn. Giles' son, Reginald de Braose, finally regained the De Braose lands and titles in Brecon, Abergavenny and Gower. Abergavenny Castle was rebuilt before Reginald died in 1228.

William Braose VII was summoned to Parliament in 1299, but upon his death in 1326, having no male heirs, Braose estates passed to his two daughters and the barony fell into abeyance.

The Bulkeley Family of Beaumaris

Bulkeley, (sometimes de Bulkeley or Buckley), is a surname of Anglo-Saxon origin. It has two possible derivations: either it means 'large mountain', or else from the Old English 'bulluc', meaning 'bullock', and 'leah', a woodland clearing, signifying a clearing where bulls or cows were pastured. Either way, the name probably derives from the parish of that name in the township Malpas in Cheshire, or the parish of Buckley in St Albans.

Some time around 1200, Robert de Bulkileh was the Lord of the Cheshire Manor of Bulkeley. However, by 1450, a significant branch of the family had settled in Anglesey.

Sir Richard Bulkeley of Beaumaris and Lewisham, (1533–1621), was a Welsh politician who sat in the House of Commons. In 1618, he established a country seat and estate at Baron Hill in Beaumaris on the island of Anglesey. He had been Constable of Beaumaris Castle since 1561 and was elected the first Mayor of the town in 1562. The following year he was elected Member of Parliament for Anglesey, and appointed its High Sheriff in 1570. He was knighted in London in 1577. The family's acquisition of land and high office made them possibly the largest landowners in Anglesey.

In 1644, the title of Viscount Bulkeley of Cashel was created in County Tipperary in the peerage of Ireland for Thomas Bulkeley, Sir Richard's son. He was one of the chief forces behind the ill-fated Anglesey Insurrection of 1648.

During the eigtheenth century, several succeeding generations of the Bulkeley Viscounts were suspected of Jacobite sympathies, though nothing seems to have been proven. Later, Thomas James Warren Bulkeley, the seventh Viscount, was created Baron Bulkeley of Beaumaris, but upon his death in 1822, his titles fell to Sir Richard Warren of Penrhyn, who succeeded to the Bulkeley estates and adopted the surname of Bulkeley.

After the First World War, (by then the family were known as Williams–Bulkeley), heavy death duties so diminished the family fortune that it proved impossible for them to continue the maintenance of the house, and they moved out to live in a smaller property. In the Second World War, Baron Hill was an army storage depot and a billet for Polish soldiers, before being converted into luxury apartments.

The Cadogan Family of Merionethshire

The earliest record of the Cadogan name is that of one Cadwgan ap Bleddyn, (1051-1111), who was Prince of Powys. It is of Brythonic Celtic origin, derived from the Old Welsh personal name, Cadwygaun. It is comprised of the Welsh word 'cad', meaning 'battle', and 'gwgan', meaning 'one who scowls'; an odd definition, that most likely described a man who rode fiercely into battle, or who had a terrifying countenance.

Other spellings of the name include Cadogan, Caddigan, Cadwgan and Caddagan. The surname is also common in the Munster and

Leinster Provinces of Ireland, where it is typically spelled O'Caedagain. It may also be related to the Irish surname Wogan.

Sir William Cadogan, (1672-1726), the first Earl Cadogan, was closely associated with the Duke of Marlborough. Born in Dublin of Welsh stock, he was created Baron Cadogan of Reading in 1716 and Viscount Caversham and Earl Cadogan in 1718. He was elected Member of Parliament for Woodstock in 1705.

Through the marriage in 1717 of Charles, the second Baron Cadogan, to Elizabeth Sloane, youngest daughter of Sir Hans Sloane, (after whom Sloane Square in London is named), the Sloane surname was incorporated into the family name for a time. Charles Cadogan was Master of the Royal Mint in 1769 and was created Viscount Chelsea in 1800. Thus Chelsea passed into the Cadogan family and the estate in Chelsea was established.

Sir Charles Cadogan, the eighth Earl Cadogan, (born in 1937), is the current incumbent of the title. He held the rank of Second-Lieutenant in the Coldstream Guards and was Deputy Lieutenant of Greater London in 1996. He is listed in the *Sunday Times* as the second richest British Peer with extensive land holdings in central London. The family estate is in Snaigow, Scotland.

The FitzOsbern Family of Chepstow

History records that William FitzOsbern, son of Duke Robert I, (and known as 'Osbern the Seneschal'), was one of the first of the Norman barons to urge William of Normandy to invade England, pledging sixty ships for the enterprise. He is also thought to have commanded the right wing of William's army at Hastings. At that time FitzOsbern, (sometimes Fitz Osbn, Fitz Osbern, Usborne or Osbourne), was Lord of Breteuil in Normandy, and after the Conquest, he was granted the Manor of Chepstow, where he immediately began building the castle as part of the Norman plan for the suppression of Wales.

The Conqueror also created him Earl of Hereford. The *Domesday Book* shows that FitzOsbern, along with Odo of Bayeux, had been given leave to distribute portions of their land to their subordinates.

Thus, Walter de Lacy, FitzOsbern's second in command, acquired the lands of South Shropshire, where he was involved with the development of Ludlow Castle, where the De Lacy family retained its lordship until the end of the thirteenth century. William FitzOsbern also built Clifford Castle on the Welsh border.

William the Conqueror also granted lordship of the Isle of Wight to FitzOsbern, who began the construction of Carisbrooke Castle; hence the connection with Osborne House, Victoria's favourite residence, evidently named after him. The lordship of the Island passed to the De Redvers family, who occupied Carisbrooke in 1101.

The surnames Osborne or Osbourne both originate from the same source and tend to be preferred in modern usage.

The Herbert Family of Powys

Herbert was originally both a Germanic personal name, (usually spelled Herebert, Herebeorht, or even Haribrecht), and emerged as an Old French name before the Conquest, with St Herbert active in Europe from the late tenth to the early eleventh centuries. According to some genealogists, Herbert, Count of Vermandois, a Norman knight, probably accompanied William from Normandy.

In its original Germanic form, its two elements were made up of 'hari', meaning 'army', and 'beraht', meaning 'bright'. In Wales it has long been the family name of the Earls of Powis (or Powys).

In 1138, during the reign of King John, the Earldom of Pembroke was first created for one Gilbert de Clare, and was resurrected after many years in abeyance when it was bestowed on William Herbert, (c.1501-1570). Known as 'Black William', he was the son of William ap Thomas, the founder of Raglan Castle, who had supported Edward IV during the Wars of the Roses. He was created Baron Herbert of Raglan in 1461, and adopted Herbert as his surname.

Sir Richard Herbert, (who died in 1540), was the first of the family known to have settled in Montgomeryshire. He had been knighted by Henry VIII in 1550 and received Montgomery Castle with the knighthood. He was also made Constable of Aberystwyth. His son,

Henry, the second Earl, was President of Wales from 1586 until his death in 1601.

Philip Herbert, fourth Earl of Pembroke, (1584-1650), along with his brother William, were both prominent courtiers of Elizabeth I, and had the distinction of having Shakespeare's first folio of collected works dedicated to them in 1623. Later, as a court favourite of James I, Philip was made a Gentleman of the Privy Chamber in 1603, the same year that he was also made a Knight of the Bath. His royal favour continued under the reign of Charles I, and he was given the honour of holding the king's spurs at his coronation in 1626.

Thomas, the eighth Earl, (c.1656-1733), was First Lord of the Admiralty from 1690 to 1692, served as Lord Privy Seal until 1699, and on two occasions was Lord High Admiral, Lord Lieutenant of Ireland. In 1689-1690, he was president of the Royal Society.

The family line of succession continued through the following centuries, with Wilton House in Wiltshire becoming the family seat upon the death of Henry Herbert, the seventeeth Earl, in 2003, at which time, his son, William Alexander Sidney Herbert, became eigtheenth Earl of Pembroke and fifteenth Earl of Montgomery.

The Mortimer Family of Wigmore

The Mortimers trace their family line back to the first Roger de Mortemer, (c.990-1087). He was known to have founded the Abbey of St Victor en Caux in Upper Normandy. He was also the first known to have taken on the name Mortimer, from the coastal village of Morte-mer-en-Brai, in the Seine-Maritime Region. He had taken possession of the village and the castle which had been built by William FitzOsbern, first Earl of Hereford.

Roger's son, Ranulf de Mortimer, (sometimes Ralf or Raoul de Mortemer), (c.1070-1104), became a Marcher Lord of Montgomery. He was also Lord of Wigmore in Herefordshire, and had acquired Wigmore Castle in 1086, after William FitzOsbern's son, Roger de Breteuil, was one of the lords who revolted against King William in 1075 and his lands and titles had been forfeited. Wigmore remained the family's principal seat until they moved to live at Ludlow Castle some time in the fourteenth century. A descendant of the family, also named Roger, married Gladys, (known as 'Gladys the Dark'), daughter of Llywelyn the Great, ruler of Wales at that time.

Later Mortimers became Earls of March, of Ulster and of Connaught, and one of the wealthiest families in England. By the end of the fourteenth century, following the murder of Richard II, they were well placed to become heirs to the throne. Schemes and plots abounded to depose Henry Bolingbroke, who had usurped the throne as Henry IV, and place the young Edward Mortimer, heir presumptive and great-grandson of Edward III, on the throne. This dispute led to the outbreak of the Wars of the Roses.

The Wars of the Roses spelled bad times for the family. When Edmund Mortimer, the fifth Earl, died childless, the male line of Mortimers at Wigmore became extinct. However, his sister Anne had married Richard Plantagenet, Duke of Cambridge, and their son Richard, Duke of York, claimed the English throne through his Mortimer ancestry, setting off the long drawn out dispute between the Houses of York and Lancaster.

Richard of York died in battle at Wakefield, but his two sons ascended the throne as Edward IV and Richard III. The House of Mortimer had become inextricably bound up in the royal families of England.

The Llywelyn Family of Gwynedd

This distinguished family name derives from Llywelyn ap Iorwerth, (in Welsh: Llywelyn Fawr), (c.1172-1240), known as Llywelyn the Great, a prince of Gwynedd who eventually became ruler of most of Wales. Following the death of his grandfather, Owain Gwynedd, in 1170, Llywelyn immediately laid claim to power, and by 1200 had become sole ruler of Gwynedd, agreed by treaty with King John of England. He ruled for the best part of forty years, holding back the Anglo-Norman invasion of Wales for much of that time. Llywelyn died in April 1240 at the Cistercian Abbey of Aberconwy, aged sixty-seven, and was buried in Llanrwst Parish Church.

Llywelyn was succeeded by his son Dafydd as prince of Gwynedd, but Henry III denied him his father's rank and authority in Wales, forcing him to agree to a treaty that restricted his power. He was also obliged to hand his illegitimate brother Gryffydd over to the king. Gryffydd had been denied any inheritance of authority or title under the prevailing Welsh laws of succession. He was killed attempting to escape from the Tower of London in 1244. Dafydd himself died without an heir in 1246 and was eventually succeeded by his nephew, Gryffydd's son, who was known as Llywelyn the Last.

The name derives in part from two old Welsh words: 'llyw', which means 'leader', and 'eilun', meaning 'the likeness of'. It first appears in Pembrokeshire in south-west Wales, in what was the ancient Kingdom of Deheubarth. An alternative suggested derivation is a compound of the names of two Celtic deities, Lugus and Belenus. An early written example of the surname is that of Roger Lewelin of Chirk in Shropshire in 1255. Another recorded spelling of the name is Tudor ap Lleyelyn, some time around 1391. The name Lewis is also a derivation, it being an Anglicised version and is a common surname throughout Wales.

The Marshal Family of Pembroke

The Marshal, (or Marshall), name comes from the Old German words 'marah', meaning 'horse' or 'mare', and 'schal', meaning 'servant'. Hence, a marshal was someone who looked after horses. The word was roughly equivalent to the French 'constable'. In time, the Field Marshal, (or Maraschel), would be placed in charge of the cavalry, eventually commander of all the forces on the field of battle.

The Marshal family trace their line back to William Marshal, (sometimes William le Mareschal), (1147-1219), a Norman soldier and influential statesman. His father was John FitzGilbert, hereditary keeper of the king's horses.

William was knighted in 1166, and by 1189, he had been made Earl of Pembroke by King John, becoming protector and retainer to the young Henry III and effective royal regent. He also held the titles of Lord of Longueville in Normandy and Earl of Leinster in Ireland.

During his lifetime, the political environment was particularly volatile, with civil war between Stephen and Matilda, each vying for the English throne. Eventually, Matilda successfully promoted Henry II, (her son by marriage to Geoffrey Plantagenet), to the throne, bringing peace to the kingdom after almost two decades of civil unrest. Some opinions go so far as to say that it was William Marshal who was responsible in the most part for saving the Plantagenet dynasty.

After many years of enmity between Marshal and King John, he came to the king's aid and accompanied him during the sealing of the Magna Carta. William Marshal died at Caversham, near Reading on 14 May 1219, becoming a member of the Order of Knight's Templar on his deathbed and directing that he be buried in the Temple Church, London. He bequeathed a manor in Hertfordshire to the Templars as a gift.

There is also a Scottish connection, with the Marshall Clan being firmly established around Glasgow, where Meledoni Mareschal is known to have lived in 1136, and later that same century, Gillecolm Marescald, who was witness to a charter by William the Lion to the Earl of Strathern. According to the Ragman Rolls of 1296, during the reign of Edward I the Keith Clan, regarded as a sept, or sub-branch of the Marshall Clan, were established as Earls Mareschal of Scotland, even though they did not adopt the Marshall surname.

The Montgomery Family of Montgomeryshire

When the Montgomerys came over from Normandy, they brought the name of the place where they originated with them: Sainte Foi de Montgomery, near Lisieux in Normandy. It was known as Monte Gomeri in 1032, De Monte Gomerico in 1040 and De Monte Gumbri in 1046. The name is a corruption of the Latin 'Mons Gomeris', meaning 'Gomer's mount'. Gomer, the son of Japhet, was an hereditary name of the Gauls.

One of the earliest bearers of the surname was Roger de Mont Gomerie, (Montgomerie or Monte Gummerie), who was born in Lisieux around 1030. An early example of the name in England is that of Hugo de Montgomeri, who is recorded in Staffordshire in the *Domesday Book*.

Following the Battle of Hastings, this same Roger de Montgomerie was also given lands on the Welsh Border by a grateful Duke William, and subsequently it became known as Montgomeryshire.

Created Earl of Shrewsbury, Roger was given a free hand by the king to take into his possession the Welsh Marches, comprising any lands he chose west of the River Severn, by force of arms if need be. Consequently, he entered the lands of Powys with a sizeable army, and seized the castle and town of Tre Valdwyn, (which in Welsh means 'the town of Baldwin'), which had been built by a man of that name, (possibly another Norman migrant). Shortly after occupation, Roger renamed the castle and the town, Montgomery. He was also created Earl of Arundel and also granted vast estates in Sussex around 1067, as well as the Earldom of Shrewsbury in Shropshire in 1071.

The name is also commonly found in south-west Scotland, the same Roger de Mundergumri, (sometimes Montgomery or Montgomerie), was granted the Manor of Eaglesham around Renfrewshire by King Malcolm. It was here where he settled a clan seat. Members of the Scottish branch went on to serve as High Stewards of Scotland. In Ireland the surname has been Gaelicised as MacIomaire and in Scotland as MacGumaraid.

The Morgan Family of Newport

A Celtic-Gaelic name of great antiquity, generally accepted as meaning 'sea chieftain' or 'of the sea', derived from the Old Welsh personal name Morcant, which is incorporated in Glamorgan, (meaning 'son of Morgan'). It is most common in Caernarvonshire in North Wales, in the old kingdom of Gwynedd. Variants on the surname spelling include Morgen, Morgain and Morgaine. The name is not solely limited to Wales; the oldest known written record of the name is in Berkshire, in England, where one John Morgan is listed in the 1214 Curia Rolls. Another John Morgane was burgess of Glasgow in 1419, and Walter Morgan is recorded in the 1273 Hundred Rolls of Oxfordshire.

Perhaps one of the most famous bearers of this family name was Sir Henry Morgan, a privateer, (though many regard him as a pirate), who became Governor of Jamaica in the seventeeth century.

Sir Charles Robinson Morgan was created Baron Tredegar in 1859, having served for many years as Member of Parliament for Breconshire. By 1905, Godrey Charles Morgan was created a Viscount and was Lord Lieutenant of Monmouth.

Frederic Charles John Morgan, the fifth Baron Tredegar, (1908–1962), was the last in line of the peerage, which became extinct on his death in 1962. The seat of the Morgans was at Tredegar House, Newport, South Wales, where they had lived since 1792.

The Nevill Family of Monmouthshire

The Nevill family name is derived from the town of Neuville in the Calvados Region of Normandy, from the Old French 'neuf', meaning 'new', and 'ville', meaning 'town'; hence, a new town or new settlement. The surname was introduced into England by the Normans, and it is first recorded in the *Domesday Book*.

The earliest known line of Nevill descent is from Walter, Earl of Herefordshire and Constable of England, the brother-in-law of Hamelyn, the Norman conqueror of Over Gwent. He became the first Lord of Abergavenny in 1090.

The family held the Monmouthshire estates until they were sold off in the twentieth century. However, these were a relatively minor part of their landed possessions. As Earls of Abergavenny they also had large land holdings in Sussex, Kent, Worcestershire, Warwickshire, Monmouthshire and Herefordshire, as well as the Manor of Sculton Burdeleys in Norfolk.

The title of Baron Abergavenny in the Nevill family dates from the fifteenth century with Edward Nevill, third Baron Bergavenny, who was the youngest son of Ralph de Nevill, first Earl of Westmorland by his second wife, Joan Beaufort, daughter of John of Gaunt, Duke of Lancaster. Nevill was knighted some time after 1426, and in 1438, Bergavenny, as he was now styled, was a Justice of the Peace for Durham. After the death of his first wife, he was summoned to Parliament in 1450 as Edwardo Nevyll de Bergavenny, by which he is held to have become Baron Bergavenny, a title he had inherited through marriage. In May 1784, George Nevill was created first Earl of Abergavenny and Viscount Nevill.

The Barony of Bergavenny was held by his successors, the Earls and Marquesses of Abergavenny, until 1938, when it passed into abeyance between the two daughters of the third Marquess. The current incumbent is Christopher George Charles Nevill, sixth Marquess of Abergavenny, who was born in April 1955.

The family's current principal residence is at Eridge in Kent, where the second Earl built a 'castle' in the early nineteenth century on the pre-existing Eridge Park hunting lodge. The castle was demolished just before the Second World War, and a modern house built, at which time the name reverted to Eridge Park.

The Paget Family of Plas Nywed

Paget, (sometimes Pagett), is a name of Old French origin, a diminutive form of the word 'page', (a page boy – ie. an attendant boy who serves or waits). The added suffix letters 'ett', signify 'little'; hence, a 'little boy', from the original Greek 'paidion', meaning a boy or child. Some have suggested, however, that it refers to the village of Pachet in Normandy, from where the earliest progenitor of the family name probably originated. It is known that William Pachet was a Norman who arrived in England some time around 1180.

Some of the earliest known written examples are Ralph Page, recorded in the 1230 Pipe Rolls of Devonshire, and John Paget whose name appears in the 1359 Court Rolls of Colchester in Essex. Other variant spellings over time have included Padgett, Paggett and Paggitt.

Its most notable family member is William Paget, born some time around 1505. He was employed as Secretary of State by Henry VIII, and built his home at Beaudesert, near Cannock Chase in Staffordshire. He became the first Baron of Beaudesert.

In 1769, Henry Bayly succeeded through his mother, to the title and estates of the Barony of Paget, on the death of Henry, eighth Baron Paget and Earl of Uxbridge, a distant cousin on his mother's side. As ninth Baron Paget, Henry took possession of the Beaudesert estate and changed his surname to Paget. When his father died in 1782, he became third Baron. Plas Newydd in Anglesey was added to his estates and he became Lord Lieutenant of Anglesey.

In 1812, his son, Henry William Paget became Earl of Uxbridge. He had raised a regiment in the 1790s, and distinguished himself at Waterloo, losing his right leg to an enemy cannnonball. When hit he was heard to remark to Wellington, "By God, sir, I've lost my leg!", to which the Iron Duke replied "By God, sir, so you have!". After the war, Paget was created first Marquess of Anglesey.

Unfortunately, in the late nineteenth century, the fifth Marquess was an inveterate spendthrift, and the main home at Beaudesert, as well as a house in London, had to be sold off to pay his debts.

George Charles Henry Victor Paget, the seventh Marquess, (1922-2013), was a British peer who served as a major in the Royal Horse Guards (Blues) in the Second World War and succeeded to the Marquessate on the death of his father Charles in 1947. Styled Lord Anglesey, he was a prolific author of military histories. His home was at Plas Newydd, which, since 1936, has been owned by the National Trust.

The Perrot Family of Pembrokeshire

Perrot, or its several variant spellings of Porritt, Parrott, Perott, Perrett and Porrett, is a name of French origin, and derives from the male given name Pierre, (or Peter). According to some accounts, the family are said to have taken their surname from Perrot Castle in Brittany, which had been built by Guillaume de Perrott in 957. His great-grandson, Sir Richard de Perrott donated ships and men to Duke William in preparation for the invasion of England.

The Perrotts initially settled in Somerset, but were granted lands in Pembrokeshire by Henry I. Later, a descendant, Sir John Perrot, Lord of Haroldston and of Langhorn, built and lived in Carew Castle. He became Lord Deputy of the Province.

Sir John, born in 1518, was a staunch Protestant during the reign of Mary, yet still managed to secure the Lordship and Castle of Carew in Pembrokeshire, by her leave. He also found favour in the court of Elizabeth I, and she appointed him as first Lord of Munster. By 1584, he had been promoted as Lord Deputy of Ireland.

Perrot had enemies. He had been made Vice-Admiral of West Wales, charged with stamping out piracy and smuggling. Local merchants conspired to have him imprisoned in the Tower in 1591 on a charge of high treason. He was found guilty and condemned to death. However, he died of an illness in 1592, (though some thought him poisoned).

Sir John's illegitimate son James failed to secure back his family's forfeited estates, but became Member of Parliament for Haverford West from 1597 to 1614. However, after opposing King Charles' Spanish marriage in 1621, he fell out of royal favour and was banished to Ireland. By 1624, he had returned as Member of Parliament for Pembrokeshire. He was also a member of the prosperous American Virginia Company. He died without issue in February 1636 and was buried at St Mary's Church in Haverford West.

In the nineteenth century, Sir Herbert Charles Perrott was created a baronet in June 1911, becoming the fifth and first Baronet Perrott. Since he left no male heirs, the baronetcies became extinct with his death in 1922.

The Taaffe Family

See: Part Ten: Ireland: The Taaffe Family of County Louth.

The Trevor Family of Brynkinalt

Trevor, (sometimes Trever or Trefor), is a popular locational name in Wales, with places of that name near Llangollen in Denbigh and in Anglesey. It comes from the word 'tre' or 'tref', meaning settlement or habitation, and either mawr', meaning large, or 'Mor', a person's name. Hence, either 'large settlement' or 'Mor's settlement'.

Trevear is also a placename in Cornwall, where the surname may, arguably, have originated, or it may have come from over the Welsh-English border in Herefordshire, where Tudor Trevor was Lord of Hereford and founder of the Tribe of the Marches.

For centuries, Trevor Hall, (now part of Wrexham District), was the seat of the Tudor Trevors, originally built by Bishop John Trevor in 1345, but largely rebuilt by John Lloyd of Glanhavon in 1715, when he married Mary Trevor, heiress to the estate.

In 1662, Marcus, (sometimes Marke), Trevor was created Baron Trevor and Viscount Dungannon in the peerage of Ireland, by Charles II, for his gallantry after wounding Oliver Cromwell at the Battle of Marston Moor.

In 1712, the baronetcy passed to Sir Thomas Trevor, who had been Solicitor General since 1692 and was Lord Privy Seal in 1726. The Duke of Wellington's mother was also a member of the Trevor family

Arthur Hill-Trevor, third Viscount Dungannon, assumed the surname of Trevor by royal licence in 1862, and in 1880 was made Baron Trevor of Brynkinalt in the County of Denbigh.

Marke Charles Hill-Trevor, Baron Trevor, the present incumbent, is director and estate manager at Brynkinalt Sporting Limited, as well as Trevor Estates Company Limited. Brynkinalt Hall, near Chirk, in the County Borough of Wrexham, where he lives with his family, has been home to the Trevor family since it was built in 1612.

The Vaughan Family of Cardigan

The Vaughan surname, (sometimes Vaughn), is derived from the Welsh 'bychan', 'wychan' or 'fychan', (pronounced 'vuh-chan'), all of which refer to a small person. The name is found throughout Wales, but is particularly prevalent in Glamorgan, Monmouthshire, Pembrokeshire, Breconshire, Denbighshire and Radnorshire.

John Vaughan of Trawsgoed, first Viscount Lisburne, (1667-1721), was created Baron Fethard, (or Fethers), and Viscount Lisburne in the peerage of Ireland in 1695, and represented Cardiganshire in Parliament from 1694 to 1698. He, and the following two generations were also Lords Lieutenant of Cardigan.

In 1776, Wilmot Vaughan, fourth Viscount Lisburne, represented Cardiganshire and Berwick-upon-Tweed in the House of Commons and held minor governmental office.

David John Francis Malet Vaughan, ninth Earl of Lisburne, (born 1945), is the current incumbent of the peerage. His family seat remains at Trawsgoed (Crosswood) in Ceredigion (Cardiganshire).

Part Ten

Ireland
Family names in Northern Ireland (Ulster)
& the Republic of Ireland (Eire)

A note about Partition

While the Republic of Ireland is no longer part of Great Britain as such, it occupies around four-fifths of the island of Ireland's land mass. As from the Act of Union on 1 January 1801, Ireland was part of the United Kingdom of Great Britain and Ireland, with the status of a Dominion.

IRELAND
Counties at the Act of Union of 1801

ATLANTIC
OCEAN

ULSTER

CONNAUGHT

MUNSTER

LEINSTER

IRISH
SEA

CELTIC SEA

KEY

Ant = Antrim
Arm = Armagh
Ca = Cavan
Car = Carlow
Cla = Clare
Cor = Cork
Don = Donegal
Dow = Down
Dub = Dublin
Fer = Fermanagh
Gal = Galway
In = Inishowen
KC = Kings County
Ker = Kerry
Ki = Kildare
Kil = Kilkenny
Lei = Leitrim
Lim = Limerick
Lo = Longford
Lon = Londonderry
Lou = Louth
May = Mayo
Me = Meath
Mon = Monaghan
QC = Queens County
Ros = Roscommon
Sli = Sligo
Tip = Tipperary
Tyr = Tyrone
Wat = Waterford
Wex = Wexford
Wic = Wicklow
WM = West Meath

A map depicting counties of Ireland in 1801.

In 1171, Ireland had been annexed to the Angevin Empire by Henry II, who declared himself 'Lord of Ireland', and an uneasy peace reigned throughout the following centuries, with rebellions in 1641, 1798 and 1803, as well as numerous other skirmishes and battles by disgruntled Irish lords.

The 1801 Act of Union saw the Kingdom of Ireland formally united with Great Britain, despite fierce local opposition. The early twentieth century saw outright hostilities break out, which culminated in the Easter Rising in Dublin in 1916. Following the declaration of Irish Independence in 1919, civil war ensued.

The former Kingdom of Ireland became the Irish Free State in 1922 as a result of the Anglo-Irish Treaty, retaining the status of a Dominion until 1937, when a new constitution was adopted. After that date, it became the Republic of Ireland, or Eire, a fully independent nation in its own right.

Many of the family entries that follow represent Ireland's ancient political status at a time before partition. Therefore, for the purposes of what follows, the entire island of Ireland is treated as one single entity.

The Babington Family

See: Part Four: The East Midlands: The Babington Family of Derby.

The Barnewall Family of Crickstown

The Barnewall family name arrived in Ireland some time during the twelfth century, though settlements are known to have existed in Northumberland and in Cambridgeshire following the Norman invasion. It probably came with Michael de Bernvale, (or De Berneval), a Norman knight from Brittany who accompanied William the Conqueror. He is thought to have taken part in the expedition to conquer Ireland in 1067, when he arrived in County Meath.

The name derives from the Old English 'beorna', meaning 'warrior', and 'wella', possibly indicating a burial place. Variations on the surname include Barnwill, Barnwall, Barnwelle and Barnewelle.

An early example of it in use as a family name is that of one William de Bernwell, recorded in the 1307 Records of Norfolk.

In 1461, Sir Robert Barnewell was created first Baron Trimlestown. He was Chief Justice of the King's Bench in Ireland. His son, Christopher, the second Baron, was implicated in the Lambert Simnel conspiracy against Henry VII, but received a royal pardon in 1488. Christopher's son John, the third Baron, served as Lord Chancellor of Ireland from 1534 until his death in 1538.

The twentieth Baron, Anthony Edward Barnewell, born in 1928, died without children in 1997 and the peerage passed to his brother, Raymond Charles Barnewall, twenty-first Baron Trimleston, who, as of 2003, lives in Surrey.

The Blayney Family of Monaghan

Blayney is an ancient Welsh family name that traces its line back to as early as the sixth century, in the person of Brockwel Ysgythrog. The name comes from the Celtic word 'blaen', signifying a place of meeting, or in its plural form, 'blaenau', frequently used to describe the tip, point or top of a mountain, (as in Blaenau Ffestiniog, the historic mining town in Merionethshire in North Wales). The family gave their name to the town of Castleblayney, created on appropriated church land granted to them by James I.

Sir Edward Blayney arrived in Ireland alongside the Earl of Essex towards the end of the sixteenth century and settled in the village of Blaney, on the southern shore of Lough Erne, County Fermanagh, in what is now Northern Ireland. He was created Baron Blayney of Monaghan in 1621.

The Welsh branch of the family line died out in 1795 with the death of Arthur Blayney of Gregynog in Montgomeryshire. Irish Blayney fortunes waxed and waned over the centuries, with Henry Vincent Blayney, the fifth baron, having his title attainted by Parliament for being a supporter of William III. The eighth baron, Reverend Charles Taylor Blaney, was the Rector of the church at Mucklow in County Tyrone in 1739, and served as Dean of Killaloe from 1750 until his death in 1761.

The eleventh Lord Blayney had Blayney Castle, (known more familiarly as Castleblayney), built in a Georgian style in 1800 to designs by Robert Woodgate.

Cadwallader Davis Blayney, the twelfth and last Baron Blayney, (1802-74), became a Tory Member of Parliament in 1820 and later joined the House of Lords. He sold the family's Irish estate in 1852 to Henry Thomas Hope, a wealthy businessman from Surrey. Thereafter the 'castle' was known as Hope Castle, though it is hardly a castle in the truest sense, more a large manor house. Hope's grandson, Francis, a man of extravagant taste, is famous for having sold the Hope Diamond as part of his family's fortune. He was declared bankrupt in 1896.

Cadwallader Blayney retired to live at the Carlton Club in London until his death, without issue, in January 1874, at which point the peerage became extinct.

The Blayney surname is still commonly found in Northern Ireland, especially around County Monaghan.

The Boyle Family of County Cork

In Ireland, the Boyle surname is a variant of O'Boyle and is derived from the Gaelic 'O'Baoighill'. Its precise meaning is vague, but it has been suggested that it might mean 'the male descendant of the rash one', though its significance is somewhat obscure. Others explain it as coming from the Irish word 'gaell', meaning 'pledge'.

As one of the fifty most common surnames in Ireland, the Boyle family were powerful chieftains in County Donegal in medieval times. They had become the Earls of Cork, and acquired extensive land in County Wexford, when a branch migrated from England in the late sixteenth century.

The Scottish Clan Boyle, who settled in lands around Kelburn Castle in Ayrshire, began as Anglo-Norman knights of the surname Beauville, and came from the town of that name near Caen. One David de Boivil, from which the Boyle surname most probably derives, is recorded as witness to a charter in 1164.

In 1660, Francis Boyle was created Baron Boyle and Viscount Shannon. His descendants were active in both Irish and English politics, with Henry Boyle, (1682-1764), being Speaker of the House of Commons in 1733. Others were Members of Parliament for County Cork and for Youghal. Over the years, the family acquired many titles and were elevated as Viscounts Boyle of Bandon and Barons Castle Martyr in the peerage of Ireland.

Richard Henry John Boyle, tenth Earl of Shannon, styled Viscount Boyle, was born in January 1960, and succeeded to the title of tenth Baron of Castle Martyr in County Cork in May 2013.

The Cadogan Family

See: Part Nine: Wales: The Cadogan Family of Merionethshire.

The Cary Family

See: Part Seven: The South-West: The Cary Family of Somerset.

The Carew Family of Wexford

Carew first appears as a surname in the County of Cornwall, shortly after the Norman Conquest. They appear to be descended from Otho through his son, Walter de Windsor and subsequently Gerald de Windsor, (sometimes Gerald FitzWalter), (1070-1136), who built Carew Castle in Pembrokeshire, where he was appointed as Constable. Gerald is thought to have adopted the name 'de Carew' some time around 1100.

The name is of Welsh and Cornish origins, ('Caeriw' in Welsh), but with variants including Cary or Carey, and in Ireland, O'Corrain.

Raymond de Carreu, (known as 'le Gros'), accompanied Richard de Clare, second Earl of Pembroke, (known as 'Strongbow'), in the invasion of Ireland in 1171. Branches of the family are known to have settled in East Cork around Garryvoe and Waterford, while another moved to the West Country and settled in Somerset, Devon and Cornwall.

In 1626, Sir George Carew of Devon became Earl of Totnes. The second Baronet, Sir Alexander Carew, (1609-44), was a member of the 'Long Parliament' in 1640, but was imprisoned in the Tower and executed during the Civil War for betraying the Parliamentarian cause. His equally unfortunate brother, John, sat in the court that tried Charles I in 1649, and after the Restoration, in light of the changing political climate, he was sentenced to death for regicide and was hanged, drawn and quartered.

In the nineteenth century, Carew fortunes fared better. Robert Shapland Carew was created Baron Carew in the peerage of Ireland in 1838, was Member of Parliament for Wexford and Lord Lieutenant of that county in 1831. The family seat of the Irish Carews was Woodstown House in County Wexford, but they also owned Castletown House in County Kildare. The family seat of the West Country branch is at Antony House, near Torpoint in Cornwall.

In April 1904, Gerald Shapland Carew, the fifth Baron Carew of Castle Borough, County Wexford, (1860-1927), married Catherine Conolly, and thereafter the surnames were combined as Conolly-Carew. The seventh Baron, Patrick Thomas Conolly-Carew, born in 1938, succeeded to the title in June 1994. He was a captain in the Royal Horse Guards and an international and Olympic show jumping rider for Ireland. As of 2003, he lived in Naas in County Kildare.

The Clotworthy Family of Antrim

The Clotworthy family name, (sometimes Clatworthy, Clatworth or Cloteworthy), appears first in Anglo-Saxon times and probably came from the village of Clatworthy in Somerset. It is recorded in the *Domesday Book* as 'Clateurde' and held by Ogis on behalf of William, it having been sequestered after the Conquest from a Saxon called Aelfgyth.

Robertus Furlong, no doubt from the village of Clatworthy, added 'de Clotworthy' to his name during the reign of Edward II, (1284-1327). The Furlong part was eventually dropped in favour of simply Clotworthy. The family settled in Devon in the South Molton and Crediton area some time around 1484. Thomas Clotworthy married Abbot Rasheigh, heiress of the Rasleigh Barton estate, and the family lived there until 1708.

In 1603, Thomas's sons, Hugh and Lewis, joined the Earl of Essex in his campaign to Antrim, where Hugh is known to have distinguished himself and was knighted as Sir Hugh Clotworthy for services to James I. Hugh married Mary of Muckamore, and their son, Sir John Clotworthy, was in 1660 created Baron of Loughneagh and Viscount Massereene, an Irish peerage which still remains in the family. He was also at one time High Sheriff of Antrim and in 1634 he was a member of the Irish House of Commons representing County Antrim.

The peerage became extinct on the death of the fourth Earl without male issue in 1816, at which time the viscountcy and baronetcy of Lough Neagh passed to his daughter Harriet Skeffington, whose husband, Thomas Foster, adopted the surname of Skeffington. In 1824, he inherited the titles of Viscount Ferrard and Baron Oriel of Collon from his mother.

Through politics and propitious marriage, the Clotworthys prospered in power and wealth, as evidenced by Clotworthy John Eyre Foster-Skeffington, fourth Viscount Ferrard who was Lord Lieutenant of Louth in 1879, and Algernon William John Clotworthy Skeffington, the fifth Viscount, who was Lord Lieutenant of Antrim in 1916.

The current peerage is held by Sir John David Clotworthy Whyte-Melville Foster Skeffington, fourteenth Viscount Massereene and seventh Viscount Ferrard, who is also styled Baron Oriel. In 1996, he oversaw the sale of Chilham Castle, the family's ancestral home in Kent. The family seat is now in North Yorkshire.

The Coote Family of Castle Cuffe

In the year 1600, Sir Charles Coote, (1581-1642), a successful soldier and administrator, arrived in Ireland as captain of the 100th Foot during the Nine Years War. He took part in the Siege of Kinsale and defeated the rebellious O'Neills. He was to be instrumental in suppressing the Irish rebellion of 1641.

After the conflict, he was appointed as Provost Marshal of Connaught and made a Baron of Castle Cuffe in Queen's County, where he was elected as Member of the Irish Parliament in 1629. Of his two sons, Charles became Earl of Mountrath in 1660, and Richard became Baron Coote of Coloony.

The Cootes inherited substantial plantation lands in the midlands of Ireland, and by 1660, Charles Coote was made Earl of Mountrath by the restored Charles II. He also built Rush Hall near Mountrath, which was the family's main home for several generations.

Succeeding family members continued in politics, with Members of Parliament for Knaresborough, for Castle Rising, and for Hedon. In 1800, Charles Henry Coote, seventh Earl of Mountrath, was created Baron Castle Coote, but upon his death in 1802, the peerage became extinct. Stanley Victor Coote, (1862–1925), was High Sheriff of Roscommon in 1900.

The Cunningham Family of Aughnamullen

See: Part Eight: Scotland: The Cunningham Family of Glencairn.

The Dalzell Family

See: Part Eight: Scotland: The Dalzell Family of Motherwell.

The Deburgh Family of County Galway

The Burgh family, (sometimes De Bourke or DeBurgh, and in Irish, Connacht), is first found in Connaught, on the west coast of Ireland in 1177, when William FitzAdelm de Burgo was made Chief Governor, with a commensurate grant of lands in the region, shortly after Henry II annexed Ireland to become part of the Angevin Empire that by the end of the twelfth century stretched from Scotland to the Pyrenees.

The surname is taken to mean a hilltop fortress, from the Old English 'burh' or 'buri', or its Anglo-Saxon derivation 'burg'. The prefix 'de' comes from the French, meaning 'of' or 'from'; hence, 'of, or from, the hilltop fortress'.

One of the first known written records of the name in use as a family name is that of Ailricus de Burc, who was listed in the *Domesday Book* in the County of Suffolk.

The second Earl of Ulster, Richard (Óg) de Burgh, (also known as Richard the Younger and sometimes as 'the Red Earl'), was born around 1259, and was also third Baron of Connaught. He became one of the most powerful men in thirteenth and fourteenth century Ireland, being a close friend of Edward I of England. His daughter Elizabeth was the second wife of Robert the Bruce of Scotland. He died in 1326 in Athassel Monastery in County Tipperary.

In 1327, William de Burgh was summoned to Parliament as Lord Burgh, as was Sir Thomas Burgh in 1487, the surname by now being simply known as Burgh, the 'de' part having been dropped. When Robert, the fourth Lord Burgh, died in 1602, the peerage fell into abeyance between his sisters, where it passed through marriage into the Leigh family, when Alexander Henry Leith succeeded as fifth Lord Burgh in May 1916. He became Lord Lieutenant of the Isle of Wight and Justice of the Peace for Hampshire. He had served as a lieutenant colonel in the Gordon Highlanders and fought in the Sudan Campaign of 1898.

Alexander Gregory Disney Leith, eighth Baron Burgh, (born in 1958), succeeded to the title in July 2001.

The De Clare Family

See: Part Five: East Anglia: The De Clare Family of Sussex.

The De Courcy Family

See: Part Seven: The South-West: The De Courcy Family of Somerset.

The FitzGerald Family of Munster

The FitzGeralds were originally an Irish-Norman or Welsh-Norman dynasty, who have been peers of Ireland since the fourteenth century. They were first found in Munster, and are sometimes referred to as the 'Geraldines'. They were established by the sons and grandsons of Gerald FitzWalter of Windsor, Lord of Manstephan, (c.1075–1135). Gerald was a Welsh knight, a participant in the Angevin invasion of

Ireland in 1169-70, and the oldest known ancestor of the FitzGerald dynasty. The prefix 'fitz' comes from the Old Norman French 'fils'. Hence, FitzGerald means 'the sons of Gerald', though it is generally reserved for those born out of wedlock.

Maurice FitzGerald, the first to use the surname, received the Barony of Offaly in 1176. He was Captain of Desmond Castle in Kinsale and for a time was Lord Justice of Ireland. The first recorded spelling of the family name is that of FitzGerald (or in its Gaelic form 'Mac Gerailt'), which was dated around 1400 in *The Annals of Ireland*.

By 1316, the FitzGeralds were Earls of Kildare, later made Marquesses of Kildare and from 1766, Dukes of Leinster. Another branch of the family were Barons, and later Earls of Desmond.

The Kildare branch of the family was very powerful and had castles in Maynooth and Kilkea. The Munster branch were located at Dingle and were known as the Knights of Kerry. They had castles in Coshmore and Coshbride in Waterford. Glin Castle, a few miles west of Foynes on the Shannon estuary, is the seat of Desmond FitzGerald, twenty-ninth Knight of Glin, whose family has been in continuous possession for seven hundred years.

In 1835, William Vesey-FitzGerald was created Baron FitzGerald. He was Member of Parliament for Clare, for Newport, for Lostwithiel and for Ennis. He was also President of the Board of Control, Lord Lieutenant of Clare and a Privy Counsellor.

Garrett FitzGerald, who was born into a political and literary family in Dublin in February 1926, and died in May 2011, was Taoiseach of the Irish Parliament, a statesman and author.

The FitzMaurice Family of Kerry

The FitzMaurice surname shares a common ancestry with the FitzGeralds, and originates in early Anglo-Norman French. In Gaelic Irish, the name is 'Mac Muiris', and they hold the title Marquesses of Lansdoone, a branch of the Lords of Lixnaw in County Kerry. The family and clan are named after Maurice, the son of Raymond le Gros, an early Cambro-Norman invader. The first record of its use as a family name is that of Thomas FitzMaurice, the first Lord of Kerry, during the reign of King Rory O'Connor. He may be the same Thomas FitzMaurice FitzGerald who was born at Banada Castle in 1229, the son of Maurice FitzGerald. It is thought that he founded the Franciscan Ardfert Friary in about 1253.

In 1537, Edmond FitzMaurice, the eleventh Baron, was created Viscount Kilmaule, though both peerages became extinct on his death in 1541.

In 1809, John Henry Petty-FitzMaurice, who had previously succeeded to the Marquessate of Lansdowne, died childless and the peerage fell to his half brother, who was known as Lord Petty. He was an influential Whig politician and served as Chancellor of the Exchequer in the English Parliament, as Home Secretary, and as Lord President of the Council on numerous occasions up to 1852.

Charles Maurice Petty-FitzMaurice, ninth Marquess of Lansdowne, (born in February 1941), is Earl of Shelburne and at the time of writing serves as Vice-Lord Lieutenant of Wiltshire.

The FitzWilliam Family of Gethampton

One of the earliest records of the family name is that of Ralph FitzWilliam, who was summoned to attend Parliament as Lord FitzWilliam in June 1295, although it is believed to have been found in Buckinghamshire where the family were granted lands by William Rufus. They are recorded as holding Gatehampton, (Gethampton), which according to the *Domesday Book* was held by Miles Crispin for the king, by which time it had become the seat of the English branch of the FitzWilliam family. Another early record of the name is that of Johannes Fitz William, who was listed in the Yorkshire Poll Tax of 1379.

A head of the family, Sir Thomas FitzWilliam, born around 1519, initially lived at Baggotrath, but later moved the family seat to Merion Castle. He was Member of Parliament for County Dublin in 1559 and Vice-Treasurer of Ireland in the same year. By 1564, he had become Sheriff of the county, and was knighted by Sir Henry Sidney at Drogheda in the autumn of 1566.

By 1600, the family had become Constables of Wicklow Castle, a frontier fortification, facing hostile Irish tribes led by the O'Byrnes. It was Sir Thomas who was responsible for setting the geographical boundaries of Wicklow County.

In 1658, William FitzWilliam was created Viscount Milton and Earl FitzWilliam, and about a century later, another William was made Lord Lieutenant of Ireland.

Both the Yorkshire and Irish branches of the family have distinguished themselves in the political arena over the centuries: they have variously been Members of Parliament for Peterborough, Northamptonshire, Malton, Wakefield, Fowey, Wilton and Wicklow, as well as being Lords Lieutenants of Ireland and of the former West Riding of Yorkshire.

William Thomas George Wentworth-FitzWilliam, tenth Earl FitzWilliam, was the last Earl FitzWilliam. He died in 1979 at Wentworth Woodhouse, Yorkshire and his peerages became extinct.

The Hamilton Family of Strabane

In April 1603, James VI of Scotland, (James I of England), conferred on the Honourable Claud Hamilton, third son of James Hamilton and second Earl of Arran, the title Lord of Paisley. His son, James Hamilton, was created Earl Abercorn and Lord of Paisley, Hamilton, Mountcastle & Kirkpatrick, (all in Scotland). His successors had the Barony of Strabane and Earldoms of Abercorn added to their collection.

By 1660, a family descendant, the sixth Earl of Abercorn, was also Baron of Dunalong in Tyrone and of Nenagh in Tipperary County. The seventh Earl, created Marquess of Abercorn in 1790, was in both the English and Irish Privy Councils, and sat in the Westminster Parliament. He was made a Knight of the Garter in 1805. The second Marquess served as Lord Lieutenant of Ireland from 1866 to 1868 and was elevated as Marquess Hamilton and made Duke of Abercorn in the peerage of Ireland.

Family members have held posts of high prestige over the years, including the Governorship of Ireland, Lords Lieutenant and Members of Parliament for Donegal, Fermanagh and South Tyrone.

The family seat is at Baronscourt Castle, a country house on the Barons Court Estate near Newtownstewart in Omagh, and the Dukes of Abercorn and their families are buried in the cemetery at Baronscourt Parish Church.

James Hamilton, Knight of the Garter, became fifth Duke of Abercorn in the peerage of Ireland on the death of his father in June 1979. The late Diana, Princess of Wales was a great-granddaughter of the third Duke of Abercorn.

The Lambart Family of County Cavan

The Lambart, (sometimes Lambard), family name derives from the Old German given name Lambert, which is composed of two elements, 'land' and 'berht', meaning 'bright land'. After the Conquest, it was usually spelled 'Landbeorht', though the name of Gozelinus Lamberti is recorded in the Yorkshire section of the *Domesday Book*, and later, Richard Lambert is entered in the Pipe Rolls of Hampshire for the year 1148.

The name can be traced back before 1004, to three brothers, Baldwin, Ralph and Hugh Lambert, and, following Hastings, a Norman knight named Haco Lambert is known to have been granted lands by the Conqueror, settling in Malham Dale in the West Riding of Yorkshire.

An early notable family member was Lord Oliver Lambart, who was created first Baron of Cavan in 1618. He had distinguished himself in the Anglo-Spanish War of 1585, and later in 1599, during the Nine Years' War, he served with Lord Essex in the Irish Campaign, commanding troops in County Wexford. In 1601, he was made Governor of Connaught and in 1613 he became High Sheriff of Cavan, also serving as Member of Parliament in the Irish House of Commons. His descendants became Viscounts Kilcoursie and Earls of the County of Cavan, Members of Parliament for Bossinney and for Kilbeggan in Ireland, as well as for Somerset South in England.

The family also boasted military men amongst its number, including Frederick Rudolph Lambart, the tenth Earl, known as

Viscount Kilcoursie, (1865-1946), who fought in the Second Boer War and who was an army commander during the First World War, a Field-Marshal and a Chief of the Imperial General Staff.

The thirteenth Earl, Roger Cavan Lambart, born in September 1944, was the last heir to the title.

The MacDonnell Family of County Clare

The MacDonnells, (sometimes McDonnells), came to County Clare and Fermanagh in Ireland in the thirteenth century, from Scottish immigrants, and in time became Earls of Antrim and Chief Heralds of Ireland. Their original name in Gaelic was Mac Donhnall, (or Mac Dhomhnaill), which means 'son of Donhnall'. The Scottish clan MacDonald is a variant on the surname.

In the sixteenth century, Sorley Boy McDonnell came from Scotland to consolidate McDonnell territory in Ireland and made his main base at Dunluce Castle. The castle is still owned by the MacDonnell family, but is nowadays managed by the Northern Irish Environment Agency.

On James I's accession in 1603, Randal MacSorley MacDonnell, fourth son of Sorley Boy MacDonnell, was granted extensive lands in the district of the Route and the Glynns, amounting to three hundred thousand acres between Larne and Coleraine. In 1618, he was created Viscount Dunluce, and in 1620 was made first Earl of Antrim. By 1645, this had been elevated to a Marquessate.

Upon Randal's death, his daughter and co-heir, Anne Katharine MacDonnell, inherited the peerages, becoming Countess of Antrim and Viscountess Dunluce in her own right. From there it passed to her sister Charlotte, who married Admiral Mark Robert Kerr and was henceforth known as Charlotte Kerr, third Countess of Antrim. Her son, Hugh, inherited the title fourth Earl and resumed the MacDonnell surname

During the English Civil War, family titles were attainted several times by Oliver Cromwell, before being finally reinstated following the Restoration of Charles II.

Randal Alexander St John McDonnell, styled Viscount Dunluce, is heir to the Earldom of Antrim. He divides his time between London and the ancestral seat, Glenarm Castle in County Antrim. He is a member of the Irish Landmark Trust, is a Trustee of the Clan Donald Lands Trust and of the Glenarm Buildings Preservation Trust.

The Murray Family

See: Part Eight: Scotland: The Murray Family of Moray.

The Needham Family of Tralee

Needham is an ancient Kerry name, originally 'O'Niadh' and commonly found in Tralee, though it probably originated in England. The Earls of Kilmorey in County Down were Needhams, descendants of Thomas de Nedeham of Derbyshire, who some time around 1330, took his surname from a place of that name. Many spellings and variants exist, including Needam, Neden, Nedin, Nedon, Needon and Needing.

The origin of the name comes from Old English 'ned', meaning 'need' and 'ham', signifying a village or settlement. Evidently, from the earliest times, the place provided a meagre subsistence for its inhabitants. The first recorded spelling of the name is that of John de Nedham, dated 1275 in the Hundred Rolls of Derbyshire, during the reign of Edward I.

In 1625, Robert Needham was created Viscount Kilmorey, and the peerage survived in the family for at least two centuries, at which time, in 1822, Francis Needham was created Viscount Newry and Morne, as well as Earl of Kilmorey.

Several succeeding generations were Members of Parliament for Newry and Morne. In 1936, Francis Charles Adelbert Henry Needham, was a Privy Counsellor and Lord Lieutenant of County Down.

The present incumbent of the peerage is Richard Francis Needham, sixth Earl of Kilmorey, who served as Under Secretary of State for Northern Ireland, (1985-92), and as Minister of State for Trade, (1992-5). The Needham estate, known as Mourne Park, is near Kilkeel in County Down.

The Nugent Family of Westmeath

The Nugents arrived in Ireland following the Norman Conquest of England. Records show that in 1172, one Gilbert de Nogent accompanied Sir Hugh de Lacy on an expedition to Ireland. He married De Lacy's daughter, and was granted the Barony of Delvin in County Westmeath as a dowry. His grandfather, Fulke de Bellesme, had been granted large estates around Winchester.

The family originated from Belesme in Normandy, where an ancestor, Evas, (or Ives), de Belesme, had been a powerful Lord and landowner up to the time of his death in 993. Evas' son, William, by a second marriage to Adelais, inherited the Lordship of Damfort and Nogent, but died without issue in 1026, so that the estate, and accompanying power base, descended through his wife, Millicent, into her family, who were Counts of Champagne, and through her kinsman, Geoffrey, to his son Rotron de Nogent. Rotron was the first known to use the family name, derived from the Nogent lordship held by the family.

The prefix 'Nogent' is attached to a number of French towns, usually situated on the banks of a river, such as Nogent-sur-Seine, Nogent-le-Rotrou and Nogent-sur-Marne. Over time the name was corrupted into its most common form – Nugent. Spelling variations include Nugent, Newgent, Neugent, Newgant, Newgeant and Nujent.

It was Rotron's son, Hugh, who had accompanied William the Conqueror and fought at Hastings. Three of his sons are known to have accompanied Hugh de Lacy, (sometimes Lacie), to Ireland in 1172.

By the sixteenth century, the Nugents had built several castles in the Westmeath region, including at Carlanstown, Loughegar, Drumcree and Donore. In 1621, Richard Nugent, seventh Baron Delvin, was created Earl of Westmeath, a title that has descended through the family for many generations.

By 1822, George Thomas John Nugent had been created Marquess of Westmeath, and within a decade he was made Lord Lieutenant of the county. Upon his death in 1871, the Marquessate became extinct and the Earldom passed to Anthony Francis Nugent.

The present incumbent is William Anthony Nugent, thirteenth Earl of Westmeath. He lives in Bradfield, Berkshire, was a captain in the Royal Artillery until 1961, and a Senior Master at St Andrew's School in Pangbourne from 1980 to 1988.

The O'Brien Family of Thomond

The O'Brien Family, (sometimes O'Brian), are a noble house that was founded in the tenth century by Brian Boru, (sometimes Boramha or Boruma), of the Irish Dalcassian tribe. O'Brian descendants ruled the Kingdom of Munster until the twelfth century.

In July 1543, Murrough O'Brien, Prince of Thomond, was created Baron Inchiquin and Earl of Thomond, with grants of estates amounting to almost forty thoudand acres in County Clare, over one thousand acres in County Limerick and more than fifteen thousand acres in County Cork. On his death, his son, Dermod, inherited the Barony of Inchiquin.

Dermod's great-great-grandson, the sixth Baron, was a prominent military leader during the Irish Confederate Wars, (1643–48), initially for the English Parliament, then changing allegiances, he became a Royalist commander during Oliver Cromwell's Irish campaign between 1649 and 1653.

In 1690, William O'Brien, the fourth Earl, was Governor of Jamaica. He married the first Countess of Orkney in 1720 and was succeeded by his son-in-law and nephew, another by the name of Murrough O'Brien, who became Marquess of Thomond in 1800. By 1843, Sir Lucius O'Brien, the fifth Baronet, was Lord Lieutenant of Clare, and in 1879, his successor, Edward Donough O'Brien also held the post.

At the time of writing, Conor Myles John O'Brien, eigtheenth Baron Inchiquin, (born 17 July 1943), retains the hereditary peerage.

The Pakenham Family (Longford)

See: Part Five: East Anglia, The Pakenham Family of Suffolk.

The Pippard Family of County Louth

Pippard, (sometimes De Pipard), is an Anglo-Norman name, brought to Ireland by Norman settlers, and probably derives from the township of Manneville la Pipard in Normandy, from where the family acquired its surname. It first appears in the east coast town of Drogheda in County Louth, Leinster, (named after Lugh, a god of the ancient Irish). It was here that one Gilbert de Angulo, (known as 'Strongbow'), was granted lands by Henry II. However, these were forfeited for his part in the rebellion against Richard I in 1195 and along with his brothers Phillip and William, he was outlawed. However, he was pardoned by King John in 1206 and his lands restored to him. One of his sons became Baron Navan, while the other became Justiciary of Ireland.

There are several other spellings of the name, including Pipard, Peppard, Pappard, De Pappard, Pepper and Peperd. It may have originated from 'peper', from the Latin word 'piper', which means pepper, a common professional name given to a pepperer or spicer. Early examples of its use as a surname include Roger Peivre and Alice Peper in the Fine Court Rolls of Essex in 1198 and 1241 respectively.

Records show that Ralph Pipard was summoned to the English Parliament as Lord Pipard in 1299, though this peerage seems to have died with him in 1301.

The Court of Chancery in Ireland lists a case where Henry Pippard sued the Mayor of Drogheda in 1759 in a dispute over a lease, a case which was brought to the House of Lords in Westminster, and in 1688, Christopher Pippard petitioned the Corporation of Drogheda for an extension on leases which he held in the town. Another Christopher Pippard, (or possibly the same man), listed as a merchant, the son of Ignatius Pippard, had his houses seized for debts.

Migrations during the potato famine of 1740-1 saw many Pippards leaving Ireland for America, where Peppard became its more common spelling and pronunciation. The late American actor, George Peppard, (1928-94), is a typical example.

The Plunket Family of County Louth

The Plunket surname, (sometimes Plunkett), is of Norman French origin and is believed to be a corruption of the word 'blanchet', meaning simply 'white'. The Gaelic form is 'Pluinceid'. It was introduced after the Anglo-Norman invasion of Ireland in 1170, and may have been derived from the village of Plouquenet in the Ile-et-Vilaine region of Brittany. The placename perhaps originally comes from the Breton 'plou', (from the Latin 'plebes', meaning 'people'). Some accounts cite the Middle English word 'blaunket', or the Old French 'blanquet', meaning a blanket, or a maker of blankets, as the most likely interpretation of the name.

A few spelling variations include Plunkit and Plonket. The name is found commonly, (although not quite exclusively), in County Louth in the Province of Leinster, on the east coast of Ireland, and in County Meath and in Dublin.

There have been a number of notable Irish Plunketts, including Thomas Plunkett, who was Chief Justice of County Louth in 1316. In June 1541, Oliver Plunkett was created Baron Louth, and by 1629, Matthew Plunkett was Lord Lieutenant of Louth & Drogheda.

Joseph Plunkett was a leader of the Easter Rising rebellion of 1916, when Irish nationalists seized several key buildings in Dublin and declared Ireland an independent republic. It took the British Army five days to regain control of the city, when Plunkett was arrested and sentenced to death by firing squad.

John Oliver Plunkett, who was born in 1952, succeeded as the seventeeth Baron Louth in 2014. The family seat is Louth Hall, near Ardee in County Louth.

The Ponsonby Family of County Kilkenny

The Ponsonbys first came to Ireland in the seventeeth century, when John Ponsonby of Hale Hall in Cumberland, (Cumbria), accompanied Oliver Cromwell. He was knighted for his service in the Parliamentarian cause and granted the estate of Kildalton in County Kilkenney, becoming its Member of Parliament. His son, William, distinguished himself at the Siege of Londonderry. He was created Baron Bessborough in 1721 and a year later was elevated as Viscount Duncannon.

The surname may be derived from the Parish of Ponsonby in the former County of Cumberland, though the family was known to have originated in Picardy in Northern France, when Ponson arrived in England with William's Conquest. With the addition of the Old English suffix 'by', Ponsonby might also mean 'the estate (or settlement) of Ponson'.

The family had high political ambitions, with several members representing constituencies in Parliament, as Members of Parliament for Derby, Harwich, Saltash, Knaresborough and Nottingham. A later William Ponsonby became Lord Lieutenant for Kilkenny in 1758, and by 1846, John William Ponsonby was Lord Lieutenant of Ireland. A notable family member was Vere Brabazon Ponsonby, who was Governor General of Canada from 1931 to 1935.

Frederick Edward Neuflize Ponsonby, the tenth Earl of Bessborough, (1913-93), styled Viscount Duncannon, was on the staff of the League of Nations, and served under Prime Minister Alec Douglas-Home as Parliamentary Secretary for Science, before becoming a Member of the European Parliament in 1973. When he died in 1993, the English earldom became extinct, while the Irish earldom of Bessborough passed to his cousin, Arthur Mountifort Longfield Ponsonby. His son, Miles, succeeded as twelfth earl in the Irish peerage, and is the present incumbent of the title.

The Preston Family of Drumahaire

The Irish Preston Family were from Drumahaire in County Antrim, and date their line back to Phillip de Preston, who was living in Preston, Lancashire in 1270, which is where their surname comes from. It derives from two Old English words 'prest', meaning 'priest', and 'ton', signifying a farmstead or settlement.

Roger Preston, was made Justice of Common Pleas in the first year of Edward III's reign and Justice of the King's Bench in 1326. A branch of the family came to Ireland when another Sir Robert Preston bought the Manor of Gormanston in County Dublin and County Meath from Almeric de Saint-Armand. Robert was the Chief Justice, Keeper of the Great Seal and Lord Chancellor of Ireland. He died in the reign of Richard II.

In August 1478, yet a third Robert Preston was created Viscount Gormanston. In the mid-seventeeth century, Jenico Preston was Lord Lieutenant of Meath. A later descendant, Jenico William Joseph Preston was Governor of the Leeward Islands, of British Guiana, and of Tasmania.

Jenico evidently remains a popular name in the family, as Jenico Nicholas Dudley Preston, seventeeth Viscount Gormanston, fourth Baron Gormanston, (born in November 1939), is the Premier Viscount of Ireland. He is an art connoisseur and lives in Kensington, London. His ancestral seat is Gormanston Castle in County Meath. It is no longer in the family's possession, though his descendants lived there for the best part of seven hundred years. Nowadays it is fully maintained by the Franciscan Order of Friars Minor, who purchased the castle some time around 1950. The Franciscans opened it, shortly afterwards, as Gormanston College, a boys' boarding school.

The Roche Family of Limerick

The first Roche surname, (sometimes Roch, De Roche, De Rupe or De LaRoche), in Ireland was found in Cork, Wexford and Limerick in Munster Province, south-west Ireland, where lands were granted to the so-called Strongbow settlers, (after Gilbert de Angulo, Earl of Pembroke, known as Strongbow). He was appointed king's Viceroy in 1173, and a large number of Norman, Flemish, English and Welsh settlers followed him into Ireland.

The family name comes from the Norman French 'roche', simply meaning 'rock' and applied to people living by a rocky outcrop or in a craggy landscape.

The earliest record of the name in Ireland is that of Richard FitzGodebert de Rhos, son of Godebert Flendrensis of Rhos of

Pembrokeshire in Wales. In 1167, he was employed by King Diarmait MacMurchada of Ireland, (sometimes MacMurrough), (1100–71), to assist in his civil war against the O'Rourkes and the O'Connors, where he commanded a mixed force of Norman, Flemish and Welsh archers.

David de Rupe, ('the Great'), who died some time before 1488, was the first to take the name De la Roche when he was granted Rosscarbery, (modern day Ross), and was recognised as Viscount Roche of Fermoy by Edward IV in 1461.

Thus the Roche family name descended through the centuries. In 1856, Edmund Burke Roche was created Baron Fermoy. He was Member of Parliament for County Cork from 1837 to 1855 and Lord Lieutenant of the county from 1857 to 1874.

Patrick Maurice Burke Roche, the sixth Baron Fermoy, who was born in October 1967, was a first cousin of the late Princess Diana of Wales. He was Page of Honour to Elizabeth the Queen Mother between 1982 and 1984, and inherited the barony when his father died in 1984.

The St Lawrence Family of Howth

The St Lawrence family descended from Christopher St Lawrence who died in 1430, a few years after he had been elevated to the peerage of Ireland as Baron Howth. The third and fourth Barons both served as Lord Chancellor of Ireland.

The family seat has been at Howth Castle in County Dublin for about 800 years. It was begun in 1177, when Almeric, the Lord of Howth, settled in Ireland. Tradition has it that he won a great battle and took the land on the Feast Day of St Lawrence, (10 August), and assumed the family name in gratitude for his victory. This so-called 'castle' would have been a fairly basic wooden stockade, but it was replaced by a stone structure later. The earliest extant parts of the present-day castle date from the mid-fifteenth century. The whole structure was extensively altered by succeeding generations, most notably in 1738, when it took on its present form. In 1911, further enhancements were added by the celebrated architect, Sir Edwin Lutyens.

The Barony of Howth continued down through the generations until, in 1767, Thomas St Lawrence, the fifteenth Baron Howth, was created Viscount St Lawrence and Earl of Howth. Later, in October 1881, William Ulick Tristram St Lawrence, the fourth Earl, was Member of Parliament for Galway. When he died in 1909, the peerage became extinct.

The family seat at Howth Castle still belongs to the female descendants of the family line, the Gaisford-St Lawrences, there having been no surviving male heirs.

The Taaffe Family of County Louth

This surname probably originated in Wales and arrived in Ireland with the Anglo-Norman invasion which took place over the decade following Hastings. The family settled in what became the modern province of Leinster, though within a century they had spread far and wide across Ireland, with Richard Taaffe occupying Lumpnagh Castle as Sheriff of Dublin in 1295. He was also Sheriff of County Louth in 1315.

The surname is generally assumed to be a derivative of the personal name Dafydd, the Welsh form of David, where 'Taff' or 'Taffy' remains a common diminutive of the name.

Sir John Taaffe was created Baron Ballymote and Viscount Taaffe of Corren in 1628, and his immediate descendant, Theobald Taaffe, the second Viscount, became Earl of Carlingford in 1661. He was killed at the Battle of the Boyne fighting against William of Orange, at which point his titles and estates were forfeited. It was only after a great deal of petitioning that they were restored to the family.

Eduard Graf von Taaffe, eleventh Viscount Taaffe, had a distinguished political career in the service of the Habsburgs, the Austrian monarchy, and served for two terms as Minister President of Austria under Francis Joseph I, and remained loyal to the Emperor. Henry Taaffe, (1895-1919), fought against Great Britain during the Great War and on the death of Richard Taaffe, the last male descendant of the family, the peerage became extinct.

The Vaughan Family

See: Part Nine: Wales: The Vaughan Family of Cardiganshire.

The Wingfield Family of County Wexford

Wingfield is the family name of the Viscounts Powerscourt in the peerage of Ireland. It first appears in Suffolk, where the ancient Saxon village of that name dates back before the Norman Conquest. The name derives from the personal name of a man, probably called Wiga, and the Old English word 'feld', a field; hence, 'the field belonging to Wiga'. There are several other places called Wingfield, notably in Bedfordshire and Derbyshire, as well as that in Suffolk. Early records show the spelling 'Winfeld' in 1200 and 'Wynnefeld' around 1002. Wingfield, also known in Suffolk, was recorded in 1035 as 'Wingefeld'.

Wingfield is also a Civil Parish in County Wexford in Ireland, where the family finally settled, and took their surname. Their family seat was eventually created at Powerscourt House, near Enniskerry in County Wicklow.

The Viscountcy of Powerscourt was first created in 1618 for Richard Wingfield, a military man who was Chief Governor of Ireland. He died without male descendants, and after a brief period of abeyance it was recreated in 1665 for Folliott Wingfield, and again in 1744 for another Richard Wingfield, who was also created Baron Wingfield.

In 1756, Edward Wingfield was Member of Parliament for Stockbridge. There followed four more generations of successive Richard Wingfields, before Mervyn Richard Wingfield, (1880-1947), was made Lord Lieutenant of Wicklow in 1910, and became a member of the ill-fated Senate of Southern Ireland.

In 2015, his titles descended to his great-grandson, Mervyn Anthony Wingfield, the eleventh Viscount Powerscourt.

Bibliography

ADDISON, William, *Understanding English Surnames*, (Batsford, London, 1978).

ANGUS-BUTTERWORTH, Lionel M, *Old Cheshire Families & Their Seats*, (E. J. Morten, 1970).

ARTHUR, William M. A, *An Etymological Dictionary of Family and Christian Names With an Essay on their Derivation and Import*, (Sheldon, Blake, Bleeker & Company, 1857).

ATKINS, Paul, *Seven Households: Life in Cheshire & Lancashire 1582-1774*, (Arley Hall Press, 2002).

Automobile Association, *Illustrated Guide to Britain*, (Drive Publications, 1976).

BAINES, Edward, *History of the County Palatine & Duchy of Lancaster*, (1836).

BARDSLEY, Charles Waering Endell, *English Surnames: Their Sources and Significations*, (Chatto & Windus, 1884).

BARDSLEY, Charles Waering Endell, *A Dictionary of English and Welsh Surnames*, (Chatto & Windus, 1901).

BARLOW, Frank, *The Feudal Kingdom of England 1042-1216*, (Longman, 1955-99).

BINDOFF, S.T, (ed.), *History of Parliament: the House of Commons 1509-1558*. (1982).

BLACK, George Fraser, *The Surnames of Scotland*, (1946).

BUCHAN, G. H, *A Brief History of the Duttons of Dutton*.

BURKE, John B, *Roll of the Battle Abbey*, (1998).

Catherine, Duchess of Cleveland & Battle Abbey, *The Battle Abbey Roll: With Some Account of the Norman lineages, 3 vols*, (J. Murray, 1889, London).

COKAYNE, G. E, *The Complete Peerage*, (Alan Sutton Publishing, 2000).

CROSBY, Alan, *A History of Lancashire*, (Phillimore 1998).

CROSBY, Alan, *A History of Cheshire*, (Phillimore, 1996).

CROSTON, James, *County Families of Lancashire and Cheshire*, (Forgotten Books).

FARRER, W. & BROWNBILL, J, (eds.), *A History of the County of Lancaster, Volume 3*, (*Victoria County History*, London, 1907).

FIENNES, Joslin, *The Origins of English Surnames*, (Robert Hale Ltd, 2015).

FLETCHER, Mike, *The Making of Manchester*, (Wharncliffe Books, 2003).

GUPPY, Henry Brougham, *Homes of Family Names in Great Britain*, (1890).

HIGHAM, N.J, *The Norman Conquest*, (Phoenix Mill UK, 1995).

Hudson's Historic Houses & Gardens, (Hudson Media Ltd, 2015).

HYLTON, Stuart, *A History of Manchester*, (Phillimore, 2004).

KENYON, Denise, *The Origins of Lancashire*, (*Origins of the Shire*), (Manchester University Press,1991).

KIDD, Charles, (ed.), *DeBrett's Peerage and Baronetage*, (DeBrett's Peerage Ltd).

Lancashire Federation of Womens' Institutes, *The Lancashire Village Book*, (Countryside Books).

LOWER, Mark Antony, *Patronymica Britannica: a Dictionary of the Family Names of the United Kingdom*, (J. R. Smith, 1860).

LOYD, Lewis C, & DOUGLAS, David C, *The Origins of Some Anglo-Norman Families*, (John Whitehead & Son Limited, 1951).

LYSONS, Daniel, *Magna Britannia: The County Palatine of Chester.*

MARTIN, Geoffrey, *Domesday Book: A Complete Translation*, (Penguin, 2003).

MARTIN, L. A, *The Victoria History of the Counties of England: Worcestershire.* (University of London Institute of Historical Research. (Dawsons of Pall Mall, 1924).

MACLYSAGHT, E, *The Surnames of Ireland*, (Irish Academic Press, 1980).

MCKIE, David, *What's in a Surname?: A Journey from Abercrombie to Zwicker*, (Windmill Books, 2014).

MCKINLEY, Richard, *Norfolk & Suffolk Surnames of the Middle Ages*, (Philmore, 1975).

ORMEROD, George, revised and expanded by HELSBY, Thomas, *History of the County Palatine and City of Chester, Volume 3*, (1882).

PINE, Leslie, *Sons of the Conqueror: Descendants of Norman Ancestry*, (1973).

RAWCLIFFE, Carole, *The Staffords, Earls of Stafford and Dukes of Buckingham 1394–1521*, (Cambridge University Press, 1978).

REANEY, P. H & WILSON, R. M, *A Dictionary of English Surnames*, (Oxford Quick Reference, 2005).

STEPHEN, Leslie (ed.), *Dictionary of National Biography*, (Smith, Elder & Co,1885).

The City & Parish of Manchester: Introduction, A History of the County of Lancaster, Vol 4, (1911).

STEPHENS, W. B, (ed.), *A History of the County of Warwick: Volume 8, the City of Coventry and Borough of Warwick*, (London, 1969).

SWANTON, Michael, *The Anglo-Saxon Chronicles*, (Translated and edited), (Psychology Press,1998).

Warwickshire Federation of Women's Institutes, *The Warwickshire Village Book*, (Countryside Books).

WILLIAMS, Richard, *Staffordshire Landed Gentry, 1086-1702: a Genealogical Account*, (Dragonby Press, 2005).

WILSON, John Marius, *Imperial Gazetteer of England and Wales*, (1870-72).

Useful Web Sources

These websites were available as reference sources at the time of writing, but considering the vagaries of the Internet, there is no guarantee that this is still the case.

Battle Abbey Roll, (battle-abbey.co.uk).

Behind the Name, (surnames.behindthename.com/names/usage/english).

Black Country Society: Surnames, (blackcountrysociety.co.uk/articles/surnames.htm).

British History Online, (british-history.ac.uk).

British Surnames, (britishsurnames.co.uk).

Family History, (familyhistory.uk.com), List of Norman Knights.

Forebears, (forebears.co.uk/surnames).

Irish Clans, (censusfinder.com/irish_surnames.htm).

Irish Roots, (Irish Surnames).

Jackson, Paul, Scribble by the Ribble: Ribblesdale Yorkshire Dales. (jacksoneditorial.co.uk).

Medieval Names Archive, (s-gabriel.org/names/english.shtml).

The Surname Database, Name Origin Research, (surnamedb.com).

Normans at the Battle of Hastings, (s-gabriel.org/names/arval/hastings.html).

Old Historic Families of Lancashire, (geni.com/projects/Old-Historic-Families-of-Lancashire).

Rampant Scotland, (rampantscotland.com).

Rare British Surnames, (blog.myheritage.com/2011/04/rare-british-surnames).

Rayment, Leigh, The Peerages of England, Scotland, Ireland, Great Britain and the United Kingdom, (leighrayment.com/peers.htm).

Scot Clans, (scotclans.com).

Scotland's People, (scotlandspeople.gov.uk).

Simpson, David, Truly Awesome Marketing, England's North East: Roots, Dialect & Place-Names, (englandsnortheast.co.uk).

Swyrich Corporation, The, House of Names (houseofnames.com).

Acknowledgements

I am indebted to the following contributors:

Alan Glassbrook for providing the information on the Glassbrook family.

Beth Seddon Busby and Daniel Seddon for providing information on the Seddon Family.

Geoff Gradwell for providing most of the information on the Grelley family.

Geoffrey Stafford for supplying a detailed genealogy of his family.

Gloria, my wife, for her patient editing and diligent scrutiny of my work, as well as her tireless encouragement.

Gordon Bold for providing details of the Bold Family.

Judith Middleton-DeFord for suggesting and supplying much of the information on the Middleton Family.

Peter Osbaldeston for providing details of his family history.

Mrs Cary Young Adams, a Whitaker descendant of Norfolk, Virginia, USA, for providing material on the Whitaker Family.

Sheila D Turton for providing a short history of the Chorlton family name.

Index